grammar clear

중학 영문법
클리어.

Level **2**

문법 개념과 내신을 한번에 끝내는
중학 영문법 클리어

문장 구조 시각화로 **핵심 문법 개념 CLEAR!**

시험포인트 및 비교포인트로 **헷갈리는 문법 CLEAR!**

더 확대된 실전테스트로 **학교 시험 대비 CLEAR!**

학습자의 마음을 읽는 동아영어콘텐츠연구팀

동아영어콘텐츠연구팀은 동아출판의 영어 개발 연구원, 현장 선생님, 그리고 전문 원고 집필자들이
공동연구를 통해 최적의 콘텐츠를 개발하는 연구조직입니다.

원고 개발에 참여하신 분들

강남숙 신영주 이유진 최현진 홍미정 홍석현

교재 검토에 도움을 주신 분들

강군필 강은주 고미선 김민성 김은영 김우경 김호성 백명숙 신영주 이상훈

이지혜 임남주 정나래 정은주 정혜승 조수진 조은혜 최재천 최현진 한지영

중학 영문법

클리어.

Level **2**

✦ STRUCTURES 구성과 특징

1 문장 시각화로 핵심 문법을 한 눈에 이해!

[교재 샘플 지면 이미지]

unit 1 현재시제, 과거시제, 미래시제

❶

1 현재시제

현재의 상태, 반복되는 습관, 일반적 사실, 변함없는 진리 등을 나타낼 때 쓴다.

We **are** middle school students.	(현재의 사실이나 상태)
I usually **watch** TV after dinner.	(반복되는 일이나 습관)
The earth **moves** around the sun.	(과학적 사실, 변함없는 진리)

◎ 현재시제로 미래의 확정된 계획이나 일정을 나타낼 수 있다.
The new semester **begins** in March.
The plane **leaves** Chicago at 11 a.m. and **arrives** in New York at 2 p.m.

2 과거시제

과거의 일이나 역사적 사실을 나타낼 때 쓰며, 동사의 과거형을 사용한다.

| Jake **went** to the movies last night. | (과거의 일이나 상태) |
| The Korean War **broke** out in 1950. | (역사적 사실) |

◎ 과거시제는 주로 과거를 나타내는 표현(yesterday, last ~, ~ ago, in+연도)과 함께 쓴다.
I **called** John *three days ago*.
I **visited** my grandparents *last month*.

3 미래시제

미래에 일어날 일이나 앞으로의 계획을 말할 때 will 또는 be going to를 써서 나타낸다.

| It | will | rain soon. | (미래에 대한 예측) |
| I | am going to | visit my uncle. | (앞으로의 계획) |

◎ will과 be going to의 의미가 차이 나는 경우
A Do you have plans for tomorrow?
→ B No. I think I **will stay** home and **watch** TV. (즉흥적으로 결정한 일)
→ B Yes. **I'm going to ride** a bike with Jimin. (미래 계획인 일)

❷

비교 point

What do you do? vs. **What are you doing?**
What do you do?는 직업을 물어볼 때 쓰고, What are you doing?은 진행 중인 일에 대해 물어볼 때 쓴다.

| What **does** your father **do**? | 너의 아버지는 무슨 일을 하시니? |
| What **is** your father **doing** now? | 너의 아버지는 지금 뭘 하고 계시니? |

012 중학영문법 링크어 LEVEL 2

---

❸

Answers p. 2

개념 우선 확인 | 옳은 핵심 고르기

1 Water boils at 100℃.
　☐ 물은 100도에서 끓는다.
　☐ 물은 100도에서 끓을 것이다.

2 The bus arrives at 8 o'clock.
　☐ 그 버스는 8시에 도착했다.
　☐ 그 버스는 8시에 도착할 것이다.

3 I'm going to meet her.
　☐ 나는 그녀를 만날 것이다.
　☐ 나는 그녀를 만나러 가고 있다.

A 괄호 안에서 알맞은 것을 고르시오.

1 He usually (plays / will play) tennis at 6 p.m.
2 Henry (goes / went) to bed early yesterday.
3 The sun (rises / rose) in the east.
4 I'm going (have / to have) lunch with Emily.
5 I (bought / will buy) a new tablet PC soon.

B 우리말과 일치하도록 괄호 안의 말을 이용하여 문장을 완성하시오.

1 나는 이틀 전에 그 식당에 자리를 예약했다. (reserve)
→ I _____ a table at the restaurant two days ago.
2 내일 아침에는 화창할 것입니다. (be)
→ It _____ sunny tomorrow morning.
3 그녀는 항상 선글라스를 낀다. (wear)
→ She always _____ sunglasses.

C 우리말과 일치하도록 밑줄 친 부분을 바르게 고쳐 쓰시오.

1 Lucy는 런던의 서점에서 일한다.
→ Lucy worked at a bookstore in London.
2 나는 저녁으로 피자를 먹을 것이다.
→ I ate pizza for dinner.
3 Ted와 그의 친구들은 지난 주말에 놀이공원에 갔다.
→ Ted and his friends go to an amusement park last weekend.

❹

30초 완성 map

시제
- 현재시제 → He now (works / worked) at a bank. / There (is / was) no air on the moon.
- 과거시제 → Jack (visits / visited) Seoul last year. / World War I (ends / ended) in 1918.
- 미래시제 → It will rain tomorrow. = It is _____ rain tomorrow.

Chapter 01 시제 013

---

❶ 핵심 문법 개념 확인

문장 구조를 시각화하여 꼭 알아야 할 핵심 기본 문법들을 이해하기 쉽게 설명

❸ 개념 우선 확인

본격적인 문제로 넘어가기 전 문법 개념 이해를 다시 한번 확인하는 단계

❷ 시험 POINT & 비교 POINT

시험에 자주 나오거나 혼동되는 문법 개념들을 다시 한번 짚어주고 복습하는 장치

❹ 30초 완성 MAP

다음 Unit으로 넘어가기 전에 map을 완성하며 해당 Unit의 문법 개념을 잘 이해했는지 확인하는 코너

2 | 서술형 집중 훈련 & 시험 출제 포인트 확인

서술형 대비 문장 쓰기
- 서술형 쓰기에 많이 나오는 4가지 유형(문장 완성, 오류 수정, 문장 전환, 영작 완성)을 집중 훈련

시험에 꼭 나오는 출제 포인트
- 시험에 꼭 나오는 중요한 문법 출제 포인트를 한번 더 확인
- 고득점 Point로 내신 고난도 문제 대비

3 | 실전 TEST로 학교 시험 완벽 대비

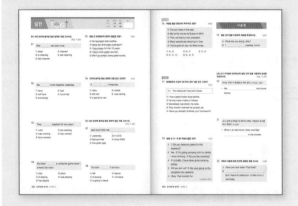

실전 TEST
- 어려워진 내신 시험에 대비하기 위한 최신 기출 유형과 고난도 유형 반영
- 서술형 문항 추가로 학교 시험 완벽 대비

+ WORKBOOK

본책 학습 뒤 Unit마다 2쪽으로 구성된 연습문제를 풀며 부족한 부분을 추가로 학습할 수 있도록 구성

- 개념 확인, 어법 선택, 어법 수정, 문장 전환, 영작 등 학습 유형별 문제 제시로 자학자습 효과 향상

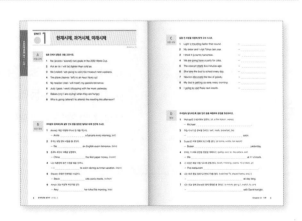

CONTENTS 차례

1 | 품사

영어 단어를 기능과 성격에 따라 나눈 것을 **품사**라고 하며, 영어에는 8가지의 품사가 있다.

명사	사람, 사물, 장소 등의 이름을 나타내는 말	Emma, uncle, friend ... cat, chair, bus, school ... Korea, Paris, time, water ...
대명사	명사를 대신해서 쓰는 말	I, you, he, she, we, they, this, that, it ...
동사	사람, 동물, 사물의 동작이나 상태를 나타내는 말 (be동사, 일반동사, 조동사)	am, are, is ... go, have, know, buy, talk ... can, may, will, must ...
형용사	명사나 대명사의 상태, 형태, 성질 등을 설명하는 말	happy, sad, kind, smart, tall, small, new, warm ...
부사	동사, 형용사, 다른 부사, 문장 전체를 꾸며주는 말	now, early, here, there ... much, really, always, ..
전치사	명사나 대명사 앞에 쓰여 시간, 장소, 방법 등을 나타내는 말	at, on, in, before, after, over, of, with, for, about ...
접속사	단어와 단어, 구와 구, 절과 절을 연결해주는 말	and, but, or, so, when, because, if ...
감탄사	기쁨, 슬픔, 놀람 등의 감정을 나타내는 말	oh, wow, oops, hooray ...

문장을 이루는 구성 요소에는 **주어**, **동사**, **목적어**, **보어**, 그리고 **수식어**가 있다.

주어

'누가, 무엇이'에 해당하며 주로 문장 맨 앞에 온다.

She did the work.   **그녀가** 그 일을 했다.

Seoul is my hometown.   **서울은** 나의 고향이다.

> 주어 자리에 올 수 있는 품사
> 명사, 대명사

동사

'~이다, ~하다'에 해당하는 말로 주어의 동작이나 상태를 나타내며, 주로 주어 다음에 온다.

Lucy **is** my friend.   Lucy는 나의 친구**이다**.

He **bought** a new bike.   그는 새 자전거를 **샀다**.

> 동사 자리에 올 수 있는 품사
> 동사

목적어

'무엇을'에 해당하며 동작의 대상이 되는 말로, 주어와 동사 다음에 온다.

Tom cooked **it** for his mom.   Tom은 엄마를 위해 **그것을** 요리했다.

He teaches **English** at school.   그는 학교에서 **영어를** 가르친다.

> 목적어 자리에 올 수 있는 품사
> 명사, 대명사

보어

주어나 목적어를 보충 설명하는 말로, 역할에 따라 동사 뒤 또는 목적어 뒤에 온다.

He looks **tired**.   그는 **피곤해** 보인다.

We called the dog **Momo**.   우리는 그 개를 **Momo라고** 불렀다.

> 보어 자리에 올 수 있는 품사
> 명사, 대명사, 형용사

수식어

문장의 다양한 위치에서 다른 구성 요소의 의미를 풍부하게 해주는 말이다.

Do you know the **tall** boy?   너는 그 **키 큰** 남자아이를 아니?

Amy **always** gets up **early**.   Amy는 **항상 일찍** 일어난다.

> 수식어 자리에 올 수 있는 품사
> 형용사, 부사

문장의 구성 요소와 품사

주어	동사	수식어	보어
The movie	**was**	**really**	**fun.**
명사	동사	부사	형용사

주어	동사	목적어	수식어
She	**plays**	**the piano**	**very well.**
대명사	동사	명사	부사

3 | 문장의 5형식

문장의 5형식은 문장의 구조에 따라 크게 5가지로 구분한 것을 말한다.

1형식 주어와 동사만으로 의미가 통하는 문장이며, 수식어(구)와 함께 쓰는 경우가 많다.

주어	동사	수식어(구)
The taxi	arrived.	
They	live	in New York.

2형식 주어, 동사, 보어로 이루어진 문장이며, 보어로는 (대)명사나 형용사가 올 수 있다.

주어	동사	보어
You	are	my best friend.
They	look	happy.

3형식 주어, 동사, 목적어로 이루어진 문장이며, 목적어는 명사(구/절), 대명사, 동명사(구), to부정사(구) 형태로 올 수 있다.

주어	동사	목적어
Emily	wants	a new bike.
They	like	to play chess.
We	knew	that he was lying.

4형식 주어와 동사 다음에 두 개의 목적어가 오는 문장으로 '~에게'의 의미인 간접목적어를 먼저 쓰고 '~을/를'의 의미인 직접목적어를 다음에 쓴다.

주어	동사	간접목적어	직접목적어
Eric	showed	us	his photos.
My uncle	bought	me	ice cream.

5형식 주어와 동사 다음에 목적어와 목적격보어가 오는 문장이다. 목적격보어는 목적어를 보충 설명하는 역할을 하며, 동사에 따라 명사, 형용사, to부정사, 분사, 동사원형의 형태로 올 수 있다.

주어	동사	목적어	목적격보어
People	called	him	Batman.
The news	made	her	angry.
He	told	me	to sit down.

구   두 개 이상의 단어가 모여 명사, 형용사, 부사처럼 쓰이는 것으로, 주어와 동사를 포함하지 않는다.

명사구   My goal is **to speak three languages.**   나의 목표는 **3개 언어를 말하는 것**이다.
                         보어

형용사구   The baby **sleeping on the bed** is my sister.   **침대 위에서 자고 있는** 아기는 나의 여동생이다.

부사구   They are playing football **in the playground.**   그들은 **운동장에서** 축구를 하고 있다.
                                 장소의 부사구

절   주어와 동사를 포함한 여러 단어가 모여 문장 안에서 명사, 형용사, 부사처럼 쓰이는 것을 말한다.

명사절   주어   동사   목적어
        What Lucy wants is   going to the concert.   **Lucy가 원하는 것**은 그 콘서트에 가는 것이다.
            주어   동사

형용사절   주어   동사   목적어
         I   read   the book **which you lent me.**   나는 **네가 나에게 빌려준** 책을 읽었다.
                               주어   동사

부사절   주어   동사   목적어   수식어구
        He   missed   the bus **because he got up late.**   그는 **늦게 일어났기 때문에** 그 버스를 놓쳤다.
                                  주어   동사

구와 절 구분하기

구와 절은 단어가 모여 문장을 구성하는 단위이다. 이 중 주어와 동사를 포함하는 것을 절이라고 한다.

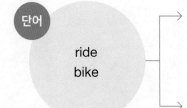

단어   ride   bike

구   My hobby is **riding my bike.**
                 명사구 (주어+동사 없음)

절   I feel good **when I ride my bike.**
                 부사절 (주어+동사 있음)

chapter

01

시제

I have lost my cat.

Q. 여자아이는 고양이를 찾았을까요?

☐ 찾았다   ☐ 못 찾았다   ☐ 알 수 없다

현재시제, 과거시제, 미래시제

1 현재시제

현재의 상태, 반복되는 습관, 일반적 사실, 변함없는 진리 등을 나타낼 때 쓴다.

We **are** middle school students.	〈현재의 사실이나 상태〉
I usually **watch** TV after dinner.	〈반복되는 일이나 습관〉
The earth **moves** around the sun.	〈과학적 사실, 변함없는 진리〉

▶ 현재시제로 미래의 확정된 계획이나 일정을 나타낼 수 있다.

The new semester **begins** in March.

The plane **leaves** Chicago at 11 a.m. and **arrives** in New York at 2 p.m.

2 과거시제

과거의 일이나 역사적 사실을 나타낼 때 쓰며, 동사의 과거형을 사용한다.

Jake **went** to the movies last night.	〈과거의 일이나 상태〉
The Korean War **broke** out in 1950.	〈역사적 사실〉

▶ 과거시제는 주로 과거를 나타내는 표현(yesterday, last ~, ~ ago, in+연도)과 함께 쓴다.

I **called** John *three days ago*.

I **visited** my grandparents *last month*.

3 미래시제

미래에 일어날 일이나 앞으로의 계획을 말할 때 will 또는 be going to를 써서 나타낸다.

It	**will**	**rain** soon.	〈미래에 대한 예측〉
I	**am going to**	**visit** my uncle.	〈앞으로의 계획〉

▶ will과 be going to의 의미가 차이 나는 경우

A Do you have plans for tomorrow?

→ B No. I think I **will stay** home and **watch** TV. (즉흥적으로 결정한 일)

→ B Yes. I'**m going to ride** a bike with Jimin. (미리 계획한 일)

비교
point

What do you do? vs. What are you doing?

What do you do?는 직업을 물어볼 때 쓰고, What are you doing?은 진행 중인 일에 대해 물어볼 때 쓴다.

What **does** your father **do**?	너희 아버지는 무슨 일을 하시니?
What **is** your father **doing** now?	너희 아버지는 지금 뭐 하고 계시니?

개념 우선 확인 | 옳은 해석 고르기

1 Water boils at 100℃.
- ☐ 물은 100도에서 끓는다.
- ☐ 물은 100도에서 끓을 것이다.

2 The bus arrives at 8 o'clock.
- ☐ 그 버스는 8시에 도착했다.
- ☐ 그 버스는 8시에 도착할 것이다.

3 I'm going to meet her.
- ☐ 나는 그녀를 만날 것이다.
- ☐ 나는 그녀를 만나고 있다.

A 괄호 안에서 알맞은 것을 고르시오.

1 He usually (plays / will play) tennis at 6 p.m.

2 Henry (goes / went) to bed early yesterday.

3 The sun (rises / rose) in the east.

4 I'm going (have / to have) lunch with Emily.

5 I (bought / will buy) a new tablet PC soon.

B 우리말과 일치하도록 괄호 안의 말을 이용하여 문장을 완성하시오.

1 나는 이틀 전에 그 식당에 자리를 예약했다. (reserve)
→ I ＿＿＿＿＿ a table at the restaurant two days ago.

2 내일 아침에는 화창할 것입니다. (be)
→ It ＿＿＿＿＿ sunny tomorrow morning.

3 그녀는 항상 선글라스를 낀다. (wear)
→ She always ＿＿＿＿＿ sunglasses.

C 우리말과 일치하도록 밑줄 친 부분을 바르게 고쳐 쓰시오.

1 Lucy는 런던의 서점에서 일한다.
→ Lucy worked at a bookstore in London.

2 나는 저녁으로 피자를 먹을 것이다.
→ I ate pizza for dinner.

3 Ted와 그의 친구들은 지난 주말에 놀이공원에 갔다.
→ Ted and his friends go to an amusement park last weekend.

30초 완성 map

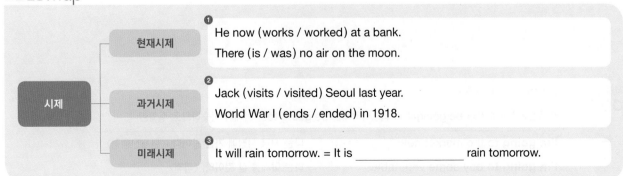

Chapter 01 시제 013

현재진행형, 과거진행형

1 현재진행형: am/are/is+동사원형-ing

현재 진행 중인 동작이나 상황을 나타낼 때 쓴다.

현재	I	**study**	English every day.	〈반복적인 습관〉
현재진행형	I	**am studying**	English now.	〈현재 진행 중인 동작〉

It **is raining** now in Seoul.
Some people **are surfing** at the beach.

▶ 현재진행형을 써서 가까운 미래의 계획을 나타낼 수 있다.

He **is coming** next week.
A What **are** you **doing** tonight?
B I'**m going** to the movies with Mina.

2 과거진행형: was/were+동사원형-ing

과거의 특정 시점에 진행 중이었던 일을 나타낼 때 쓴다.

과거	I	**took**	a shower last night.	〈과거에 일어난 일〉
과거진행형	I	**was taking**	a shower at that time.	〈과거에 진행 중이었던 일〉

When I saw Bill, he **was talking** on the phone.
What **were** you **doing** at 9 p.m. yesterday?

3 진행형으로 쓸 수 없는 동사

진행형은 동작을 나타내는 동사에만 쓸 수 있으며, 상태를 나타내는 동사는 진행형으로 쓰지 않는다.

상태를 나타내는 동사

- **소유**: have, belong 등
- **감정**: like, hate, love 등
- **지각**: see, hear, smell, sound, taste 등
- **인식**: know, understand, believe 등

He **has** a lot of money.　　*cf.* He **is having** lunch now.
↳ is having (×)　　　　　　　　　　↳ '먹다'의 의미로 쓰인 have는 진행형으로 쓸 수 있다.

시험 **point**

be going to 구분하기

현재진행형으로 쓰인 be going과 미래를 나타내는 be going to는 형태가 비슷하므로 주의한다.

I'**m going** to the market now.	나는 지금 시장에 **가는 중이다.** 〈현재진행형〉
I'**m going to** buy some vegetables.	나는 야채를 **살 것이다.** 〈미래〉

개념 우선 확인 | **옳은 해석 고르기**

1 It was raining.
- ☐ 비가 오는 중이다.
- ☐ 비가 오는 중이었다.

2 I'm going to the park now.
- ☐ 나는 지금 공원에 갈 것이다.
- ☐ 나는 지금 공원에 가는 중이다.

3 He is having pizza.
- ☐ 그는 피자를 가지고 있다.
- ☐ 그는 피자를 먹고 있다.

A 괄호 안에서 알맞은 것을 고르시오.

1 I (believe / am believing) you.

2 The students (take / are taking) a math test now.

3 He (checks / is checking) his email every morning.

4 My little sister (hates / is hating) spiders.

5 Jenny (does / was doing) her homework when I called.

B 밑줄 친 부분을 어법에 맞게 고쳐 쓰시오.

1 I <u>am having</u> three sisters.

2 What <u>were</u> you reading now?

3 We <u>are understanding</u> your situation.

4 It <u>is snowing</u> a lot in winter.

5 She <u>is sleeping</u> when we arrived home.

C 우리말과 일치하도록 괄호 안의 말을 이용하여 문장을 완성하시오.

1 우리는 지금 야구 경기장에 가고 있다. (go)

  → We ＿＿＿＿＿＿ ＿＿＿＿＿＿ to the baseball stadium now.

2 두 소년이 K-pop 음악에 맞춰 춤을 추고 있었다. (dance)

  → Two boys ＿＿＿＿＿＿ ＿＿＿＿＿＿ to K-pop music.

3 나는 영자 신문을 읽고 있다. (read)

  → I ＿＿＿＿＿＿ ＿＿＿＿＿＿ an English newspaper.

4 Jack은 그때 수영장에서 수영을 하고 있었다. (swim)

  → Jack ＿＿＿＿＿＿ ＿＿＿＿＿＿ in the pool at that time.

30초 완성 map

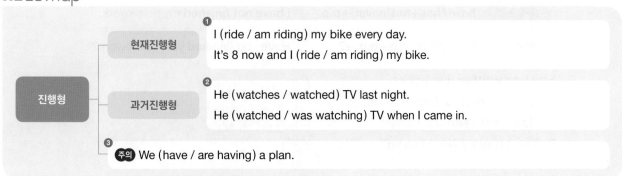

	현재진행형	❶ I (ride / am riding) my bike every day. It's 8 now and I (ride / am riding) my bike.
진행형	과거진행형	❷ He (watches / watched) TV last night. He (watched / was watching) TV when I came in.
	❸ 주의 We (have / are having) a plan.	

unit 3 현재완료의 개념

1 현재완료의 의미

「have/has+과거분사형(p.p.)」으로 나타내며 과거에 일어난 일이 현재까지 영향을 미칠 때 쓴다.

I **lived** here 10 years ago.

(과거에 이곳에 살았음)

I **have lived** here for 10 years.

(과거부터 현재까지 이곳에 살고 있음)

2 과거시제 vs. 현재완료

과거시제	현재완료
I **lost** my bicycle yesterday. 〈과거에 잃어버림. 현재 상황은 알 수 없음〉 He **lived** in London last year. 〈과거에 런던에 살았음. 현재 상황은 알 수 없음〉	I **have lost** my bicycle. 〈과거부터 현재까지 잃어버린 상태〉 He **has lived** in London for a year. 〈과거부터 현재까지 런던에 살고 있음〉
▼	▼
과거시제는 과거에 일어난 일을 나타내므로 특정 과거 시점을 나타내는 표현(yesterday, last ~, ~ ago 등)이나 when과 함께 쓸 수 있다.	현재완료는 과거에 시작된 일이 현재와 연관성을 갖는다는 것을 나타내므로 특정 과거 시점을 나타내는 표현과 함께 쓸 수 없다.

I **made** dinner *yesterday*. (○) / I **have made** dinner *yesterday*. (×)
When **did** you **make** dinner? (○) / *When* **have** you **made** dinner? (×)

3 현재완료의 형태

긍정문	have/has+p.p.	I **have finished** my homework.
부정문	have/has+not(never)+p.p.	I **have not finished** my homework.
의문문	Have/Has+주어+p.p. ~?	**Have** you **finished** your homework?

She **has written** five books.
It **hasn't rained** for two months.
A **Have** you **seen** her lately?
B Yes, I **have**. / No, I **haven't**.

현재완료의 줄임말
have not → haven't
has not → hasn't

개념 우선 확인 | 옳은 문장 고르기

1 나는 작년에 그 영화를 봤다.
- ☐ I watched the movie last year.
- ☐ I have watched the movie last year.

2 3일 동안 비가 오고 있다.
- ☐ It rained for three days.
- ☐ It has rained for three days.

A 괄호 안에서 알맞은 것을 고르시오.

1 They (built / have built) the house two years ago.

2 We have (knew / known) each other for a long time.

3 She (have / has) played the piano since 2020.

4 I (met / have met) Daniel at the soccer stadium in 2017.

5 When (did you go / have you gone) to Jeju-do?

B 밑줄 친 부분을 어법에 맞게 고쳐 쓰시오. (옳으면 ○ 표시할 것)

1 Jake <u>has won</u> the lottery last month.

2 Alex <u>used</u> this iPad for three years. He is still using it.

3 I <u>ate</u> hamburgers with my friends yesterday.

4 <u>Did</u> you ever played chess?

5 She <u>never has eaten</u> Thai food before.

C 우리말과 일치하도록 괄호 안의 말을 이용하여 과거시제 또는 현재완료 문장을 완성하시오.

1 나는 지난 주말에 그 박물관을 방문했다. (visit)

→ I _____ the museum last weekend.

2 그 작가는 3년 동안 그 소설을 써 왔다. (write)

→ The author _____ the novel for three years.

3 그녀는 어제 이후로 나에게 전화하지 않고 있다. (call)

→ She _____ me since yesterday.

30초 완성 map

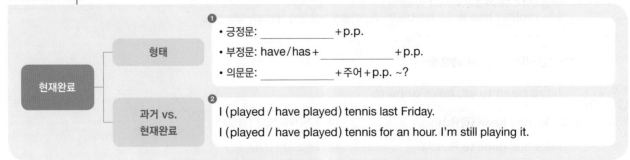

❶
- 긍정문: _____ + p.p.
- 부정문: have/has + _____ + p.p.
- 의문문: _____ + 주어 + p.p. ~?

❷
I (played / have played) tennis last Friday.
I (played / have played) tennis for an hour. I'm still playing it.

형태

과거 vs. 현재완료

현재완료

현재완료의 쓰임

1 **계속: 계속 ~해 왔다**

과거부터 현재까지 계속되는 상황을 나타내며, 주로 since(~ 이래로), for(~ 동안) 등과 함께 쓴다.

| I | have studied | Spanish | since 2010. |

I **have had** a headache *for* two hours.
He **has lived** in Seoul *since* last year.

▶ for 다음에는 기간을 나타내는 말이 오고, since 다음에는 시점을 나타내는 말이 온다.

We have known each other **for** *a long time*.
I have known her **since** *2020*.

2 **경험: ~한 적이 있다**

과거부터 현재까지의 경험을 나타내며, 주로 ever(지금까지), never(~하지 않은), once(한 번), before(전에) 등과 함께 쓴다.

| I | have been | to Jeju-do | before. |

He **has** *never* **lost** a game.
Have you *ever* **tried** Mexican food?

3 **완료: 막 ~했다**

과거에 시작된 일이 현재 시점에 완료되었음을 나타내며, 주로 just(방금), yet(아직), already(이미) 등과 함께 쓴다.

| I | have *already* watched | the movie. |

We **have** *just* **arrived** here.
I **have** not **read** the book *yet*.

4 **결과: ~했다 (그 결과 현재 …하다)**

과거에 일어난 일의 결과가 현재까지 영향을 미치는 상태를 나타낸다.

| I | have lost | my father's watch. |

They **have gone** to Italy. (이탈리아에 가 버려서 그들은 현재 여기에 없는 상태)
My brother **has sold** his bike. (자전거를 팔아서 현재 자전거가 없는 상태)

비교 point

have been to vs. have gone to

| Mike **has been to** Russia. | ~에 가 본 적이 있다 〈경험〉 |
| Mike **has gone to** Russia. | ~에 가 버렸다 〈결과〉 |

개념 우선 확인 | **옳은 의미 고르기**

1 I have learned Chinese for two years.
- ☐ 2년 전에 중국어를 배웠다
- ☐ 2년 동안 중국어를 배워 왔다

2 She has lost her ring.
- ☐ 반지를 잃어버려서 지금 없다
- ☐ 반지를 잃어버렸다가 찾았다

A

밑줄 친 현재완료의 쓰임에 ✔ 표시하시오.

계속: ㉙ 경험: ㉚ 완료: ㉛ 결과: ㉜

1 The little girl <u>has just stopped</u> crying.   ㉙ ㉚ ㉛ ㉜

2 I <u>have never been</u> late for school.   ㉙ ㉚ ㉛ ㉜

3 We <u>have been</u> friends since elementary school.   ㉙ ㉚ ㉛ ㉜

4 Mina <u>has moved</u> to another city.   ㉙ ㉚ ㉛ ㉜

B

괄호 안에서 알맞은 것을 고르시오.

1 She has taught math (for / since) five years.

2 He hasn't finished the work (already / yet).

3 Amy has (been / gone) to Hawaii once.

C

〈보기〉와 같이 두 문장을 현재완료를 이용하여 한 문장으로 쓰시오.

> 보기   I had a toothache yesterday. I still have it.
> → I <u>have had</u> a toothache since yesterday.

1 My dad went to New York. He is not here now.

→ My dad _____ to New York.

2 Jacob started to work for the company three years ago. He still works there.

→ Jacob _____ for the company for three years.

3 I watched the movie two months ago. I watched the movie again yesterday.

→ I _____ the movie twice.

30초 완성 map

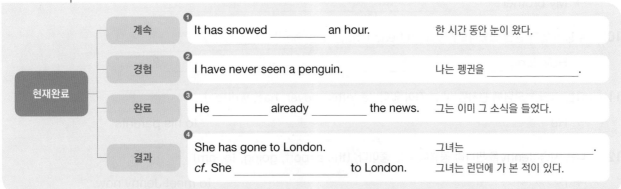

계속	❶ It has snowed _____ an hour.	한 시간 동안 눈이 왔다.
경험	❷ I have never seen a penguin.	나는 펭귄을 _____.
완료	❸ He _____ already _____ the news.	그는 이미 그 소식을 들었다.
결과	❹ She has gone to London.	그녀는 _____.
	cf. She _____ _____ to London.	그녀는 런던에 가 본 적이 있다.

현재완료

서술형 대비 문장 쓰기

Answers p. 2

□ 빈칸 완성 괄호 안의 말을 이용하여 빈칸 완성하기

01 Steve는 항상 검정색 재킷을 입는다. (wear)

→ Steve always _____ a black jacket.

02 그 빵집은 다음 주에 개업할 예정이다. (open)

→ The bakery _____ _____ _____ _____ next week.

03 그 학생들은 학교 버스를 기다리는 중이었다. (wait)

→ The students _____ _____ for the school bus.

04 그녀는 전에 유럽에 가 본 적이 없다. (be, never)

→ She _____ _____ _____ to Europe before.

✓ 오류 수정 어법에 맞게 문장 고쳐 쓰기

05 We <u>didn't see</u> Ben since Monday.

→ We _____ Ben since Monday.

06 James <u>is sleeping</u> when I entered his room.

→ James _____ when I entered his room.

07 Lucy <u>is having</u> blue eyes.

→ Lucy _____ blue eyes.

08 When <u>have you taken</u> these photos?

→ When _____ these photos?

☰ 배열 영작 괄호 안의 말을 바르게 배열하기

09 내 남동생은 내년에 중학생이 될 것이다. (be, next year, a middle school student, will)

→ My brother _____.

10 두통이 얼마 동안 있었나요? (you, a headache, have, had)

→ How long _____?

11 그는 그의 부모님께 편지를 써 본 적이 없다. (a letter, never, has, written)

→ He _____ to his parents.

12 나는 지금 Jenny를 만나러 공항에 가는 중이다. (the airport, going, to, am)

→ I_____ to meet Jenny now.

시험에 나오는 출제 포인트

Answers p. 2

출제 포인트 **1** 미래를 나타내는 표현들을 익히자!

다음 중 미래를 나타내는 문장이 <u>아닌</u> 것은?

① He is going to the park now.
② It's going to be warm this week.
③ We will have a music festival.
④ The bus leaves in 5 minutes.
⑤ She is coming back this Friday.

출제 포인트 **2** 진행형으로 쓸 수 없는 동사를 기억하자!

괄호 안에서 알맞은 것을 고르시오.

(1) They (love / are loving) each other.

(2) Jack (fixes / is fixing) my bike now.

(3) He (knows / is knowing) a lot about football.

출제 포인트 **3** 현재완료는 특정 과거 시점을 나타내는 표현과 함께 쓸 수 없다!

빈칸에 들어갈 말로 알맞은 것은?

> I have visited Disneyland _____.

① last year
② yesterday
③ in 2017
④ three times
⑤ two years ago

고득점 POINT 「since+시점」 vs. 「for+기간」

우리말과 일치하도록 빈칸에 알맞은 말을 쓰시오.

(1) 미나는 2019년 이래로 서울에 살고 있다.
 → Mina has lived in Seoul _____ 2019.
(2) Peter는 1년 동안 서울에 살고 있다.
 → Peter has lived in Seoul _____ a year.

출제 포인트 **4** 현재완료의 여러 가지 쓰임을 구분하자!

현재완료의 쓰임이 나머지와 <u>다른</u> 것은?

① David has never eaten Korean food.
② They have never been to India.
③ I have learned English for five years.
④ She has read the book three times.
⑤ Have you ever ridden a horse?

고득점 POINT have been to vs. have gone to

우리말과 일치하도록 괄호 안에서 알맞은 것을 고르시오.

(1) 그는 파리에 가 본 적이 있다.
 → He has (been / gone) to Paris.
(2) 그는 파리에 가 버렸다. (그래서 현재 여기에 없다.)
 → He has (been / gone) to Paris.

[01-04] 빈칸에 들어갈 말로 알맞은 것을 고르시오.

|8점, 각 2점|

01

> She _____ her room now.

① clean   ② cleaned
③ is cleaning   ④ are cleaning
⑤ has cleaned

02

> We _____ lunch together yesterday.

① have   ② had
③ will have   ④ have had
⑤ are having

03

> They _____ together for two years.

① work   ② are working
③ was working   ④ has worked
⑤ have worked

04

> My sister _____ a computer game when I entered her room.

① play   ② plays
③ is playing   ④ was playing
⑤ has played

05 밑줄 친 현재완료의 형태가 잘못된 것은? |3점|

① He <u>has been</u> there before.
② <u>Have</u> you ever <u>seen</u> a penguin?
③ I <u>have knew</u> him for 10 years.
④ I <u>have</u> never <u>eaten</u> raw fish.
⑤ She <u>has written</u> some great novels.

06 빈칸에 들어갈 말로 알맞은 것을 <u>모두</u> 고르면? |2점|

> It _____ tomorrow.

① rains   ② rained
③ will rain   ④ was raining
⑤ is going to rain

[07-08] 빈칸에 들어갈 말로 알맞지 <u>않은</u> 것을 고르시오.

|6점, 각 3점|

07

> Jack and I first met _____.

① yesterday   ② in 2015
③ last summer   ④ since 2020
⑤ two years ago

08

> The train _____ in an hour.

① left   ② leaves
③ is leaving   ④ will leave
⑤ is going to leave

[09-10] 어법상 틀린 것을 고르시오. |8점, 각 4점|

09
① She is knowing the answer.
② Water freezes at 0 °C.
③ I take a yoga class once a week.
④ We're going to the party tonight.
⑤ The train arrives in Busan at 5 p.m.

10
① I have already read the book.
② He has gone to the concert.
③ I have moved here last year.
④ She has never been abroad.
⑤ Have you heard of the musical?

11 빈칸에 들어갈 말이 나머지와 다른 것은? |3점|

① It has snowed _____ two hours.
② She has taught English _____ 2008.
③ I have lived here _____ seven years.
④ He has been in the hospital _____ a week.
⑤ We have been friends _____ a long time.

고난도

12 어법상 옳은 문장을 모두 고르면? |5점|

① They are coming next week.
② The man is having five cars.
③ I've lost my wallet yesterday.
④ She was having lunch at that time.
⑤ When have you visited London?

13 빈칸에 들어갈 말이 순서대로 바르게 짝지어진 것은? |3점|

- I _____ to the amusement park last weekend.
- I _____ a horse twice.

① am going – rode
② went – was riding
③ have gone – rode
④ went – have ridden
⑤ have gone – have ridden

14 우리말을 영어로 잘못 옮긴 것은? |4점|

① 그녀는 보통 저녁에 개를 산책시킨다.
  → She usually walks her dog in the evening.
② 우리는 그 전쟁이 1945년에 끝났다는 것을 안다.
  → We know that the war ended in 1945.
③ 나는 오늘 밤에 영화 보러 갈 것이다.
  → I'm going to the movies tonight.
④ 그는 그때 전화 통화를 하고 있었다.
  → He was talking on the phone at that time.
⑤ 최근에 그녀를 본 적이 있니?
  → Did you seen her recently?

15 문장의 시제가 나타내는 의미가 나머지와 다른 것은? |4점|

① It's raining hard.
② They're watching TV now.
③ He's leaving for New York soon.
④ Mom is cooking in the kitchen.
⑤ She's studying for the exam.

16 어법상 옳은 문장끼리 짝지어진 것은? |5점|

> ⓐ The sun rises in the east.
> ⓑ My family moves to Busan in 2010.
> ⓒ They will elect a new president.
> ⓓ Many people are believing in God.
> ⓔ I have gone to Jeju-do three times.

① ⓐ, ⓑ　　　② ⓐ, ⓒ　　　③ ⓒ, ⓓ
④ ⓐ, ⓒ, ⓔ　　⑤ ⓑ, ⓓ, ⓔ

17 현재완료의 쓰임이 〈보기〉와 같은 것을 <u>모두</u> 고르면? |5점|

> 보기　The restaurant has just closed.

① I have eaten Indian food before.
② He has never made a mistake.
③ Somebody has stolen my bike.
④ They haven't started the project yet.
⑤ Have you already finished your homework?

18 밑줄 친 ①~⑤ 중 어법상 <u>틀린</u> 것은? |4점|

> A ① <u>Do you have any plans for this weekend?</u>
> B Yes, ② <u>I'm going camping with my family.</u> I love camping. ③ <u>Do you like camping?</u>
> A ④ <u>Actually, I have never gone camping before.</u>
> B Will you join us? ⑤ <u>We were going to the campsite this weekend.</u>
> A Okay. That sounds fun.
>
> * campsite 캠핑장

서 술 형

19 괄호 안의 말을 이용하여 대화를 완성하시오. |3점|

> A What are you doing, Jiho?
> B I ＿＿＿＿＿＿＿＿＿ cookies. (bake)

[20-21] 우리말과 일치하도록 괄호 안의 말을 이용하여 문장을 완성하시오. |6점, 각 3점|

20 우리는 전에 이 영화를 본 적이 없다. (never, see)

> → We ＿＿＿＿＿＿＿＿＿＿＿＿＿ this movie before.

21 내가 집에 도착했을 때 엄마와 아빠는 주방에서 요리를 하고 계셨다. (cook)

> → When I arrived home, Mom and Dad ＿＿＿＿＿＿＿＿＿＿＿ in the kitchen.

22 대화의 흐름에 맞게 빈칸에 알맞은 말을 쓰시오. |3점|

> A Have you ever eaten Thai food?
> B ＿＿＿＿＿, ＿＿＿＿＿ ＿＿＿＿＿. But I heard it's delicious. I'd like to try it someday.

23 우리말과 일치하도록 〈조건〉에 맞게 영작하시오. |5점|

> 나는 이번 여름 방학에 중국어를 배울 것이다.

> 조건 다음 중에서 필요한 단어만을 골라 영작할 것
> (I, Chinese, go, learn, am, was, to, going)

→ _____

this summer vacation.

24 그림의 내용과 일치하도록 문장을 완성하시오. |5점|

Yesterday   Now

→ She _____ _____ _____

_____ yesterday.

25 다음을 읽고, 괄호 안의 동사를 알맞은 형태로 바꿔 글을 완성하시오. |6점, 각 2점|

> My family _____(travel) to China to see the Great Wall last month. The Great Wall of China _____(be) the longest wall in the world. It _____(be) a really great experience. * the Great Wall of China 만리장성

[26-27] 우리말과 일치하도록 밑줄 친 부분을 바르게 고쳐 쓰시오. |6점, 각 3점|

26 너는 언제 그 책을 도서관에 반납했니?

When have you returned the book to the library?

→ _____

27 Kevin은 그의 숙제를 아직 끝내지 못했다.

Kevin doesn't have finished his homework yet.

→ _____

28 다음 표는 지민이의 오늘 하루 일과 중 일부이다. 표를 참고하여 문장을 완성하시오. |6점, 각 2점|

Time	Activities
7:00 a.m.	get up
10:00 a.m. ~ 12:00 p.m. NOW	watch a movie
3:00 p.m.	play tennis
8:00 p.m.	do his homework

(1) He _____ at 7 in the morning.

(2) He _____ for two hours.

(3) He _____ at 8 in the evening.

chapter

02

조동사

Q. 아기 염소들에게 해줄 말로 적절한 것은?

☐ You must not open the door.

☐ You don't have to open the door.

can, may, will

1 조동사의 쓰임

조동사는 동사에 다양한 의미를 더해 주는 역할을 하며, 항상 「조동사+동사원형」의 형태로 쓰인다.

He		rides	a bike.	그는 자전거를 **탄다**.
	can	**ride**		그는 자전거를 **탈 수 있다**.

2 can

능력	~할 수 있다(= be able to)	She **can** play the piano. = She **is able to** play the piano. I **can't** solve the problem. = I'**m not able to** solve the problem.
허가	~해도 좋다(= may)	You **can** use my umbrella. **Can** I ask a question?
요청	~해 주시겠어요?	**Can**(**Could**) you close the door? ＊ could는 can보다 정중한 표현이다.

> 능력의 can의 과거는 could나 was/were able to로 나타내고, 미래는 will be able to로 나타낸다.
>
> We **could**(**were able to**) see stars in the sky. 〈과거: ~할 수 있었다〉
> You **will be able to** swim well. 〈미래: ~할 수 있을 것이다〉

3 may

허가	~해도 좋다(= can)	You **may** stay here with us. **May** I use your phone?
불확실한 추측	~일지도 모른다	It's cloudy. It **may**(**might**) rain today. ＊ might는 may보다 약한 추측을 나타낸다.

4 will

예정	~할 것이다	I **will** visit my grandparents next week. ＊ will의 부정은 won't(= will not)로 나타낼 수 있다.
요청	~해 주시겠어요?	**Will**(**Would**) you do me a favor? ＊ would는 will보다 정중한 표현이다.

시험 **point**

조동사를 쓸 때 주의할 점

조동사는 두 개를 연달아 쓸 수 없다.

We (will can / will be able to) travel to space someday.

개념 우선 확인 | 옳은 해석 고르기

1 He can play the guitar.
☐ 그는 기타를 칠 것이다.
☐ 그는 기타를 칠 수 있다.

2 That may be true.
☐ 그것은 사실일 것이다.
☐ 그것은 사실일지도 모른다.

3 Will you help me?
☐ 나를 도와줄래?
☐ 내가 도와줄까?

A   밑줄 친 조동사의 의미에 ✔ 표시하시오.

1 I can speak Chinese.   ☐ 능력   ☐ 허가

2 It will rain a lot tomorrow.   ☐ 요청   ☐ 예정

3 After the class is over, you may go home.   ☐ 허가   ☐ 추측

4 Could you take me to the subway station?   ☐ 능력   ☐ 요청

B   우리말과 일치하도록 괄호 안에서 알맞은 것을 고르시오.

1 저와 결혼해 주시겠어요?
→ (May / Will) you marry me?

2 너는 스노보드를 탈 수 있니?
→ (Can / Will) you ride a snowboard?

3 그는 지금 집에 없을지도 모른다.
→ He (won't / may not) be home now.

C   우리말과 일치하도록 조동사와 괄호 안의 말을 이용하여 문장을 완성하시오.

1 내가 너의 태블릿 PC를 사용해도 되니? (use)
→ _____ _____ _____ your tablet PC?

2 나는 그의 이름을 잊지 않을 것이다. (forget)
→ I _____ _____ his name.

3 나는 그 문제를 쉽게 풀 수 있었다. (solve)
→ I _____ _____ _____ _____ the problem easily.

30초 완성 map

조동사		
can	❶ I can swim. = I am _____ _____ swim.	나는 수영을 할 수 있다.
	_____ _____ help me?	나를 도와줄래?
	주의 You will (can / be able to) finish the work.	너는 그 일을 끝낼 수 있을 것이다.
may	❷ She _____ be hungry.	그녀는 배가 고플지도 모른다.
	_____ I sit here? = Can I sit here?	제가 여기에 앉아도 될까요?
will	❸ I _____ see a doctor tomorrow.	나는 내일 병원에 갈 것이다.

unit 2   must, should, had better, used to

1 must

의무	~해야 한다 (= have to)	You **must** wear a helmet. = You **have to** wear a helmet.
		You **must not** swim here. 〈금지〉 You **don't have to** hurry. 〈불필요〉 ＊ must not은 '~해서는 안 된다'는 의미이고, 　don't have to는 '~할 필요가 없다'는 의미이다.
강한 추측	~임에 틀림없다	Emily stayed up all night. She **must** be tired.

> 의무의 must(have to)의 과거형은 had to이고, 미래형은 will have to이다.
>
> I **had to** get up early this morning. 〈과거: ~해야만 했다〉
> I **will have to** return the book tomorrow. 〈미래: ~해야만 할 것이다〉

2 should

| 의무 | (마땅히) ~해야 한다 | You **should** help your friends. |
| 충고 | ~하는 게 좋다 | I think you **should** see a doctor. |

3 had better

| 충고, 권고 | ~하는 게 좋겠다 | You **had better** take the subway.
You **had better not** smoke. |

> had better의 부정은 had better not으로 쓰며, '~하지 않는 게 좋겠다'의 의미이다.

4 used to

> used to는 '(과거에는) ~했으나 현재는 그렇지 않다'는 뜻을 포함한다.

| 과거의 습관 | ~하곤 했다
(= would) | I **used to** write in my diary.
= I **would** write in my diary. |
| 과거의 상태 | (과거에) ~이 있었다 | There **used to** be an apple tree here. |

주의 used to가 과거의 상태를 나타낼 때는 would로 바꿔 쓸 수 없다.
There **used to** be a fountain here.
　　　　↘ would (×)

비교 point

must not vs. don't have to

must와 have to의 부정형은 각각 의미가 다르므로 주의해야 한다.

1 You (must not / don't have to) go out. It's dangerous.

2 You (must not / don't have to) bring your umbrella. It's sunny.

개념 우선 확인 | 옳은 해석 고르기

1 He must be a genius.
  ☐ 그는 천재임에 틀림없다.
  ☐ 그는 천재일지도 모른다.

2 You must not lie.
  ☐ 너는 거짓말을 해서는 안 된다.
  ☐ 너는 거짓말을 할 필요가 없다.

3 You had better leave now.
  ☐ 너는 지금 떠나는 게 좋겠다.
  ☐ 너는 지금 떠나도 된다.

A 괄호 안에서 알맞은 것을 고르시오.

1 He (must / had to) attend the meeting yesterday.

2 You look tired. I think you (should / would) go home early today.

3 You (must not / don't have to) swim here. The water is deep.

4 This bag (must / may) be Amy's. I can see her name on it.

B 우리말과 일치하도록 〈보기〉에서 알맞은 말을 골라 문장을 완성하시오. (단, 한 번씩만 사용할 것)

보기   should   had better   used to

1 우리는 지금 표를 사는 게 좋겠다.
  → We _____ buy the tickets now.

2 내 남동생은 내 장난감을 망가뜨리곤 했다.
  → My brother _____ break my toys.

3 우리는 야생동물을 보호해야 한다.
  → We _____ protect wild animals.

C 우리말과 일치하도록 괄호 안의 말을 이용하여 문장을 완성하시오.

1 너는 지금 Tom에게 전화하지 않는 게 좋겠다. (call, had better)
  → You _____ Tom now.

2 그녀는 그것에 대해 걱정할 필요가 없다. (worry, have to)
  → She _____ about that.

3 너는 공공장소에서는 큰 소리로 이야기해서는 안 된다. (talk loudly, must)
  → You _____ in public places.

30초 완성 map

조동사

must ❶
He must go. = He _____ _____ go. — 그는 가야 한다.
They _____ _____ rich. — 그들은 부자임에 틀림없다.
You (must not / don't have to) go there. — 너는 그곳에 갈 필요가 없다.

should ❷
You should study English. — 너는 영어를 _____.

had better ❸
You _____ _____ _____ go there. — 너는 그곳에 가지 않는 게 좋겠다.

used to ❹
There (used to / would) be a bank here. — (과거에) 이곳에 은행이 있었다.

서술형 대비 문장 쓰기

☐ 빈칸 완성   괄호 안의 말과 조동사를 이용하여 빈칸 완성하기

01 제가 들어가도 될까요? (come)

   → _____ _____ _____ in?

02 너는 밤에 외출하지 않는 게 좋겠다. (go)

   → You _____ _____ _____ _____ out at night.

03 그는 그 질문에 답하지 않아도 된다. (answer)

   → He _____ _____ _____ _____ the question.

04 Tom은 서울에 살았지만, 지금은 부산에 산다. (live)

   → Tom _____ _____ _____ in Seoul, but now he lives in Busan.

✓ 오류 수정   어법에 맞게 문장 고쳐 쓰기

05 He is wearing a ring. <u>He has to be</u> married.

   → He is wearing a ring. _____ married.

06 <u>You will able to speak</u> English well soon.

   → _____ English well soon.

07 It's a secret. <u>You had not better tell</u> anybody.

   → It's a secret. _____ anybody.

08 <u>There would be a theater</u> in my town, but now there isn't.

   → _____ in my town, but now there isn't.

☰ 배열 영작   괄호 안의 말을 바르게 배열하기

09 조금 더 천천히 말씀해 주시겠어요? (speak, you, could)

   → _____ more slowly?

10 그는 은행에서 돈을 빌려야 했다. (to, some money, had, borrow)

   → He _____ from the bank.

11 너는 너의 건강에 신경을 써야 한다. (of, take, should, care, you)

   → _____ your health.

12 나는 오늘 밤에 너에게 전화할 수 없을 것이다. (not, call, able, be, will, to)

   → I _____ you tonight.

시험에 꼭 나오는 출제 포인트

Answers p. 4

출제 포인트 ① can, must와 바꿔 쓸 수 있는 표현을 기억하자!

두 문장의 의미가 같도록 빈칸에 알맞은 말을 쓰시오.

(1) I can carry these boxes alone.

→ I _____ _____ _____

_____ these boxes alone.

(2) He must get up early.

→ He _____ _____ _____

up early.

> **고득점 POINT** 추측의 의미로 쓰인 must는 have/has to로 바꿔 쓸 수 없다.
>
> **밑줄 친 부분을 have/has to로 바꿔 쓸 수 없는 것은?**
>
> ① You <u>must</u> tell the truth.
> ② We <u>must</u> do our best.
> ③ She <u>must</u> be a smart girl.
> ④ I <u>must</u> return the books tomorrow.
> ⑤ He <u>must</u> finish the work today.

출제 포인트 ② 여러 가지 의미를 가진 조동사에 주의하자!

밑줄 친 부분의 의미가 〈보기〉와 같은 것을 모두 고르면?

보기	You <u>may</u> sit here.

① <u>May</u> I take your order?
② <u>Can</u> he read and write?
③ You <u>can</u> use this computer.
④ It <u>may</u> rain today.
⑤ That <u>may</u> not be true.

> **고득점 POINT** 과거의 상태를 나타내는 조동사
>
> **밑줄 친 부분을 어법에 맞게 고쳐 쓰시오.**
>
> There <u>would</u> be a lot of flowers in the garden.
>
> → _____

출제 포인트 ③ must not과 don't have to의 의미를 구분하자!

우리말과 일치하도록 must 또는 have to를 이용하여 문장을 완성하시오.

(1) 너는 저곳에 앉으면 안 된다.

→ You _____ sit there.

(2) 너는 그 문제에 대해 걱정할 필요가 없다.

→ You _____ worry about the problem.

출제 포인트 ④ had better의 부정문에서 not의 위치에 주의하자!

다음 문장을 부정문으로 바꿔 쓰시오.

You had better go home now.

→ _____

유형	문항수	배점	점수
객관식	18	60	
서술형	10	40	

[01-03] 빈칸에 들어갈 말로 알맞은 것을 고르시오.
|6점, 각 2점|

01

You look tired. You _____ get some rest.

① will　　　　　② should
③ used to　　　 ④ must not
⑤ had better not

02

It's Sunday. You _____ go to school.

① must　　　　 ② used to
③ will not　　　 ④ had better
⑤ don't have to

03

I _____ have a pet dog when I was young.

① can　　　　 ② will
③ must　　　　④ used to
⑤ had better

04 밑줄 친 부분과 바꿔 쓸 수 있는 것은?　　|2점|

You <u>must</u> be quiet in the library.

① can　　　　 ② may
③ will　　　　 ④ have to
⑤ are able to

05 빈칸에 들어갈 말로 알맞은 것은?　　|3점|

너는 이 강에서 수영해서는 안 된다.
→ You _____ swim in this river.

① must not　　 ② should
③ don't have to ④ aren't able to
⑤ will not

06 빈칸에 들어갈 말이 나머지와 <u>다른</u> 것은?　　|4점|

① You had _____ not believe him.
② We don't have _____ hurry up.
③ I have _____ finish the work alone.
④ She used _____ read a lot of books.
⑤ I'm not able _____ answer the question.

07 빈칸에 들어갈 말로 알맞은 것을 <u>모두</u> 고르면?　　|3점|

A Excuse me. _____ you pass me the salt, please?
B Sure. Here you are.

① Will　　　　 ② May　　　　 ③ Could
④ Must　　　　⑤ Should

08 밑줄 친 부분의 의미가 나머지와 <u>다른</u> 것은?　　|4점|

① I <u>can</u> play chess.
② He <u>can</u> sing beautifully.
③ You <u>can</u> use my computer.
④ We <u>can</u> see stars at night.
⑤ She <u>can</u> speak five languages.

09 밑줄 친 부분을 의미가 같도록 바꿔 쓸 때, 알맞지 <u>않은</u> 것은? |4점|

① <u>May</u> I sit here? (→ Can)
② He <u>can</u> fly a drone. (→ is able to)
③ There <u>used to</u> be a school here. (→ would)
④ You <u>must</u> try again. (→ have to)
⑤ I <u>could</u> dance well when I was young.
　　(→ was able to)

10 빈칸에 공통으로 들어갈 말로 알맞은 것은? |2점|

• You _____ better stay home.
• We _____ to apologize to him.

① had　　　② used　　　③ went
④ should　　⑤ would

11 어법상 <u>틀린</u> 문장을 <u>모두</u> 고르면? |4점|

① You must drive safely.
② It will be going to rain tomorrow.
③ You don't have to bring your passport.
④ He will be able to solve the problem.
⑤ They have to leave early yesterday.

12 괄호 안의 말을 이용하여 우리말을 영작할 때 네 번째 오는 단어는? |3점|

너는 혼자 여행하지 않는 게 좋겠다.
(not, you, alone, had, travel, better)

① had　　　② not　　　③ alone
④ better　　⑤ travel

13 밑줄 친 부분의 의미가 같은 것끼리 짝지어진 것은? |5점|

ⓐ They have a nice house, so they <u>must</u> be rich.
ⓑ We <u>must</u> have a dream because it will make us happy.
ⓒ I <u>must</u> get some sleep.
ⓓ She <u>must</u> be very sick.
ⓔ You <u>must</u> be home before dark.

① ⓐ, ⓑ　　　② ⓐ, ⓒ　　　③ ⓑ, ⓓ
④ ⓐ, ⓓ, ⓔ　　⑤ ⓑ, ⓒ, ⓔ

14 밑줄 친 부분의 의미가 〈보기〉와 같은 것은? |4점|

보기　You <u>may</u> use my phone.

① <u>May</u> I leave now?
② He <u>may</u> call you tomorrow.
③ We <u>may</u> miss the train.
④ The rumor <u>may</u> be true.
⑤ You <u>may</u> not believe this story.

15 다음 중 우리말을 영어로 <u>잘못</u> 옮긴 것은? |4점|

① 제가 지금 집에 가도 될까요?
　→ May I go home now?
② 그는 나한테 화난 게 틀림없다.
　→ He must be angry with me.
③ 우리는 지금 떠나서는 안 된다.
　→ We don't have to leave now.
④ 나는 스키타러 가곤 했다.
　→ I used to go skiing.
⑤ 너는 아침 식사를 해야 한다.
　→ You should have breakfast.

16 다음 우리말을 바르게 영작한 것은? |3점|

> 우리는 제시간에 그곳에 도착할 수 있을 것이다.

① We can get there in time.
② We are able to get there in time.
③ We will can get there in time.
④ We can able to get there in time.
⑤ We will be able to get there in time.

17 짝지어진 두 문장의 의미가 서로 <u>다른</u> 것은? |4점|

① I can cook spaghetti.
= I am able to cook spaghetti.
② May I have your name?
= Can I have your name?
③ Can you wait outside?
= Could you wait outside?
④ You must not cross the street here.
= You don't have to cross the street here.
⑤ Kevin must clean his room.
= Kevin has to clean his room.

고난도
18 다음은 동물원에 방문한 학생들을 위한 안내문이다. 내용상 빈칸에 들어갈 말로 <u>가장</u> 알맞은 것은? |5점|

> Hello, students. Welcome to the zoo. During the tour, you will be able to see many kinds of animals. They look cute, but some of them are dangerous. So you should be careful. You _____ touch or feed them. I hope you will enjoy the tour.

① will   ② won't   ③ may
④ had better   ⑤ must not

[19-20] 우리말과 일치하도록 빈칸에 알맞은 말을 쓰시오.
|4점, 각 2점|

19 나는 예전에 조부모님과 함께 살았었다. (live)

→ I _____ _____ _____ with my grandparents.

20 Jessica는 전화를 받지 않고 있어. 그녀는 바쁜 게 틀림없어. (busy)

→ Jessica is not answering the phone. She _____ _____ _____.

21 우리말과 일치하도록 괄호 안의 말을 바르게 배열하여 문장을 완성하시오. |3점|

> Harry는 그의 고양이를 돌보아야 한다.
> (care, his cat, has, take, of, to)

→ Harry _____.

고난도
22 어법상 <u>틀린</u> 부분을 <u>두 곳</u> 찾아 바르게 고쳐 쓰시오.
|6점, 각 3점|

> You had not better buy that lamp. I think it's too expensive. We will able to find a better one.

(1) _____ → _____
(2) _____ → _____

23 다음 그림을 설명하는 문장을 〈조건〉에 맞게 완성하시오.

|4점|

10 years ago   now

> 조건 1. 조동사와 a swing을 이용할 것
>   2. 5단어로 쓸 것

→ There _____

in my backyard 10 years ago.

24 다음 문장을 지시대로 바꿔 쓰시오.

|4점, 각 2점|

(1)
> You can enjoy fun activities here.
> (미래시제로)

→ You _____ fun

activities here.

(2)
> You must rent a car. (과거시제로)

→ You _____ rent a

car.

25 밑줄 친 우리말을 〈조건〉에 맞게 영작하시오.

|4점|

> It's already 11 o'clock. 너는 잠자리에 드는 것이
> 좋다.

> 조건 1. 충고의 표현과 go to bed를 이용할 것
>   2. 5단어로 쓸 것

→ _____

26 두 문장의 의미가 같도록 빈칸에 알맞은 말을 쓰시오.

|3점|

> Dinosaurs could not live in cold weather.

→ Dinosaurs _____ _____ _____

_____ live in cold weather.

27 〈보기〉의 단어와 알맞은 조동사를 이용하여 문장을 완성하시오.

|6점, 각 3점|

보기	lose	cross	take

(1) It's sunny today. You _____ _____

_____ _____ an umbrella.

(2) It's a red light. You _____ _____

_____ the road.

28 다음은 도서관에서 지켜야 할 규칙을 메모한 것이다. 〈보기〉에서 알맞은 조동사를 골라 문장을 완성하시오.

|6점, 각 2점|

×	(1) eat or drink (2) talk on the phone
O	(3) read books quietly

보기	should	should not

(1) We _____

_____ in the library.

(2) We _____

_____ in the library.

(3) We _____

_____ in the library.

chapter

3

to부정사

I was happy to win the game.

Q. 위 문장이 의미하는 것은?

☐ 경기에서 이기는 것은 행복했다.

☐ 나는 경기에서 이겨서 행복했다.

to부정사의 명사적 용법

1 명사적 용법의 to부정사

to부정사는 명사처럼 문장의 주어, 목적어, 보어 역할을 할 수 있다.

(1) 주어 역할: ~하는 것은

To ride a bike	is	exciting.
To visit new places	is	fun.

자전거를 **타는 것은** 재미있다.

새로운 곳을 **방문하는 것은** 재미있다.

↳ to부정사 주어는 항상 단수 취급한다.

▶ 주어로 쓰인 to부정사(구)는 가주어 it으로 바꿔 쓸 수 있다.

To fly a kite is fun.
= **It** is fun **to fly** a kite.
　　가주어　　　　진주어

(2) 목적어 역할: ~하는 것을

I	want	**to eat** chocolate.
He	plans	**to study** abroad.

나는 초콜릿 **먹는 것을** 원한다.

그는 해외에서 **공부하는 것을** 계획한다.

▶ to부정사의 부정은 to 바로 앞에 not을 써서 표현한다.
He decided **not to go** there.

> to부정사를 목적어로 쓰는 동사
> want, hope, decide, plan 등

(3) 보어 역할: ~하는 것(이다)

My goal	is	**to pass** the exam.
His hope	is	**to become** an actor.

내 목표는 그 시험을 **통과하는 것**이다.

그의 바람은 배우가 **되는 것**이다.

2 의문사+to부정사

문장에서 주어, 보어, 목적어 역할을 하며, 의문사에 따라 의미가 달라진다.

how+to부정사	어떻게 ~할지	**what+to부정사**	무엇을 ~할지
when+to부정사	언제 ~할지	**where+to부정사**	어디에(서) ~할지

▶ 「의문사+to부정사」는 「의문사+주어+should+동사원형」으로 바꿔 쓸 수 있다.

I don't know **what to say** to her. = I don't know **what I should say** to her.
Please tell me **how to use** it. = Please tell me **how I should use** it.

주의 「why+to부정사」로는 쓰지 않는다.

시험 point

가주어 it이 있는 문장의 해석

to부정사(구) 대신 주어 자리에 쓰인 가주어 it은 의미가 없는 형식적인 주어이므로 '그것'으로 해석하지 않는다.

It is not easy **to climb the mountain.** → 그 산을 등반하는 것은 쉽지 않다.

개념 우선 확인 | 옳은 표현 고르기

1 나는 너와 함께 가기를 원한다.
- ☐ I want go with you.
- ☐ I want to go with you.

2 내 직업은 영어를 가르치는 것이다.
- ☐ My job is teach English.
- ☐ My job is to teach English.

3 무엇을 해야 할지 모르겠다.
- ☐ I don't know what to do.
- ☐ I don't know to do what.

A 밑줄 친 to부정사의 역할에 ✔ 표시하시오.　　　주어: ㉠　목적어: ㉫　보어: ㉲

1 It is hard to get up early.　　　㉠　㉫　㉲

2 His dream is to become a movie star.　　　㉠　㉫　㉲

3 We hope to see him again.　　　㉠　㉫　㉲

4 To go there alone is very dangerous.　　　㉠　㉫　㉲

B 두 문장의 의미가 같도록 빈칸에 알맞은 말을 쓰시오.

1 To watch sci-fi movies is interesting.
→ _____ is interesting _____ _____ sci-fi movies.

2 To live without water is impossible.
→ _____ is impossible _____ _____ without water.

3 I can't decide what I should buy.
→ I can't decide _____ _____ _____.

4 Tom doesn't know how he should fix the car.
→ Tom doesn't know _____ _____ _____ the car.

C 우리말과 일치하도록 괄호 안의 말을 이용하여 문장을 완성하시오.

1 그녀의 꿈은 전 세계를 여행하는 것이다. (be, travel)
→ Her dream _____ _____ _____ around the world.

2 우리는 어디에서 살지 선택할 필요가 있다. (choose, live)
→ We need to _____ _____ _____ _____.

3 그는 수업에 빠지지 않기로 결심했다. (miss, decide)
→ He _____ _____ _____ _____ class.

30초 완성 map

to부정사 명사적 용법

역할
❶
- 주어: It is fun **to play games**.　　　_____ 재미있다.
- 목적어: I want **to buy new shoes**.　　　나는 _____ 원한다.
- 보어: Her dream is **to be a singer**.　　　그녀의 꿈은 _____ 이다.

의문사+ to부정사
❷
He showed me _____ _____ _____ it.
= He showed me how I should do it.

to부정사의 형용사적·부사적 용법

1 형용사적 용법의 to부정사

to부정사는 명사나 대명사를 수식하는 형용사 역할을 할 수 있으며 '~할', '~하는'으로 해석한다.

(1) 명사+to부정사

I have a book	**to read**.	읽을 책
They need something	**to drink**.	마실 무언가
They need something cold	**to drink**.	마실 차가운 무언가

> -thing, -one, -body로 끝나는 대명사를 형용사와 to부정사가 같이 수식할 때는 「대명사+형용사+to부정사」의 순서로 쓴다.

(2) 명사+to부정사+전치사

to부정사의 수식을 받는 명사가 전치사의 목적어일 경우 to부정사 뒤에 전치사를 써야 한다.

I need a friend	**to play** with.	놀 친구 (← play with a friend)	a pen to write with 쓸 펜 a friend to talk to 말할 친구 a chair to sit on 앉을 의자 a hotel to stay in 머물 호텔
He bought a house	**to live** in.	살 집 (← live in a house)	

2 부사적 용법의 to부정사

to부정사는 동사, 형용사, 문장 전체를 수식하는 부사 역할을 할 수 있다.

(1) 목적: ~하기 위해

He went to America	**to learn** English.	그는 영어를 **배우기 위해** 미국에 갔다.
I turned on the TV	**to watch** the show.	나는 그 쇼를 **보기 위해** TV를 켰다.

> 목적의 의미를 명확히 나타내기 위해 to 대신 in order to를 쓸 수 있다.

(2) 감정의 원인: ~해서, ~하여

I'm happy	**to see** you again.	나는 너를 다시 **만나서** 행복해.
We were surprised	**to hear** the news.	우리는 그 소식을 **듣고** 놀랐다.

(3) 결과: (…해서) ~하다

The girl grew up	**to be** a famous singer.	그 소녀는 자라서 유명한 가수가 **되었다**.
He lived	**to be** 100 years old.	그는 100세까지 **살았다**.

(4) 판단의 근거: ~하다니

He must be smart	**to get** perfect scores.	만점을 **받다니** 그는 똑똑한 게 틀림없다.
You are silly	**to believe** the rumor.	그 소문을 **믿다니** 너는 어리석구나.

개념 우선 확인 | **옳은 표현 고르기**

1 나는 마실 무언가를 샀다.
☐ I bought something to drink.
☐ I bought to drink something.

2 그는 버스를 잡기 위해 달렸다.
☐ He ran to catch the bus.
☐ He caught the bus to run.

A   〈보기〉에서 알맞은 말을 골라 **to부정사**를 이용하여 문장을 완성하시오.

> 보기   eat   buy   hear   be   see

1 I'm hungry. I need to buy something _____.

2 Picasso lived _____ 92.

3 He bought a ticket _____ the musical.

4 We were shocked _____ the news.

5 I don't have enough money _____ it.

B   밑줄 친 부분을 어법에 맞게 고쳐 쓰시오.

1 I need a pen <u>to write on</u>.

2 Is there <u>fun anything to do</u>?

3 We are looking for a bench <u>to sit</u>.

C   우리말과 일치하도록 괄호 안의 말을 이용하여 문장을 완성하시오.

1 우리는 그 콘서트에 가서 행복했다. (happy, go)

→ We were _____ to the concert.

2 너는 이야기할 누군가가 필요하다. (someone, talk)

→ You need _____.

3 나는 그녀의 생일을 축하하기 위해 케이크를 만들었다. (celebrate, birthday)

→ I made a cake _____.

4 그 소년은 자라서 훌륭한 축구 선수가 되었다. (be, a great soccer player)

→ The boy grew up _____.

30초 완성 map

to부정사	형용사적 용법	❶ I have (work to do / to do work). We bought a house (to live / to live in).	나는 해야 할 일이 있다. 우리는 살 집을 구입했다.
	부사적 용법	❷ I studied hard **to be a doctor**. I was sad **to hear the news**. You are very kind **to help me**.	(의사가 되기 위해 / 의사가 되다니) (그 소식을 듣기 위해 / 그 소식을 들어서) (나를 도와주다니 / 나를 도와주기 위해)

1 to부정사의 의미상 주어

to부정사의 행위의 주체를 나타낼 때는 to부정사 앞에 「for+목적격」으로 의미상 주어를 쓴다.

It was easy		**to solve** the problem.	그 문제를 **푸는 것**은 쉬웠다.
	for him	**to solve** the problem.	**그가** 그 문제를 **푸는 것**은 쉬웠다.

▶ 사람의 성격이나 성향을 나타내는 형용사(kind, rude, polite, foolish, honest, wise, careful 등) 다음에 의미상의 주어가 올 때는 「of+목적격」으로 쓴다.

It was nice **of you** to help us.

2 too+형용사/부사+to부정사: 너무 ~해서 …할 수 없는

I'm	too busy.		나는 / 너무 바쁘다.
I'm	**too** busy	**to call** him back.	나는 / 너무 바쁘다 / 그에게 다시 전화하기에는. → 나는 **너무 바빠서** 그에게 다시 **전화할 수 없다**.

▶ too 자체에 '너무 지나치게'라는 의미가 있어서 뒤에 to부정사를 붙이면 전체 문장이 부정의 의미를 갖게 된다. 따라서 이 문장은 「so+형용사/부사+that+주어+can't+동사원형」으로 바꿔 쓸 수 있다.

= I'm **so** busy **that** I **can't call** him back.

문장이 과거시제일 때는 「so+형용사/부사+that+주어+couldn't+동사원형」으로 써야 한다.

I was **too** busy **to wash** the dishes.

= I was **so** busy **that** I **couldn't wash** the dishes.

3 형용사/부사+enough+to부정사: ~할 만큼 충분히 …한/하게

He is	rich enough.		그는 충분히 부유하다.
He is	rich **enough**	**to buy** the car.	그는 그 차를 **살 만큼 충분히** 부유하다.

▶ enough는 '충분히'라는 의미의 부사로 쓰여 형용사나 부사를 뒤에서 꾸며 준다. 이 문장에 to부정사를 덧붙이면 '충분히 …해서 …하다'는 의미가 되어 「so+형용사/부사+that+주어+can+동사원형」으로 바꿔 쓸 수 있다.

= He is **so** rich **that** he **can buy** the car.

의미상 주어가 있는 to부정사 구문을 that절로 전환할 때는 의미상 주어가 that절의 주어가 된다.

It is warm **enough** for us **to go** swimming.

= It is **so** warm **that** we **can go** swimming.

시험 point

to부정사 구문의 어순

「형용사/부사+enough+to부정사」 구문에서 enough는 수식하는 형용사나 부사 뒤에 와야 한다.

Jack is (strong enough / enough strong) to carry it alone.

개념 우선 확인 | 옳은 해석 고르기

1 It's hard for Jack to get up early.
- ☐ Jack을 위해 일찍 일어나는 것은 힘들다.
- ☐ Jack은 일찍 일어나는 것이 힘들다.

2 The box is too heavy to move.
- ☐ 그 상자는 너무 무거워서 옮길 수 없다.
- ☐ 그 상자는 매우 무겁지만 옮길 만하다.

A 괄호 안에서 알맞은 것을 고르시오.

1 The dress is too expensive (for / of) her to buy.

2 This soup is (too / enough) hot to eat.

3 The ladder is (long enough / enough long) to reach the roof.

4 It was wise (for / of) you to make a study plan.

B 두 문장의 의미가 같도록 빈칸에 알맞은 말을 쓰시오.

1 Jenny was so shy that she couldn't speak in front of people.

→ Jenny was _____ _____ _____ _____ in front of people.

2 The little boy is so smart that he can solve any problem.

→ The little boy is _____ _____ _____ _____ any problem.

3 She is tall enough to be a model.

→ She is _____ _____ _____ _____ _____ be a model.

4 It was too noisy for us to fall asleep.

→ It was _____ _____ _____ _____ _____ fall asleep.

C 우리말과 일치하도록 괄호 안의 말을 배열하여 문장을 완성하시오.

1 내가 그에게 돈을 빌려준 것은 어리석었다. (me, lend, foolish, of, to)

→ It was _____ him money.

2 그 소방관들은 너무 바빠서 점심을 먹을 수가 없었다. (busy, too, have, lunch, to)

→ The firefighters were _____.

3 그 영화는 다시 볼 만큼 충분히 재미있다. (enough, watch, interesting, to)

→ The movie is _____ again.

30초 완성 map

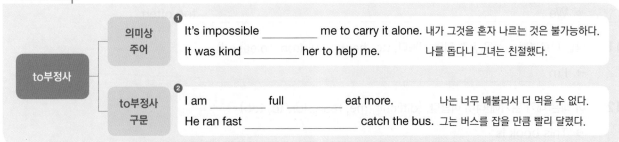

to부정사	의미상 주어	❶ It's impossible _____ me to carry it alone. 내가 그것을 혼자 나르는 것은 불가능하다.
		It was kind _____ her to help me. 나를 돕다니 그녀는 친절했다.
	to부정사 구문	❷ I am _____ full _____ eat more. 나는 너무 배불러서 더 먹을 수 없다.
		He ran fast _____ _____ catch the bus. 그는 버스를 잡을 만큼 빨리 달렸다.

Answers p. 6

빈칸 완성   두 문장의 의미가 같도록 빈칸 완성하기

01   To exercise every day is not easy.

→ _____ is not easy _____ _____ every day.

02   Let's decide when we should leave for vacation.

→ Let's decide _____ _____ _____ for vacation.

03   I was so busy that I couldn't help you yesterday.

→ I was _____ _____ _____ _____ you yesterday.

04   The man is rich enough to buy the island.

→ The man is _____ _____ _____ he _____ _____ the island.

오류 수정   어법에 맞게 문장 고쳐 쓰기

05   My brother is <u>enough old to sleep</u> alone.

→ My brother is _____ alone.

06   Please lend me <u>a pen to write</u>.

→ Please lend me _____.

07   It was honest <u>for you to admit</u> your mistake.

→ It was honest _____ your mistake.

08   I have <u>interesting something to tell</u> you.

→ I have _____ you.

배열 영작   괄호 안의 말을 바르게 배열하기

09   그의 직업은 개를 훈련시키는 것이다. (dogs, to, is, train)

→ His job _____.

10   우리는 패스트푸드를 너무 자주 먹지 않기로 동의했다. (fast food, not, agreed, eat, to)

→ We _____ too often.

11   나는 너로부터 소식을 듣게 되어 기쁘다. (to, hear, you, from, pleased)

→ I'm _____.

12   이 책은 내가 읽기에 너무 어렵다. (difficult, me, read, for, to, too)

→ This book is _____.

시험에 꼭 나오는 출제 포인트

Answers p. 6

출제 포인트 **1** to부정사의 의미를 이해하고 쓰임을 구분하자!

밑줄 친 to부정사의 쓰임이 나머지와 다른 것은?

① I decided to study English hard.
② She wanted to win the prize.
③ My dream is to be a tour guide.
④ He has a lot of homework to do.
⑤ Her goal is to walk an hour every day.

> **고득점 POINT** 가주어 it을 이용한 문장
>
> **두 문장의 의미가 같도록 빈칸에 알맞은 말을 쓰시오.**
>
> To get a perfect score is hard.
>
> → It _____ _____ _____ _____ a perfect score.

출제 포인트 **2** 형용사적 용법의 to부정사에서 전치사가 필요한지 확인하자!

다음 중 어법상 틀린 문장은?

① There wasn't a chair to sit.
② We have enough time to prepare.
③ I need a friend to talk to.
④ Do you have anything to read?
⑤ He didn't have toys to play with.

> **고득점 POINT** -thing, -body, -one으로 끝나는 대명사를 수식하는 to부정사의 위치
>
> **괄호 안의 말을 이용하여 우리말을 영작하시오.**
>
> 입을 따뜻한 무언가가 있나요? (warm, anything, wear)
>
> → Do you have _____ ?

출제 포인트 **3** to부정사의 의미상 주어를 알맞은 형태로 쓰자!

우리말과 일치하도록 빈칸에 알맞은 의미상 주어를 쓰시오.

(1) 그렇게 하다니 당신은 용감했다.

→ It was brave _____ _____ to do that.

(2) 그녀가 현명한 판단을 하는 것이 필요하다.

→ It's necessary _____ _____ to make a wise decision.

출제 포인트 **4** to부정사 구문은 「so ~ that ...」 구문으로 바꿔 쓸 수 있다!

두 문장의 의미가 같도록 빈칸에 알맞은 말을 쓰시오.

(1) I was too tired to do my homework.

→ I was _____ tired that I _____ _____ my homework.

(2) Jake is strong enough to carry the box.

→ Jake is _____ _____ _____ he _____ carry the box.

> **고득점 POINT** to부정사 구문의 의미상 주어는 「so ~ that ...」 구문에서 that절의 주어가 된다.
>
> **두 문장의 의미가 같도록 빈칸에 알맞은 말을 쓰시오.**
>
> The shoes are too expensive for her to buy.
>
> → The shoes are so expensive that _____ _____ them.

유형	문항수	배점	점수
객관식	18	60	
서술형	10	40	

[01-03] 빈칸에 들어갈 말로 알맞은 것을 고르시오.
|6점, 각 2점|

01
It is exciting _____ a roller coaster.

① ride ② rode
③ to ride ④ riding
⑤ to riding

02
It was easy _____ to win the game.

① me ② of me
③ to me ④ for me
⑤ with me

03
He was _____ to go out.

① tired ② so tired
③ too tired ④ tired enough
⑤ very tired

04 밑줄 친 부분의 쓰임이 나머지와 다른 것은? |4점|

① There are a lot of things to do.
② She has many friends to help her.
③ We need something cold to drink.
④ Give me some paper to write on.
⑤ He turned on the TV to watch the news.

05 빈칸에 들어갈 말이 순서대로 바르게 짝지어진 것은? |3점|

• It is _____ for us to arrive in time.
• It is _____ of you to help us.

① careful – kind
② difficult – easy
③ impossible – easy
④ careful – great
⑤ impossible – kind

06 밑줄 친 부분의 쓰임이 〈보기〉와 같은 것은? |4점|

> 보기 Kate called me to ask some questions.

① I have a funny story to tell you.
② He did his best to achieve his goal.
③ You need to understand the situation.
④ It is hard to find water in the desert.
⑤ We're looking for a bench to sit on.

[07-08] 밑줄 친 부분이 어법상 틀린 것을 고르시오.
|8점, 각 4점|

07
① He ran to catch the train.
② I don't have any friends to play.
③ She is looking for something to eat.
④ I decided not to go camping.
⑤ It is important to exercise regularly.

08
① It is enough warm to eat outside.
② We didn't know how to get there.
③ He saved money to buy a flight ticket.
④ I have a lot of homework to finish today.
⑤ It's difficult for me to speak English.

09 다음 우리말을 영작할 때, 필요하지 <u>않은</u> 단어는? |3점|

> 물 위를 걷는 것은 불가능하다.

① to   ② walk   ③ is
④ that   ⑤ impossible

10 밑줄 친 It(it)의 쓰임이 〈보기〉와 같은 것을 <u>모두</u> 고르면?
　|3점|

> 보기　It is boring to play alone.

① It is spring now.
② It is not my bag.
③ Is it exciting to travel abroad?
④ It is far from here to the bank.
⑤ It is not a good idea to take a bus.

11 빈칸에 들어갈 말이 나머지와 <u>다른</u> 것은? |3점|

① It is fun _____ me to ride a skateboard.
② It was rude _____ him to say like that.
③ It is important _____ us to follow the rules.
④ It is natural _____ her to get angry.
⑤ It looked impossible _____ them to
complete the project.

12 우리말과 일치하도록 할 때 빈칸에 들어갈 말로 알맞은 것을 <u>모두</u> 고르면? |2점|

> 나는 다음에 무엇을 해야 할지 모르겠어.
> → I don't know _____ next.

① to do what
② what to do
③ something to do
④ what I can do
⑤ what I should do

13 밑줄 친 부분의 쓰임이 같은 것끼리 짝지어진 것은? |5점|

> ⓐ I studied hard <u>to get</u> good grades.
> ⓑ He must be kind <u>to have</u> so many friends.
> ⓒ We were happy <u>to meet</u> him again.
> ⓓ She went to the market <u>to buy</u> some fruit.
> ⓔ You must be honest <u>to tell</u> the truth.

① ⓐ, ⓑ   ② ⓐ, ⓓ   ③ ⓑ, ⓒ
④ ⓒ, ⓓ   ⑤ ⓒ, ⓔ

[14-15] 우리말을 영어로 바르게 옮긴 것을 고르시오.
　|6점, 각 3점|

14 　그 바지는 너무 길어서 내가 입을 수 없다.

① The pants are long for me to wear.
② The pants are so long for me to wear.
③ The pants are enough long for me to wear.
④ The pants are too long for me to wear.
⑤ The pants are long enough for me to wear.

15 　너는 감기에 걸리지 않도록 조심해야 한다.

① You should be careful to catch a cold.
② You should not be careful to catch a cold.
③ You should be careful not to catch a cold.
④ You should be careful to not catch a cold.
⑤ You should be careful not to catching a cold.

16 짝지어진 두 문장의 의미가 서로 <u>다른</u> 것은? |4점|

① I went to the library to return the books.
   = I went to the library in order to return the books.

② To read English novels is difficult.
   = It is difficult to read English novels.

③ Please tell me where to put these boxes.
   = Please tell me where I should put these boxes.

④ The shoes are too small for me to wear.
   = The shoes are so small that I can wear them.

⑤ She is rich enough to buy the house.
   = She is so rich that she can buy the house.

17 다음 대화의 빈칸에 들어갈 말로 알맞은 것은? |4점|

A What's wrong?
B I'm trying to do my math homework, but
   _____.
A Don't worry. I can help you.
B Thanks!

① it's too easy for me to do alone
② it's too difficult for me to do alone
③ it's difficult enough for me to do alone
④ it's too difficult for you to do alone
⑤ it's easy enough for you to do alone

고난도
18 다음 중 어법상 옳은 문장의 개수는? |5점|

ⓐ I want warm something to wear.
ⓑ Let me know when to turn off the oven.
ⓒ I need someone to talk.
ⓓ She is enough smart to pass the test.
ⓔ To make friends is not easy.

① 1개　　② 2개　　③ 3개
④ 4개　　⑤ 5개

[19-20] 주어진 문장과 같은 의미가 되도록 빈칸에 알맞은 말을 쓰시오. |6점, 각 3점|

19
We have to decide where to stay.

→ We have to decide _____ _____
_____ _____.

20
He was wise enough to make a good decision.

→ He was _____ wise _____
_____ _____ make a good decision.

[21-22] 다음 문장에서 어법상 <u>틀린</u> 부분을 찾아 바르게 고쳐 쓰시오. |6점, 각 3점|

21
It was foolish for her to forget her father's birthday.

_____ → _____

22
I have something to say important.

_____ → _____

23 우리말과 일치하도록 〈보기〉에서 필요한 말을 골라 영작하시오. |4점|

영어로 나 자신을 표현하는 것은 나에게 어렵다.

보기 difficult, me, is, express, of, to, myself, for, not

→ It _____

in English.

26 우리말과 일치하도록 괄호 안의 말을 바르게 배열하여 문장을 완성하시오. |6점, 각 3점|

(1) 그 피자는 우리가 나눠 먹을 만큼 충분히 크다.
(enough, share, us, to, for, large)

→ The pizza is _____

_____.

(2) 이야기할 현명한 누군가가 있는 것은 도움이 된다.
(to, to, talk, someone, wise)

→ It's helpful to have _____

_____.

24 다음 두 문장을 〈조건〉에 맞게 한 문장으로 쓰시오. |5점|

It is very cold. We can't go out.

조건 1. 「too ~ to부정사」 구문을 이용할 것
2. 의미상 주어를 포함할 것

→ _____

27 다음 우리말을 〈조건〉에 맞게 영작하시오. |5점|

나는 무엇을 입어야 할지 결정할 수 없다.

조건 1. 「의문사+to부정사」 구문을 이용할 것
2. can, decide, wear를 포함하여 6단어로 쓸 것

→ _____

28 다음 표지판의 의미를 〈조건〉에 맞게 영작하시오. |4점|

조건 1. 가주어를 이용할 것
2. dangerous, swim here를 포함하여 6단어로 쓸 것

→ _____

25 우리말과 일치하도록 어법상 틀린 부분을 찾아 바르게 고쳐 쓰시오. |4점|

네가 그의 이메일에 답장하지 않은 것은 무례했다.
→ It was rude of you to not answer his email.

_____ → _____

chapter

04

동명사

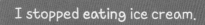

Q. 여자아이의 말이 의미하는 것은?

☐ 나는 아이스크림 먹는 것을 멈췄다.

☐ 나는 아이스크림을 먹으려고 멈췄다.

1 동명사의 역할

동명사는 「동사원형+-ing」의 형태로 문장 안에서 명사처럼 주어, 목적어, 보어 역할을 한다.

(1) 주어 역할: ~하는 것은, ~하기는

Surfing	is	fun.

서핑하는 것은 재미있다.

Taking pictures	is	my hobby.

사진을 **찍는 것은** 나의 취미이다.

> **주의** 동명사 주어는 단수 취급하므로 뒤에는 단수 동사가 와야 한다.
> Learning foreign languages **is** not easy.
> ↘ are (×)

(2) 목적어 역할: ~하는 것을

He	enjoys	**reading** mysteries.

그는 추리소설 **읽는 것을** 즐긴다.

I	don't like	**staying** home alone.

나는 혼자 집에 **있는 것을** 좋아하지 않는다.

> ▶ 동명사는 동사뿐 아니라 전치사의 목적어 역할을 할 수도 있다.

Thank you **for inviting** me.
I'm afraid **of riding** roller coasters.

(3) 보어 역할: ~하는 것(이다)

My hobby	is	**riding** my bike.

내 취미는 자전거를 **타는 것**이다.

Her job	is	**teaching** math.

그녀의 직업은 수학을 **가르치는 것**이다.

2 자주 쓰는 동명사 구문

keep -ing	계속해서 ~하다	**feel like -ing**	~하고 싶다
be busy -ing	~하느라 바쁘다	**be worth -ing**	~할 가치가 있다
can't help -ing	~하지 않을 수 없다	**be used to -ing**	~하는 데 익숙하다
spend+시간/돈+-ing	~하는 데 시간/돈을 쓰다	**look forward to -ing**	~하기를 고대하다

My sister **is busy doing** her homework.
This museum **is worth visiting**.
I'm **looking forward to going** to the concert.

시험 point

look forward to 구문을 쓸 때 주의할 점

look forward to의 to는 전치사이므로 뒤에는 명사나 동명사가 와야 한다.

He looked forward to (see / seeing) her again.

개념 우선 확인 | 밑줄 친 부분의 옳은 해석 고르기

1 I finished <u>reading the book</u>.
☐ 그 책을 읽는 중에
☐ 그 책을 읽는 것을

2 My hobby is <u>watching movies</u>.
☐ 영화를 보는 중인
☐ 영화를 보는 것

A 밑줄 친 동명사의 역할에 ✔ 표시하시오.

주어: 주　목적어: 목　보어: 보

1 She likes <u>playing</u> computer games.　　주　목　보

2 <u>Mastering</u> a language is difficult.　　주　목　보

3 My little sister is afraid of <u>sleeping</u> alone.　　주　목　보

4 Her job is <u>counseling</u> students at school.　　주　목　보

5 <u>Drinking</u> too much soda is bad for your teeth.　　주　목　보

B 어법상 틀린 부분을 찾아 바르게 고쳐 쓰시오.

1 Thank you for invite me to your party.

2 Riding roller coasters are really exciting.

3 I'm worried about to take the math test.

4 I'm looking forward to hear from you soon.

C 우리말과 일치하도록 괄호 안의 말을 이용하여 문장을 완성하시오.

1 그는 컴퓨터를 고치는 데 두 시간을 보냈다. (spend, hours, fix)

→ He _____ his computer.

2 나는 새로운 사람들을 만나는 데 익숙하다. (used, meet)

→ I _____ new people.

3 이 책은 여러 번 읽을 가치가 있다. (worth, read)

→ This book _____ several times.

4 누군가가 계속해서 문을 두드렸다. (knock, keep)

→ Someone _____ at the door.

30초 완성 map

동명사

역할
❶
• 주어: Making sandwiches (is / are) easy.
• 목적어: She enjoys (watching / to watch) horror movies.
• 보어: My hobby is (fly / flying) my drone.

동명사 구문
❷
I don't feel like (going / to go) out.
I can't help (fall / falling) in love with her.

동명사와 to부정사

1 동명사만 목적어로 취하는 동사

| enjoy, finish, stop, practice, mind, avoid, quit, give up 등 | + | 동명사 |

I finished **doing** my homework.
Do you mind **opening** the window?
My dad gave up **smoking** last year.

2 to부정사만 목적어로 취하는 동사

| want, hope, expect, plan, promise, agree, decide, manage 등 | + | to부정사 |

I want **to watch** the movie again.
He planned **to travel** around the world.
We didn't expect **to win** the game.

3 동명사와 to부정사를 모두 목적어로 취하는 동사

(1) 의미 차이가 없는 경우

| like, love, hate, begin, start, continue 등 | + | 동명사/to부정사 |

Billy likes **swimming** in the river. = Billy likes **to swim** in the river.

(2) 의미 차이가 있는 경우

remember /forget	+동명사	(과거에) ~한 것을 기억하다/잊다
	+to부정사	(미래에) ~할 것을 기억하다/잊다
try	+동명사	(시험 삼아, 한번) ~해 보다
	+to부정사	~하려고 노력하다〔애쓰다〕

I remember **meeting** her last year.	(과거에) 그녀를 **만났던 것을** 기억한다
Remember **to meet** her at 3 p.m.	(앞으로) 그녀를 **만날 것을** 기억한다
He forgot **going** there with me.	(과거에) 그곳에 **갔던 것을** 잊었다
He forgot **to go** there with me.	(앞으로) 그곳에 **가야 할 것을** 잊었다
I tried **losing** weight, but I gave up.	**한번 살을 빼려고 해 보다**
I tried **to lose** weight, but it was hard.	**살을 빼려고 노력했다**

비교
point 「stop+-ing」 vs. 「stop+to부정사」

She stopped **talking**.	**말하는 것을 멈추다**
She stopped **to talk** on the phone.	**말하기 위해 멈추다**

개념 우선 확인 | **옳은 표현 고르기**

1 춤추는 것을 연습하다	2 돕기로 약속하다	3 방문했던 것을 기억하다
☐ practice dancing	☐ promise helping	☐ remember visiting
☐ practice to dance	☐ promise to help	☐ remember to visit

A 괄호 안에서 알맞은 것을 고르시오.

1 My mom enjoys (baking / to bake) cookies.

2 Daniel decided (quitting / to quit) his job.

3 I finished (cleaning / to clean) my room.

4 We agreed (meeting / to meet) again on Friday.

B 괄호 안의 말을 적절한 형태로 바꿔 문장을 완성하시오.

1 I hope _____ backpacking in Europe. (go)

2 Suddenly, Olivia began _____. (cry)

3 I don't mind _____ for you here. (wait)

4 They continued _____ board games. (play)

5 Do you remember _____ in this river last summer? (swim)

C 우리말과 일치하도록 괄호 안의 말을 이용하여 문장을 완성하시오.

1 그녀는 꽃에 물 주는 것을 잊어버렸다. (forget, water)

→ She _____ the flowers.

2 나는 그 문을 열려고 노력했지만, 열 수 없었다. (try, open)

→ I _____ the door, but I couldn't.

3 나는 어렸을 때 파리에 살았던 것을 기억한다. (remember, live)

→ I _____ in Paris when I was young.

4 나는 패스트푸드 먹는 것을 중단했다. (stop, eat)

→ I _____ fast food.

30초 완성 map

동명사와 to부정사	목적어 형태 구분	❶ He finished (to do / doing) the work. I want (to read / reading) the book.
	의미 차이 구분	❷ Don't forget _____ off the light. (turn) 불을 끄는 것을 잊지 마세요. Do you remember _____ her last week? (meet) 지난주에 그녀를 만났던 것을 기억하니?

서술형 대비 문장 쓰기

Answers p. 7

☐ 빈칸 완성 괄호 안의 말을 이용하여 빈칸 완성하기

01 나는 패션 잡지 읽는 것을 즐긴다. (read, enjoy)

→ I _____ fashion magazines.

02 나에게 그것을 설명해 줘서 고마워. (explain, thanks for)

→ _____ it to me.

03 그는 진실을 말하기로 결심했다. (tell, decide)

→ He _____ the truth.

04 너는 작년에 캠핑 갔던 것을 기억하니? (go, remember)

→ Do you _____ camping last year?

✓ 오류 수정 어법에 맞게 문장 고쳐 쓰기

05 Eating vegetables <u>are good for your health</u>.

→ Eating vegetables _____.

06 I don't feel like <u>to do anything today</u>.

→ I don't feel like _____.

07 My grandmother is <u>looking forward to see us</u>.

→ My grandmother is _____.

08 What do you plan <u>doing this weekend</u>?

→ What do you plan _____?

☰ 배열 영작 괄호 안의 말을 바르게 배열하기

09 엄마는 나를 이해하려고 노력하신다. (understand, tries, to, me)

→ Mom _____.

10 소라는 친구들과 수다를 떠는 데 3시간을 보냈다. (three hours, chatting, spent, with)

→ Sora _____ her friends.

11 그는 그 사고에 대해 이야기하는 것을 좋아하지 않는다. (talk, doesn't, to, like)

→ He _____ about the accident.

12 네 비밀번호 바꾸는 것을 잊지 마. (forget, change, to, don't)

→ _____ your password.

시험에 꼭 나오는 출제 포인트

Answers p. 8

**출제 포인트 ** 동명사의 역할을 구분하자!

밑줄 친 동명사의 역할이 〈보기〉와 같은 것을 모두 고르면?

> 보기   I enjoy listening to music.

① He avoided drinking too much coffee.
② His hobby is swimming.
③ Making pizza is not difficult.
④ John doesn't mind traveling alone.
⑤ My dream is becoming an actor.

> **고득점 POINT** 동명사 주어는 항상 단수 취급한다.
>
> **어법상 틀린 부분을 찾아 바르게 고쳐 쓰시오.**
> Meeting new people are interesting.
> _____ → _____

**출제 포인트 ** 자주 쓰는 동명사 구문을 익히자!

우리말과 일치하도록 괄호 안의 말을 이용하여 문장을 완성하시오.

(1) 그는 저녁을 요리하느라 바쁘다. (busy, cook)

　→ He _____ dinner.

(2) 그녀는 웃지 않을 수 없었다. (laugh, help)

　→ She _____.

> **고득점 POINT** to부정사의 to vs. 전치사 to
>
> **괄호 안의 말을 이용하여 문장을 완성하시오.**
> 나는 소풍 가는 것을 고대하고 있다. (go)
> → I'm looking forward to _____ on a picnic.

**출제 포인트 ** 목적어로 동명사 또는 to부정사를 취하는 동사를 구분하자!

빈칸에 들어갈 말로 알맞지 않은 것은?

> Jennifer _____ playing the piano.

① enjoyed　　② planned　　③ stopped
④ gave up　　⑤ practiced

**출제 포인트 ** 목적어의 형태에 따라 의미가 달라지는 동사를 기억하자!

우리말과 일치하도록 괄호 안의 말을 이용하여 문장을 완성하시오.

나는 TV에서 그 가수를 봤던 것을 기억한다. (remember, see)

→ I _____ the singer on TV.

[01-03] 빈칸에 들어갈 말로 알맞은 것을 고르시오.
|6점, 각 2점|

01

The baby stopped _____.

① cry
② to crying
③ cries
④ cried
⑤ crying

02

They agreed _____ the schedule.

① change
② changed
③ changing
④ to change
⑤ to changed

03

I feel like _____ home tonight.

① stay
② to stay
③ staying
④ to staying
⑤ stayed

04 밑줄 친 부분의 역할이 나머지와 다른 것은? |4점|

① She enjoys reading comic books.
② I practice playing the drums every day.
③ He suddenly stopped talking.
④ Do you mind opening the window?
⑤ My hobby is taking pictures of flowers.

05 빈칸에 공통으로 들어갈 말로 알맞지 않은 것은? |3점|

• I _____ to learn Chinese.
• I _____ working with Brian.

① like
② expect
③ hate
④ started
⑤ continued

[06-07] 어법상 틀린 것을 고르시오. |8점, 각 4점|

06 ① The dog began barking loudly.
② This museum is worth visiting again.
③ Do you mind turning on the TV?
④ I spent an hour reading the book.
⑤ I'm looking forward to see the movie.

07 ① Playing online games is fun.
② Thank you for helping my friend.
③ We couldn't help laughing at his jokes.
④ He promised coming back soon.
⑤ I hate getting up early in the morning.

08 다음 중 빈칸에 들어갈 말로 알맞지 않은 것은? |3점|

Mia _____ to take care of sick animals.

① hopes
② wants
③ avoids
④ decided
⑤ planned

09 다음 중 어법상 옳은 문장의 개수는? |4점|

ⓐ Keeping promises are important.
ⓑ She's good at speaking English.
ⓒ Don't forget saving the file later.
ⓓ I avoid to eat junk food these days.
ⓔ My hobby is growing plants.

① 1개 ② 2개 ③ 3개
④ 4개 ⑤ 5개

10 빈칸에 들어갈 말이 순서대로 바르게 짝지어진 것은? |3점|

• He decided _____ the truth.
• I will practice _____ English.

① tell – speak
② to tell – speak
③ to tell – speaking
④ telling – to speak
⑤ telling – speaking

11 빈칸에 들어갈 말로 알맞은 것을 모두 고르면? |3점|

Paul _____ playing the violin.

① likes ② wants ③ enjoys
④ expects ⑤ stopped

12 밑줄 친 부분이 어법상 틀린 것은? |3점|

① We agreed buying a new car.
② The baby began crying loudly.
③ They'll continue to talk after lunch.
④ I gave up going to the gym.
⑤ Do you plan to study until late tonight?

13 다음 중 우리말을 영어로 잘못 옮긴 것은? |4점|

① 문 잠그는 것을 기억해.
→ Remember locking the door.
② 그녀는 하늘을 보기 위해 멈추었다.
→ She stopped to look at the sky.
③ 우리는 영어로 의사소통하려고 노력했다.
→ We tried to communicate in English.
④ 나는 엄마에게 전화하는 것을 잊어버렸다.
→ I forgot to call my mom.
⑤ 나는 혼자 일하는 것에 익숙하다.
→ I'm used to working alone.

최신기출

14 다음 우리말을 영작할 때, 밑줄 친 ①~⑤ 중 어법상 틀린 것은? |3점|

그 가수는 전화를 받기 위해 노래하기와 춤추기를 연습하는 것을 멈췄다.

→ The singer stopped to practice singing
①   ②   ③
and dancing to answer the phone.
④   ⑤

고난도

15 빈칸에 taking이 들어갈 수 없는 것은? |5점|

Sumin's hobby is ___①___ pictures.
She is good at ___②___ beautiful pictures.
However, she broke her camera last week.
She couldn't continue ___③___ pictures.
Fortunately, her father bought her a new
camera for her birthday. She was able to
start ___④___ pictures again. She planned
___⑤___ her father's picture first.

16 다음 우리말을 영어로 바르게 옮긴 것은? |3점|

> 그는 밤에 운전하는 것에 익숙하지 않다.

① He used not to driving at night.
② He is not used to drive at night.
③ He is not used to driving at night.
④ He does not used to drive at night.
⑤ He does not used to driving at night.

17 우리말과 일치하도록 할 때, 빈칸에 들어갈 말로 알맞은 것은? |3점|

> 나는 같은 실수를 하지 않으려고 노력했다.
> → I tried _____.

① make the same mistake
② to make the same mistake
③ making the same mistake
④ not to make the same mistake
⑤ not to making the same mistake

고난도

18 (A)~(C)에 들어갈 말이 바르게 짝지어진 것은? |5점|

> • Reading comic books (A) is / are fun.
> • I hope (B) seeing / to see you soon.
> • I couldn't help (C) crying / to cry .

	(A)		(B)		(C)
①	is	·····	seeing	·····	to cry
②	are	·····	seeing	·····	crying
③	is	·····	to see	·····	crying
④	are	·····	to see	·····	to cry
⑤	is	·····	seeing	·····	crying

서 술 형

19 괄호 안의 말을 알맞은 형태로 써서 문장을 완성하시오. |3점|

> The author finished _____ his new novel. (write)

[20-21] 우리말과 일치하도록 괄호 안의 말을 바르게 배열하시오. |6점, 각 3점|

20
> Alex는 방을 청소하는 데 한 시간을 썼다.
> (spent, his room, an hour, cleaning)
>
> → Alex _____
> _____.

21
> 저의 상황을 이해하려고 노력해 주셔서 감사합니다.
> (trying, my situation, understand, to)
>
> → Thank you for _____
> _____.

22 밑줄 친 우리말을 〈조건〉에 맞게 영작하시오. |4점|

> A Are you going to watch the movie again?
> B Yes. 그것은 여러 번 볼 가치가 있어.

> 조건 1. it을 주어로 할 것
>   2. worth, many times를 포함하여 6단어로 쓸 것

> → _____

23 어법상 틀린 부분을 찾아 바르게 고쳐 쓰시오. |3점|

> Making good friends are very important.

_____ → _____

26 다음 두 문장을 동명사를 이용하여 한 문장으로 쓰시오. |3점|

> I turned off the computer. I remember it.

→ I remember _____ .

24 그림을 보고, 〈조건〉에 맞게 문장을 완성하시오. |4점|

> 조건 1. 동명사를 이용할 것
> 2. busy, her homework를 포함하여 5단어로 쓸 것

→ Jenny _____

_____ right now.

고난도

27 어법상 틀린 문장 두 개를 찾아 기호를 쓰고, 바르게 고쳐 쓰시오. |8점, 각 4점|

> ⓐ Please stop talking. I need time to think.
> ⓑ We're looking forward to visiting Hawaii.
> ⓒ I gave up try to persuade my parents.
> ⓓ Do you enjoy eating alone?
> ⓔ He doesn't mind to work on weekends.
>
> * persuade 설득하다

( ) → _____

_____

( ) → _____

_____

고난도

25 다음 우리말과 일치하도록 〈조건〉에 맞게 문장을 완성하시오. |5점|

> 우리 아빠는 담배를 끊기로 결심하셨다.
>
> 조건 1. decide, quit, smoke를 이용할 것
> 2. 과거시제로 쓸 것

→ My dad _____ .

28 그림의 상황에 맞게 빈칸에 알맞은 말을 써서 문장을 완성하시오. |4점|

I had to bring my textbook, but I forgot.

→ He forgot _____ .

chapter

5

분사와 분사구문

Q. 각 표현에 알맞은 그림은?

- falling leaves □ ① □ ②
- fallen leaves □ ① □ ②

unit 1 현재분사와 과거분사

1 분사의 종류

분사는 동사원형에 -ing나 -ed를 붙인 형태로 형용사처럼 쓰인다.

현재분사: 동사원형+-ing	과거분사: 동사원형+-ed
능동(~하는) **surprising** news	수동(~된) **surprised** people
진행(~하고 있는) a **crying** girl	완료(~한) **fallen** leaves

surprise
놀라게 하다

→ **surprising** 놀라운
→ **surprised** 놀란

Look at the **shining** star in the sky!
They found the **hidden** treasure.

2 분사의 역할

분사는 형용사처럼 명사를 수식하거나 주어나 목적어를 보충 설명하는 보어 역할을 한다.

(1) 명사 수식

a **dancing** boy   **춤추는** 소년 〈분사만 있는 경우 – 명사 앞에서 수식〉

a window **broken** by a baseball   야구공에 의해 **깨진** 창문 〈수식어구와 함께 쓰인 경우 – 명사 뒤에서 수식〉

(2) 보어

The movie was **exciting**.   그 영화는 **재미있었다**. 〈주어(The movie)를 보충 설명〉

3 감정을 나타내는 분사

주어가 '어떤 감정을 일으키는' 경우에는 현재분사를 쓰고, '어떤 감정을 느끼게 되는' 경우에는 과거분사를 쓴다.

interesting 흥미로운	**interested** 흥미를 느끼는	**surprising** 놀라운	**surprised** 놀란
exciting 흥미진진한	**excited** 신이 난	**boring** 지루한	**bored** 지루해하는
shocking 충격적인	**shocked** 충격 받은	**satisfying** 만족스러운	**satisfied** 만족하는
amazing 놀라운	**amazed** 놀란	**pleasing** 기쁘게 하는	**pleased** 기쁜

His speech was **boring**.   You look **bored**.
Your idea sounds **interesting**.   She is **interested** in science.

비교 point

현재분사 vs. 동명사

둘 다 「동사원형+-ing」로 형태는 같지만 쓰임이 다르므로 주의해야 한다.

	현재분사	동명사
명사 앞	명사 수식(~하는) a **sleeping** cat 잠자고 있는 고양이	명사의 용도나 목적 설명 a **sleeping** bag 침낭 (= a bag for sleeping)
be동사 뒤	진행형(~하는 중인) He is **running**. 그는 달리고 있다.	보어(~하기, ~하는 것) His hobby is **running**. 그의 취미는 달리기이다.

개념 우선 확인 | 옳은 표현 고르기

1 깨진 유리
- ☐ breaking glass
- ☐ broken glass

2 Amy와 이야기하고 있는 남자아이
- ☐ a boy talking with Amy
- ☐ a boy talked with Amy

3 충격적인 사건
- ☐ a shocking event
- ☐ a shocked event

A 괄호 안에서 알맞은 것을 고르시오.

1 I want to eat (frying / fried) chicken.

2 Do you know the (crying / cried) girl?

3 We're (pleasing / pleased) to see him again.

4 It's important to have a (satisfying / satisfied) job.

5 The ring (finding / found) under the bed was mine.

B 괄호 안의 말을 이용하여 문장을 완성하시오.

1 That was a really _____ story. (amaze)

2 I bought a bag _____ in Italy. (make)

3 She was _____ to hear the news. (shock)

4 He likes the picture _____ by his daughter. (draw)

5 The cat _____ on the sofa is so cute. (sleep)

C 우리말과 일치하도록 괄호 안의 말을 이용하여 문장을 완성하시오.

1 James는 그의 잃어버린 강아지를 찾고 있다. (lose, puppy)

→ James is looking for _____ _____ _____.

2 나는 영어로 쓰인 편지 한 통을 발견했다. (letter, write)

→ I found _____ _____ _____ in English.

3 나는 무대에서 드럼을 치고 있는 그 남자를 안다. (man, play)

→ I know _____ _____ _____ the drums on the stage.

30초 완성 map

분사	현재분사	❶ **singing** birds	_____ 새들
	과거분사	❷ a man **caught** by the police	경찰에게 _____ 남자
	감정을 나타내는 분사	❸ We were (exciting / excited) to watch the movie. The game was (exciting / excited).	

1 분사구문

분사구문이란 「접속사+주어+동사」로 이루어진 부사절을 분사를 이용하여 부사구로 간단히 나타낸 것이다.

부사절	주절
~~Because~~ ~~we~~ arrived late, ① ② ③	we sat in the back row. ②

↓

Arriving late,	we sat in the back row.
늦게 도착했기 때문에	우리는 뒷줄에 앉았다.

분사구문 만드는 방법
① 접속사 생략
② 부사절과 주절의 주어가 같으면 부사절 주어 생략
③ 부사절의 동사를 현재분사 (동사원형+-ing)로 바꾸기

~~When she~~ entered the room, she found a present on the bed.
→ **Entering** the room, she found a present on the bed. 방에 들어갔을 때 그녀는 침대 위의 선물을 발견했다.

▶ 부사절의 동사가 진행형인 경우, be동사는 생략하고 현재분사로 시작한다.

~~While I was~~ taking a walk, I saw a rainbow in the sky.
→ **Taking** a walk, I saw a rainbow in the sky. 산책을 하다가, 나는 하늘의 무지개를 보았다.

2 분사구문의 여러 가지 의미

분사구문은 시간, 이유, 동시 동작 등의 의미를 가지므로 문맥을 잘 파악하여 해석하는 것이 중요하다.

(1) 시간: ~할 때(when), ~하는 동안(while), ~후에(after), ~전에(before)

Seeing my brother, I waved to him. 내 남동생을 봤을 때 나는 그에게 손을 흔들었다.
(= **When I saw** my brother, I waved to him.)

(2) 이유: ~ 때문에(because, since, as)

Feeling tired, he took a nap. 피곤했기 때문에 그는 낮잠을 잤다.
(= **Because he felt** tired, he took a nap.)

Having a toothache, I went to the dentist. 치통이 있었기 때문에 나는 치과에 갔다.
(= **As I had** a toothache, I went to the dentist.)

(3) 동시 동작: ~하면서(as, while)

Smiling at me, she walked toward me. 나에게 미소 지으면서 그녀는 나를 향해 걸어왔다.
(= **As she was smiling** at me, she walked toward me.)

▶ 의미를 명확히 나타내기 위해 분사구문의 접속사를 생략하지 않는 경우도 있다.

After breaking the window, he ran away. 창문을 깬 후 그는 달아났다.
(= **After he broke** the window, he ran away.)

시험 point

부사절의 동사가 be동사인 문장의 분사구문

부사절의 동사가 be동사이고 부사절과 주절의 시제가 같을 때는 being(be동사 원형+-ing)을 써서 분사구문으로 나타낸다.

Since I was busy, I forgot to call him. → **Being** busy, I forgot to call him.

개념 우선 확인 | 밑줄 친 부분의 옳은 해석 고르기

1 <u>Having no time</u>, I couldn't help you.
- ☐ 시간이 없어도
- ☐ 시간이 없었기 때문에

2 <u>Finishing my homework</u>, I started to watch TV.
- ☐ 숙제를 끝낸 후에
- ☐ 숙제를 끝내지 않아도

A 밑줄 친 부분을 분사구문으로 바꿔 쓸 때, 빈칸에 알맞은 말을 쓰시오.

1 <u>While he walked his dog</u>, he met Sumin.

→ _____ his dog, he met Sumin.

2 <u>Because she had a headache</u>, she took some medicine.

→ _____ a headache, she took some medicine.

3 <u>As they were hungry</u>, they went to a fast-food restaurant.

→ _____ hungry, they went to a fast-food restaurant.

B 자연스러운 문장이 되도록 빈칸에 알맞은 분사구문을 〈보기〉에서 골라 그 기호를 쓰시오.

| 보기 | ⓐ Before spending money | ⓑ After having dinner |
| | ⓒ Staying in New York | ⓓ Studying hard for the test |

1 _____, we visited a lot of places.

2 _____, she got a good grade.

3 _____, I washed the dishes.

4 _____, you should think carefully.

C 두 문장의 의미가 같도록 밑줄 친 부분을 부사절로 바꿔 문장을 완성하시오.

1 After <u>washing her hands</u>, she started cooking.

→ After _____, she started cooking.

2 <u>Being rich</u>, he can buy the expensive car.

→ Because _____, he can buy the expensive car.

3 <u>Playing the piano</u>, he sang a song.

→ As _____, he sang a song.

30초 완성 map

분사구문

형태 ➊
When she saw a rat, she screamed. 〈부사절〉
→ _____, she screamed. 〈분사구문〉 쥐를 보았을 때 그녀는 비명을 질렀다.

의미 ➋
Hearing the news, she began to cry. 그 소식을 _____ 그녀는 울기 시작했다.
Waking up late, I missed the bus. 늦게 _____ 나는 버스를 놓쳤다.

서술형 대비 문장 쓰기

Answers p. 9

☐ **빈칸 완성** 괄호 안의 말을 이용하여 빈칸 완성하기

01 David는 부서진 의자를 고쳤다. (break)

→ David fixed the _____ chair.

02 나는 액션 영화가 흥미롭다고 생각한다. (interest)

→ I think action movies are _____.

03 그 말하는 앵무새는 축제에서 매우 인기 있었다. (talk)

→ The _____ parrot was very popular at the festival.

04 우리는 그녀의 갑작스러운 죽음에 충격을 받았다. (shock)

→ We were _____ by her sudden death.

↻ **문장 전환** 밑줄 친 부사절을 분사구문으로 바꿔 쓰기

05 <u>Because we left early</u>, we arrived on time.

→ _____, we arrived on time.

06 <u>As they ate popcorn</u>, they watched a movie.

→ _____, they watched a movie.

07 <u>When she arrived in Busan</u>, she called her aunt.

→ _____, she called her aunt.

08 <u>While I was playing soccer</u>, I hurt my knee.

→ _____, I hurt my knee.

≡ **배열 영작** 괄호 안의 말을 바르게 배열하기

09 네 머리 위로 날아가고 있는 풍선을 봐. (your head, over, the balloon, flying)

→ Look at _____.

10 유나는 일본어로 쓰인 책을 읽고 있다. (a book, written, reading, is)

→ Yuna _____ in Japanese.

11 버스에서 내릴 때 그는 지갑을 떨어뜨렸다. (the bus, he, getting off, dropped)

→ _____, _____ his wallet.

12 시간이 거의 없기 때문에 우리는 서둘러야 한다. (little, we, have to, time, having)

→ _____, _____ hurry.

시험에 꼭 나오는 출제 포인트

Answers p. 9

출제 포인트 수식하는 말과의 관계가 능동인지 수동인지 구분하자!

우리말과 일치하도록 괄호 안의 말을 이용하여 문장을 완성하시오.

(1) 너는 춤추는 로봇을 본 적 있니? (dance)

　　→ Have you ever seen a _____ robot?

(2) 나는 도난 당한 지갑을 찾았다. (steal)

　　→ I found my _____ wallet.

> **고득점 POINT** 수식어구와 함께 쓰인 분사의 위치
>
> **우리말과 일치하도록 괄호 안의 말을 바르게 배열하시오.**
>
> 나무에 앉아 있는 새들이 노래하고 있다.
>
> (sitting, the birds, are, in the tree, singing)
>
> → _____

출제 포인트 「동사원형+-ing」가 동명사인지 현재분사인지 구분하자!

밑줄 친 부분의 쓰임이 나머지와 <u>다른</u> 것은?

① Look at the <u>crying</u> kid.
② The game was really <u>exciting</u>.
③ My favorite exercise is <u>running</u>.
④ What is he <u>talking</u> about?
⑤ The boys <u>playing</u> basketball look happy.

출제 포인트 감정을 나타내는 현재분사와 과거분사를 구분하자!

우리말과 일치하도록 괄호 안에서 알맞은 말을 고르시오.

(1) 그는 영화를 만드는 것에 관심이 있다.

　　→ He is (interesting / interested) in making movies.

(2) 이 책은 매우 인기 있지만, 나에게는 지루하다.

　　→ This book is very popular, but it's (boring / bored) to me.

> **고득점 POINT** 감정을 일으키는 경우에는 현재분사를 쓰고, 감정을 느끼는 경우에는 과거분사를 쓴다.
>
> **우리말과 일치하도록 괄호 안의 말을 이용하여 문장을 완성하시오.**
>
> 우리는 그 충격적인 소식을 듣고 매우 놀랐다.
>
> (surprise, shock)
>
> → We were very _____ to hear the _____ news.

출제 포인트 분사구문 만드는 법을 익히자!

두 문장의 의미가 같도록 빈칸에 알맞은 분사구문을 쓰시오.

(1) Because she was tired, she didn't go out with us.

　　→ _____, she didn't go out with us.

(2) After I had dinner, I went for a walk with my dog.

　　→ _____, I went for a walk with my dog.

[01-03] 빈칸에 들어갈 말로 알맞은 것을 고르시오.
|6점, 각 2점|

01

The boy _____ on the stage is Justin.

① dance ② to dance
③ danced ④ dancing
⑤ to dancing

02

She bought a novel _____ in English.

① write ② to write
③ wrote ④ written
⑤ writing

03

_____ sleepy, I went to bed early.

① Be ② To be
③ Being ④ I was
⑤ To being

04 밑줄 친 부분의 의미로 가장 적절한 것은? |3점|

Having no time, Alice couldn't eat breakfast this morning.

① Before she had no time
② Since she had no time
③ As she having no time
④ After she had no time
⑤ While she was having no time

05 두 문장의 의미가 같도록 할 때, 빈칸에 들어갈 말로 알맞은 것은? |3점|

While I was watching the movie, I fell asleep.
= _____ the movie, I fell asleep.

① Watch ② Watched ③ Watching
④ To watching ⑤ To watch

최신기출

06 다음 두 문장을 분사를 이용하여 한 문장으로 나타낼 때, 필요하지 않은 것은? |3점|

Look at the woman. She is playing the guitar.

① she ② the ③ woman
④ playing ⑤ guitar

07 빈칸에 들어갈 말로 알맞은 것을 모두 고르면? |3점|

_____ lunch, I went to the library.

① Having ② I had
③ After I had ④ I having
⑤ After having

08 밑줄 친 부분이 어법상 옳은 것은? |3점|

① That movie looks bored.
② I saw a bird flied in the sky.
③ She is exciting about the trip.
④ Being crying badly, the baby woke up.
⑤ Did you see the boy running in the park?

09 빈칸에 들어갈 말이 순서대로 바르게 짝지어진 것은? |3점|

> A How was the movie?
> B It was really _____! I was _____ by the special effects.

① amazing – surprising
② amazing – surprised
③ amazed – surprised
④ amazed – surprising
⑤ amazed – surprise

13 밑줄 친 부분의 쓰임이 〈보기〉와 다른 것은? |4점|

> 보기   The man waiting for me is my uncle.

① There is a kite flying in the sky.
② His job is teaching Korean to foreigners.
③ This is a really surprising story.
④ There is a boy swimming in the pool.
⑤ Look at the cat sleeping on the roof.

[10-12] 밑줄 친 부분이 어법상 틀린 것을 고르시오.
|9점, 각 3점|

10 ① I felt tired after a long walk.
② Your plan sounds interesting.
③ Look at the man lying on the grass.
④ His speech was long and bored.
⑤ The ending of the story was satisfying.

고난도

14 다음 중 어법상 옳은 문장의 개수는? |5점|

> ⓐ Don't wake the sleeping baby.
> ⓑ The musical was bored.
> ⓒ He is interested in taking photos.
> ⓓ She bought a car made in Germany.
> ⓔ I was shocking to see my report card.
> * report card 성적표

① 1개　　　　② 2개　　　　③ 3개
④ 4개　　　　⑤ 5개

11 ① Having a cold, I took some medicine.
② I know the girl wearing a red coat.
③ Eating popcorn, I watched TV.
④ I found a broken watch on the street.
⑤ Smiled brightly, she walked toward me.

15 우리말과 일치하도록 할 때, 빈칸에 들어갈 말로 알맞은 것은? |4점|

> 너는 전화 통화를 하고 있는 그 남자를 아니?
> → Do you know _____?

① the talking man on the phone
② the talked man on the phone
③ the man talking on the phone
④ the man talked on the phone
⑤ the man is talking on the phone

12 ① The store sells used items.
② I ate fried chicken for dinner.
③ Do you like the sound of the fallen rain?
④ She bought an expensive bag made in Italy.
⑤ We went to the sea to watch the rising sun.

16 밑줄 친 부분의 쓰임이 〈보기〉와 같은 것의 개수는? |5점|

> 보기 They looked at the shining stars.

ⓐ Let's swim in the swimming pool.
ⓑ Your idea is very interesting.
ⓒ Do you know the crying girl?
ⓓ My hobby is learning new languages.
ⓔ I don't enjoy listening to classical music.

① 1개   ② 2개   ③ 3개
④ 4개   ⑤ 5개

17 밑줄 친 부분을 부사절로 바꿀 때, 알맞지 않은 것은? |4점|

① Brushing her teeth, she went to bed.
  → After she brushed her teeth
② Listening to music, I cleaned my room.
  → Since I was listening to music
③ Having a cold, he didn't come to school.
  → Because he had a cold
④ Saying goodbye, she got on the train.
  → As she was saying goodbye
⑤ Wanting to lose weight, I started exercising.
  → Because I wanted to lose weight

18 밑줄 친 부분이 어법상 옳은 것끼리 짝지어진 것은? |5점|

ⓐ Can you see the cat hiding in the box?
ⓑ Be careful of the breaking glass.
ⓒ I don't want to listen to the bored lecture.
ⓓ Are you satisfied with your test score?
ⓔ I was amazing at the beautiful view.

① ⓐ, ⓒ   ② ⓐ, ⓓ   ③ ⓑ, ⓔ
④ ⓒ, ⓓ   ⑤ ⓒ, ⓔ

서술형

[19-20] 괄호 안의 말을 이용하여 문장을 완성하시오.
|6점, 각 3점|

19
The ending of the movie was _____.
(shock)

20
They walked on the _____ leaves.
(fall)

[21-22] 밑줄 친 부분을 분사구문으로 바꿔 쓰시오.
|6점, 각 3점|

21
When I traveled abroad, I enjoyed trying street food.
→ _____, I enjoyed trying street food.

22
Because he was angry, he didn't say anything.
→ _____, he didn't say anything.

23 그림의 내용과 일치하도록 〈보기〉에서 알맞은 단어를 골라 대화를 완성하시오. |5점|

보기	cap	glasses	hold	wear

A Which one is your brother?
B The boy _____ is my
   brother.

최신기출

24 〈보기〉에서 알맞은 접속사를 골라 밑줄 친 부분을 부사절로 바꿔 쓰시오. |4점|

보기	before	while	since

<u>Knowing a shortcut</u>, I was able to get there in time.   * shortcut 지름길

→ _____,
   I was able to get there in time.

고난도

25 밑줄 친 ⓐ~ⓓ 중 어법상 틀린 것을 찾아 기호를 쓰고, 바르게 고쳐 쓰시오. |5점|

Last night, I was ⓐ <u>taking</u> a walk near the forest. Suddenly, somebody screamed, "Fire! Fire!" There was a ⓑ <u>burning</u> cabin in the forest. ⓒ <u>Seeing</u> the fire, I called 119. Soon firefighters arrived. After the fire, there was nothing ⓓ <u>leaving</u> in the cabin.

(   ) → _____

26 주어진 문장과 의미가 같도록 빈칸에 알맞은 말을 쓰시오. |4점|

As he was making spaghetti, he sang a song.

→ _____ _____, he sang a song.

고난도

27 다음 우리말을 〈조건〉에 맞게 영작하시오. |5점|

우리는 그 소식을 듣고 기뻐했다.

조건 1. please, hear, the news를 이용할 것
     2. 7단어로 쓸 것

→ _____

고난도

28 어제 수민(Sumin)이가 한 일을 순서대로 나타낸 그림을 보고, 〈조건〉에 맞게 영작하시오. |5점|

had lunch   **rode her bicycle**

조건 1. 접속사 after를 포함한 분사구문을 이용하여
        7단어로 쓸 것
     2. 과거시제로 쓸 것

→ _____

_____

chapter

.6

수동태

The cat **was chased by** the mouse.

① ②

Q. 위 문장의 내용과 일치하는 그림은?

☐ ① ☐ ②

수동태의 기본 개념

1 능동태와 수동태

능동태는 주어가 어떤 행위를 하는 경우에 쓰고, 수동태는 주어가 어떤 행동을 당하거나 영향을 받는 경우에 쓴다.

| Romeo | **loves** | Juliet | 로미오는 줄리엣을 **사랑한다**. 〈능동태〉 |
| Juliet | **is loved** | by Romeo. | 줄리엣은 로미오에 의해 **사랑받는다**. 〈수동태〉 |

2 수동태의 형태와 의미

수동태는 「be동사+p.p.」의 형태로 나타내며, '(주어)가 어떤 행동을 받다/당하다'의 의미이다. 수동태 문장에서는 동사 뒤에 「by+목적격」을 써서 행위자를 나타낸다.

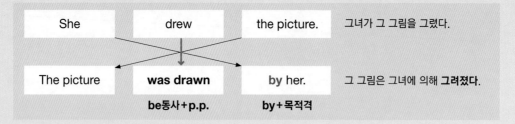

She	drew	the picture.	그녀가 그 그림을 그렸다.
The picture	**was drawn**	**by** her.	그 그림은 그녀에 의해 **그려졌다**.
	be동사+p.p.	by+목적격	

The novel **is read** by many teenagers.
The light bulb **was invented** by Thomas Edison.

> 행위자가 막연한 일반인이거나 분명하지 않을 때, 행위자보다 상황이나 행동이 더 중요할 때는 「by+목적격」을 생략할 수 있다.
> English **is spoken** all over the world. 〈행위자가 일반인일 때〉
> My bike **was stolen** yesterday. 〈행위자가 분명하지 않을 때〉
> Five people **were killed** in the accident. 〈상황이 중요할 때〉

3 수동태의 시제

(1) 현재시제: am/are/is+p.p.

| Computers | **are used** | everywhere. | 컴퓨터는 모든 곳에서 **사용된다**. |

The kitchen **is cleaned** every day.

(2) 과거시제: was/were+p.p.

| The movie | **was released** | yesterday. | 그 영화는 어제 **개봉되었다**. |

All flights **were canceled** because of the storm.

(3) 미래시제: will be+p.p.

| The festival | **will be held** | next month. | 그 축제는 다음 달에 **열릴 것이다**. |

The fence **will be painted** by my dad.

개념 우선 확인 | 밑줄 친 부분의 옳은 해석 고르기

1 The actor is loved by many fans.
   ☐ 사랑한다
   ☐ 사랑받는다

2 A frog was caught by a boy.
   ☐ 잡았다
   ☐ 잡혔다

A 괄호 안에서 알맞은 것을 고르시오.

1 These cookies (baked / were baked) yesterday.

2 The photo (took / was taken) by a famous photographer.

3 A lot of tourists (visit / are visited) the museum every year.

4 The 34th Olympic Games (will held / will be held) in Los Angeles.

B 다음 문장을 수동태로 바꿔 쓰시오.

1 People use the Internet almost every day.
   → The Internet _____ _____ (by people) almost every day.

2 The teacher respected Emma's opinion.
   → Emma's opinion _____ _____ _____ the teacher.

3 Big animals eat small animals.
   → Small animals _____ _____ _____ big animals.

4 He will translate this book.
   → This book _____ _____ _____ _____ _____.

C 우리말과 일치하도록 괄호 안의 말을 이용하여 문장을 완성하시오.

1 그 건물은 2002년에 지어졌다. (build)
   → The building _____ in 2002.

2 그의 새 앨범이 다음 달에 출시될 것이다. (release)
   → His new album _____ next month.

3 그 노래는 전 세계에서 많은 사람들에 의해 불려진다. (sing)
   → The song _____ many people around the world.

30초 완성 map

| 수동태 | 형태 | ❶ Someone stole my wallet. 〈능동태〉 → My wallet _____ _____ _____ someone. 〈수동태〉 |
| | 시제 | ❷ • 현재: The song _____ by many people. (love) • 과거: These books _____ by Jim. (write) • 미래: The work _____ by Amy. (finish) |

수동태의 여러 가지 형태

1 수동태의 부정문과 의문문

(1) 수동태의 부정문: be동사+not+p.p.

| This building | **was designed** | by Gaudi. | 그 건물은 가우디에 의해 **설계되었다.** 〈긍정문〉 |
| This building | **was not designed** | by Gaudi. | 그 건물은 가우디에 의해 **설계되지 않았다.** 〈부정문〉 |

Rome **was not built** in a day.
The tickets **aren't sold** on the website.
These pictures **were not painted** by Picasso.

(2) 수동태의 의문문: Be동사+주어+p.p. ~? / 의문사+be동사+주어+p.p. ~?

		These photos	**were taken**	by Lucy.	이 사진들은 Lucy에 의해 **찍혔다.**
	Were	these photos	**taken**	by Lucy?	이 사진들은 Lucy에 의해 **찍혔니?**
When	**were**	these photos	**taken**	by Lucy?	**언제** 이 사진들은 Lucy에 의해 **찍혔니?**

Was the book **written** by J.K. Rowling?
How is cheese **made**?
Why was the window **opened**?

2 조동사가 있는 수동태

조동사가 있는 문장의 수동태는 「조동사+be+p.p.」로 쓴다.

| He | **can** | **repair** | the car. | 그는 그 차를 **수리할 수 있다.** 〈능동태〉 |
| The car | **can** | **be repaired** | by him. | 그 차는 그에 의해 **수리될 수 있다.** 〈수동태〉 |

The work **must be finished** by tomorrow.
Everyone **should be treated** equally.

▶ 조동사가 있는 수동태 문장의 부정문은 「조동사+not+be+p.p.」로 쓴다.

This opportunity **should not be missed**.
Knives **may not be used** by children.

개념 우선 확인 | 옳은 문장 고르기

1 그 경기는 취소되지 않았다.

☐ The game did not cancel.
☐ The game was not canceled.

2 약속은 지켜져야만 한다.

☐ Promises should kept.
☐ Promises should be kept.

A 괄호 안에서 알맞은 것을 고르시오.

1 When (did / was) the cake baked?

2 (Was / Were) the movie ticket bought by him?

3 The classroom (should cleaned / should be cleaned) every day.

4 The essay (didn't / wasn't) written by Paul.

B 다음 문장을 수동태로 바꿔 쓰시오. (단, 줄임말로 쓸 것)

1 I didn't make the chocolate.

→ The chocolate _____ _____ by me.

2 Did you write the report?

→ _____ _____ _____ _____ by you?

3 People should not break the law.

→ The law _____ _____ _____ (by people).

C 우리말과 일치하도록 괄호 안의 말을 이용하여 문장을 완성하시오.

1 네 자전거는 Jack이 고칠 수 있어. (can, fix)

→ Your bike _____ _____ _____ by Jack.

2 그 도둑은 경찰에게 잡혔니? (catch)

→ _____ the thief _____ _____ the police?

3 그 옷은 차가운 물에서 세탁되어야 한다. (must, wash)

→ The clothes _____ _____ _____ in cold water.

4 텔레비전은 언제 발명되었나요? (when, invent)

→ _____ _____ the television _____ ?

30초 완성 map

수동태의 형태	부정문	❶ Tom didn't break the window. → The window _____ _____ _____ by Tom.
	의문문	❷ Did Tom break the window? → _____ _____ _____ _____ by Tom?
	조동사+수동태	❸ Milk (should kept / should be kept) in the refrigerator.

1 동사구의 수동태

동사구 전체를 하나의 동사처럼 취급하여 수동태로 만든다. 동사구의 동사만 「be동사+p.p.」 형태로 바꾸고 나머지는 그대로 쓴다.

| Kids | look up to | teachers. | 아이들은 선생님을 존경한다. 〈능동태〉 |
| Teachers | **are looked up to** | by kids. | 선생님은 아이들에 의해 **존경받는다.** 〈수동태〉 |

Volunteers looked after the dogs.
→ The dogs **were looked after** by volunteers.
She may put off our plans again.
→ Our plans may **be put off** again (by her).

2 수동태로 쓰지 않는 동사

(1) **목적어가 없는 자동사:** appear, disappear, seem, happen, arrive, consist 등
Suddenly a rainbow **appeared**.
       ↘ was appeared (×)
Accidents can **happen** anywhere.
       ↘ be happened (×)

(2) **상태나 소유를 나타내는 타동사:** have, become, resemble, possess, fit 등
I **have** an old camera.   An old camera is had by me. (×)
Paul **resembles** his father a lot.   His father is resembled a lot by Paul. (×)

3 by 이외의 전치사를 쓰는 수동태 표현

be filled with	~으로 가득 차다	**be tired** of	~에 싫증이 나다
be satisfied with	~에 만족하다	**be worried** about	~에 대해 걱정하다
be covered with	~으로 덮여 있다	**be interested** in	~에 흥미가(관심이) 있다
be pleased with	~에 기뻐하다	**be surprised** at(by)	~에 놀라다

She **is satisfied** with her life in New York.
The mountain **is covered** with snow.
I'm **interested** in classical music.
We **were surprised** at the news.

시험 point

동사구가 있는 문장의 수동태 전환 시 주의할 점

「by+목적격」이 동사구 바로 다음에 나올 때 전치사가 연이어 나올 수 있으므로 형태에 주의한다.

We took care of the bird.
→ The bird (was taken care by / was taken care of by) us.

개념 우선 확인 | 옳은 문장 고르기

1 그는 친구들의 놀림을 받았다.
- ☐ He was laughed at his friends.
- ☐ He was laughed at by his friends.

2 그 정원은 꽃으로 가득 차 있다.
- ☐ The garden is filled by flowers.
- ☐ The garden is filled with flowers.

A 〈보기〉에서 알맞은 전치사를 골라 문장을 완성하시오.

보기	of	with	in	at

1 Emily is interested _____ K-pop.

2 I was surprised _____ his behavior.

3 I am tired _____ eating salad every day.

4 They were pleased _____ his success.

B 밑줄 친 부분을 어법에 맞게 고쳐 쓰시오.

1 A rabbit was run over a car.

2 He brought up by his grandmother.

3 The singer was appeared on the stage.

4 Many good things can be happened to us.

C 우리말과 일치하도록 괄호 안의 말을 이용하여 문장을 완성하시오.

1 그녀는 수학 시험에 대해 걱정한다. (worry)

→ She _____ _____ _____ the math test.

2 그 오래된 가구는 먼지로 덮여 있었다. (cover)

→ The old furniture _____ _____ _____ dust.

3 우리의 여행은 미뤄질 것이다. (put off)

→ Our trip _____ _____ _____ _____.

4 그 고양이는 내 여동생에 의해 돌보아졌다. (take care of)

→ The cat _____ _____ _____ _____ _____ my sister.

30초 완성 map

수동태
- 동사구 수동태 — ❶ He (looked up to / was looked up to) by everyone.
- 수동태로 쓰지 않는 동사 — ❷ The cat (appeared / was appeared) on the roof.
  I (don't resemble / am not resembled with) my parents.
- by 이외의 전치사를 쓰는 수동태 — ❸ I'm tired _____ cold weather.
  We're satisfied _____ the results.

빈칸 완성 괄호 안의 말을 이용하여 빈칸 완성하기

01 그 크리스마스 트리는 학생들에 의해 장식되었다. (decorate)

→ The Christmas tree _____ _____ _____ the students.

02 이 책은 그 작가가 쓴 것이 아니었다. (write)

→ This book _____ _____ _____ _____ the author.

03 그 들판은 아름다운 꽃들로 덮여 있었다. (cover)

→ The field _____ _____ _____ beautiful flowers.

04 이 상자는 여러 가지로 사용될 수 있다. (can, use)

→ This box _____ _____ _____ in many ways.

문장 전환 수동태 문장으로 바꿔 쓰기

05 Lucy waters the flowers every morning.

→ _____ every morning.

06 The doctor looked after many patients.

→ _____ by the doctor.

07 The earthquake destroyed buildings and roads. * earthquake 지진

→ _____ by the earthquake.

08 The company will introduce a new smartwatch.

→ _____ by the company.

영작 완성 우리말에 맞게 문장 완성하기

09 이 꽃병은 내가 깨뜨리지 않았다. (break)

→ This vase _____.

10 컴퓨터는 언제 발명되었나요? (invent, computers)

→ When _____?

11 그 회의 시간은 변경되지 않아야 한다. (change, should)

→ The meeting time _____.

12 Katie는 그녀의 현재 직업에 만족한다. (satisfy, current job)

→ Katie _____.

시험에 꼭 나오는 출제 포인트

출제 포인트 1 수동태 문장에서 동사의 형태에 주의하자!

다음 문장을 수동태로 바꿔 쓰시오.

(1) Carl Benz invented the car.

→ The car _____ _____ _____ Carl Benz.

(2) He carried the heavy boxes.

→ The heavy boxes _____ _____ _____ _____.

출제 포인트 2 수동태의 부정문과 의문문의 형태에 주의하자!

밑줄 친 부분이 어법상 틀린 것은?

① Where <u>was</u> the movie <u>shot</u>? * shoot (영화를) 촬영하다
② When <u>was</u> the package <u>delivered</u>?
③ The picture <u>wasn't taken</u> by Peter.
④ The pizza <u>didn't made</u> by my mom.
⑤ <u>Was</u> the frog <u>kissed</u> by the princess?

출제 포인트 3 조동사가 있는 수동태의 형태를 기억하자!

다음 문장을 수동태로 바꿔 쓰시오.

We must change the law.

→ The law _____ _____ _____
by us.

> **고득점 POINT** 조동사가 있는 수동태의 부정문
>
> **밑줄 친 부분을 어법에 맞게 고쳐 쓰시오.**
>
> Promises <u>should be not broken</u>.
>
> → _____

출제 포인트 4 by 이외의 전치사를 쓰는 수동태 표현을 기억하자!

우리말과 일치하도록 빈칸에 알맞은 전치사를 쓰시오.

(1) 그 가게는 꽃으로 가득 차 있다.

The store is filled _____ flowers.

(2) 너는 그 시험에 대해 걱정하고 있니?

Are you worried _____ the test?

> **고득점 POINT** 동사구의 수동태
>
> **우리말과 일치하도록 괄호 안의 말을 이용하여 문장을 완성하시오.**
>
> 나의 알람 시계는 엄마에 의해 꺼졌다. (turn off)
> → My alarm clock _____
> my mom.

[01-03] 빈칸에 들어갈 말로 알맞은 것을 고르시오.

|6점, 각 2점|

01

The art gallery _____ by many tourists.

① visits
② visited
③ is visited
④ is visiting
⑤ has visited

02

Fortunately, the flight _____.

① not canceled
② didn't cancel
③ was canceling
④ not be canceled
⑤ wasn't canceled

03

These photos _____ last year.

① are taken
② was taken
③ were taken
④ have taken
⑤ were taking

04 다음 중 밑줄 친 부분을 생략할 수 있는 것은? |3점|

① Hangul was created by King Sejong.
② English is spoken by people in Canada.
③ The cookies were made by Kate.
④ The picture was painted by Jack's dad.
⑤ The window was broken by my neighbor yesterday.

05 다음 문장을 수동태로 바르게 바꾼 것은? |2점|

A little boy wrote the poem.

① The poem written by a little boy.
② The poem is written by a little boy.
③ The poem did written by a little boy.
④ The poem was written by a little boy.
⑤ The poem were written by a little boy.

06 빈칸에 들어갈 말이 순서대로 바르게 짝지어진 것은?|3점|

• The earth should be protected _____ us.
• We are tired _____ waiting in line.

① by – of
② with – of
③ of – with
④ of – in
⑤ by – in

[07-08] 어법상 옳은 것을 고르시오. |8점, 각 4점|

07
① Why the plan was delayed?
② Emma is interested with musicals.
③ What language is spoken in Egypt?
④ The twins are resembled their mother.
⑤ Children should be taken care by parents.

08
① Did she surprised at the news?
② The word doesn't used these days.
③ Alex was laughed at by his friends.
④ Good things will be happened someday.
⑤ Many houses was damaged by the flood.

09 수동태로 바꿀 수 <u>없는</u> 문장은?　　　　|4점|

① She has a diamond ring.
② We will visit the museum.
③ I looked up to the professor.
④ They didn't believe the rumor.
⑤ Did Jack take these photos?

최신기출

10 다음 우리말을 영작할 때, 밑줄 친 ⓐ~ⓔ 중 어법상 <u>틀린</u> 것은?　　　　|3점|

> 그 컴퓨터는 하루 안에 수리될 수 없다.
> The computer <u>can't</u> <u>is</u> <u>fixed</u> <u>in</u> <u>one day</u>.
> 　　　　　　 ⓐ 　 ⓑ 　 ⓒ 　 ⓓ 　 ⓔ

① ⓐ　　② ⓑ　　③ ⓒ　　④ ⓓ　　⑤ ⓔ

최신기출

11 괄호 안의 말을 배열하여 우리말을 영작할 때 다섯 번째 오는 단어는?　　　　|3점|

> 그 영화는 언제 개봉될 예정인가요?
> (be, will, when, the, film, released)

① be　　　　② the　　　　③ will
④ film　　　⑤ released

12 빈칸에 들어갈 말이 나머지와 <u>다른</u> 것은?　　　　|4점|

① The room is filled _____ balloons.
② The roof is covered _____ snow.
③ I'm not satisfied _____ the product.
④ Are you worried _____ something?
⑤ We were pleased _____ her success.

13 주어진 문장을 수동태로 <u>잘못</u> 바꾼 것은?　　　　|4점|

① A car ran over something.
　→ Something was run over by a car.
② My sister looked after the puppy.
　→ The puppy was looked after by my sister.
③ My grandparents brought me up.
　→ I was brought up by my grandparents.
④ The principal put off the meeting.
　→ The meeting was put off by the principal.
⑤ Jane turned off the TV.
　→ The TV turned off by Jane.

14 다음 우리말을 영어로 바르게 옮긴 것은?　　　　|3점|

> 너는 K-pop에 관심이 있니?

① Do you interested in K-pop?
② Do you interested with K-pop?
③ Are you interested at K-pop?
④ Are you interested in K-pop?
⑤ Are you interested with K-pop?

고난도

15 어법상 <u>틀린</u> 것을 <u>모두</u> 고르면?　　　　|5점|

① The book was covered with dirt.
② The airplane will be arrived soon.
③ When should the report be done?
④ The store is had by my aunt.
⑤ The living room must be cleaned today.

16 빈칸 ⓐ~ⓓ에 들어갈 말이 아닌 것은? |4점|

- I'm tired ___ⓐ___ your complaining.
- Don't be worried ___ⓑ___ your future.
- Ms. Kim is satisfied ___ⓒ___ her job.
- They were surprised ___ⓓ___ the news.

① at　　　② in　　　③ of
④ with　　⑤ about

17 밑줄 친 부분을 잘못 고친 것은? |4점|

① Jenny is resembled her mother a lot.
　　　(→ resembles)
② The planet discovered in 1988.
　　　(→ was discovered)
③ This room will painted tomorrow.
　　　(→ will paint)
④ The actor was appeared on the stage.
　　　(→ appeared)
⑤ Eggs should keep in the refrigerator.
　　　(→ should be kept)

18 빈칸 ⓐ와 ⓑ에 들어갈 말이 바르게 짝지어진 것은? |4점|

A I heard that BTS will have a concert soon.
B Really? I really want to go to it.
A The tickets will ___ⓐ___ online.
B But many people will try to ___ⓑ___ them. I don't think I can get one.

① sell – buy　　　② sell – be bought
③ sold – buy　　　④ be sold – buy
⑤ be sold – be bought

서 술 형

[19-20] 다음 문장을 수동태로 바꿀 때 빈칸에 알맞은 말을 쓰시오. |6점, 각 3점|

19

A superhero saved the world.

→ The world _____
a superhero.

20

Many Americans look up to Abraham Lincoln.

→ Abraham Lincoln _____
many Americans.

[21-22] 우리말과 일치하도록 괄호 안의 말을 바르게 배열하시오. |6점, 각 3점|

21

인터넷은 언제 발명되었나요?
(the Internet, when, invented, was)

→ _____
_____ ?

22

정크 푸드는 아이들에게 판매되어서는 안 된다.
(children, be, to, not, sold, should)

→ Junk food _____
_____ .

23 다음 그림과 일치하도록 〈보기〉에서 알맞은 단어를 골라 문장을 완성하시오. (필요하면 형태를 바꿀 것)

|4점, 각 2점|

(1) 　　(2)

Photo by Lisa Kim　　Book by John Brown

보기	break	take	read	write

(1) The photo ＿＿＿＿ ＿＿＿＿ ＿＿＿＿

　　Lisa Kim.

(2) The book ＿＿＿＿ ＿＿＿＿ ＿＿＿＿

　　John Brown.

24 우리말과 일치하도록 괄호 안의 말을 이용하여 문장을 완성하시오.

|4점|

월드컵이 내년에 개최될 것이다. (will, hold)

→ The World Cup ＿＿＿＿＿＿＿＿＿＿＿＿＿＿

　　next year.

25 표를 보고, 빈칸에 알맞은 말을 넣어 대화를 완성하시오.

|4점, 각 2점|

	Designer	**Built**
The Eiffel Tower	Gustave Eiffel	-
The Leaning Tower of Pisa	-	12th century

A　Who designed the Eiffel Tower?

B　The Eiffel Tower (1) ＿＿＿＿＿＿＿＿

　　＿＿＿＿＿＿ ＿＿＿＿＿＿ Gustave Eiffel.

A　When was the Leaning Tower of Pisa built?

B　The Leaning Tower of Pisa (2) ＿＿＿＿＿＿

　　＿＿＿＿＿＿ in the 12th century.

26 우리말과 일치하도록 괄호 안의 단어를 이용하여 문장을 완성하시오.

|6점, 각 3점|

그 제품에 만족하지 않으신다면, 일주일 이내에 환불 받을 것입니다.

↓

If you (1) ＿＿＿＿ ＿＿＿＿ ＿＿＿＿

＿＿＿＿ the product, the money (2) ＿＿＿＿

＿＿＿＿ ＿＿＿＿ within a week.

(satisfy, refund, will)

27 다음 우리말을 〈조건〉에 맞게 영작하시오. |5점|

그 전쟁에서 많은 사람들이 죽었다.

| 조건 | 1. a lot of people, kill, in, the war를 이용할 것 (필요하면 형태를 바꿀 것)
2. 총 9단어로 쓸 것 |

→ ＿＿＿＿＿＿＿＿＿＿＿＿＿＿＿＿＿＿

＿＿＿＿＿＿＿＿＿＿＿＿＿＿＿＿＿＿

28 밑줄 친 ⓐ~ⓓ 중 어법상 틀린 것을 찾아 기호를 쓰고, 바르게 고쳐 쓰시오.

|5점|

A jewelry shop in my town ⓐ was robbed yesterday. The robbers ⓑ were not caught on the CCTV camera, but the police ⓒ found some fingerprints there. The robbers ⓓ will catch soon. *rob (가게를) 털다　fingerprint 지문

(＿＿) → ＿＿＿＿＿＿＿＿＿＿＿＿

chapter

07

대명사

There are few people at the beach.

Q. 위 문장이 나타내는 해변은?

☐ ①   ☐ ②

부정대명사 I (one, another, other)

1   one

앞에서 언급된 것과 같은 종류의 사물이나 사람을 가리킬 때는 one이나 ones를 쓴다.

I lost my phone. I should buy a new **one**.

⟨one = a phone⟩

I lost my shoes. I should buy new **ones**.

⟨ones = shoes⟩

▶ 앞에서 언급된 것과 동일한 대상을 가리킬 때는 it이나 them을 쓴다.

I lost *my phone*, but I found **it** under my bed. ⟨it = my phone⟩
I bought *new sunglasses*. I'm wearing **them** today. ⟨them = new sunglasses⟩

2   one, another, the other

정해진 범위 안에서 대상을 '하나씩' 가리킬 때 사용한다.

(1) 둘 중에서

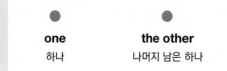

one	**the other**	I have two caps.
하나	나머지 남은 하나	**One** is yellow, and **the other** is blue.

(2) 셋 중에서

one	**another**	**the other**	There are three flavors.
하나	또 다른 하나	나머지 남은 하나	**One** is vanilla, **another** is chocolate, and **the other** is strawberry.

3   some, others, the others

여러 대상을 묶어서 가리킬 때 사용한다.

some	**others**	There are a lot of students in the playground.
몇몇	다른 몇몇	**Some** play football. **Others** play basketball.

some	**the others**	There are eight roses in the vase.
몇몇	나머지 모두	**Some** are red, and **the others** are white.

비교 point

another vs. the other

여러 대상 중 '또 다른 하나'를 가리킬 때는 another를, 두 대상이나 여러 대상 중 '나머지 하나'를 가리킬 때는 the other를 쓴다.

1   I have two bags. One was made in Italy, and (another / the other) was made in France.

2   I don't like the design of this bag. Can you show me (another / the other)?

1 There are two cars. The red _____ is hers.

☐ it   ☐ one   ☐ ones

2 I have two pets. One is a cat, and _____ is a dog.

☐ another   ☐ other   ☐ the other

A   괄호 안에서 알맞은 것을 고르시오.

1 My sneakers are too old. I need new (one / ones).

2 My uncle bought me a smartwatch. I love (one / it).

3 Some enjoy outdoor activities, but (others / another) don't.

4 One of the twins is a girl, and (another / the other) is a boy.

5 There are three rooms in my house. One is my parents', (other / another) is my brother's, and the other is mine.

B   빈칸에 알맞은 부정대명사를 〈보기〉에서 골라 쓰시오. (단, 한 번씩만 사용할 것)

보기	one	another	others	the other

1 I don't like this color. Can you show me _____?

2 **A** Is there a bank near here?   **B** Yes, there's _____ around the corner.

3 She can speak two languages. One is French, and _____ is Japanese.

4 Some like action movies, and _____ like horror movies.

C   우리말과 일치하도록 괄호 안의 말과 부정대명사를 이용하여 문장을 완성하시오.

1 그 감독은 작년에 또 다른 영화를 만들었다. (make, movie)

→ The director _____ last year.

2 내 자전거가 고장 났다. 나는 새것을 하나 사고 싶다. (new)

→ My bike is broken. I want to buy _____.

3 나는 많은 책을 가지고 있다. 몇 권은 만화책이고, 나머지는 모두 소설이다. (novel)

→ I have many books. Some are comic books, and _____.

30초 완성 map

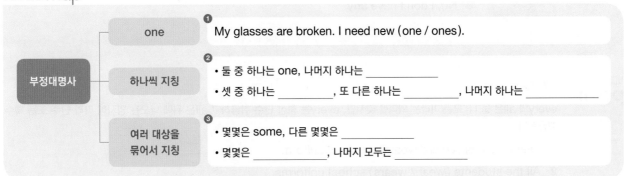

부정대명사	one	❶ My glasses are broken. I need new (one / ones).
	하나씩 지칭	❷ • 둘 중 하나는 one, 나머지 하나는 _____ • 셋 중 하나는 _____, 또 다른 하나는 _____, 나머지 하나는 _____
	여러 대상을 묶어서 지칭	❸ • 몇몇은 some, 다른 몇몇은 _____ • 몇몇은 _____, 나머지 모두는 _____

부정대명사 II (each, every, both, all, some, any)

1 each, every

each는 '각각(의)'이라는 의미이고, every는 '모든'이라는 의미이다. 둘 다 단수 취급한다.

each	**Each** person was given a bottle of water.
	Each of the students has a different goal.
every	**Every** employee has to attend the meeting.

2 both, all

both는 '둘 다(의)'라는 의미이고, 항상 복수 취급한다. all은 '모두, 모든 (것)'이라는 의미이고, 뒤에 나오는 명사에 따라 단수 또는 복수 취급한다.

both	**Both** windows are broken.	
	Both (of) my parents are teachers.	
all	**All** (of) my friends have smartphones.	〈all (of)+복수명사 → 복수 취급〉
	All (of) the money was stolen last night.	〈all (of)+단수명사 → 단수 취급〉

▶ 「both of+대명사」, 「all of+대명사」로 쓰는 경우에는 of를 생략할 수 없다.

All of us were surprised at the news.

3 some, any

'약간(의), 조금(의)'이라는 의미이며, some은 긍정문이나 권유하는 의문문에 주로 쓰고, any는 부정문과 의문문에 주로 쓴다.

some	I bought **some** bread and cookies.
	A Would you like **some** ice cream? B Yes, I'd like **some**.
any	I don't have **any** money.
	A Do you have **any** questions? B No, I don't have **any**.

비교 point

every vs. all

every와 all은 둘 다 '모든'이라는 의미를 갖지만, every는 항상 단수 취급하고 all은 뒤에 나오는 명사에 따라 단수 또는 복수 취급한다.

1 Every student (wear / wears) a school uniform.

2 All the students (wear / wears) school uniforms.

1 모든 사람
- ☐ some people
- ☐ every person

2 내 남동생들 둘 다
- ☐ all my brothers
- ☐ both my brothers

3 우리 모두
- ☐ all us
- ☐ all of us

A 괄호 안에서 알맞은 것을 고르시오.

1 Please read each (sentence / sentences) carefully.

2 I'd like to have (any / some) chocolate.

3 All the people in this town (was / were) shocked by the accident.

4 I have a cat and a dog. (Both / Each) of them are cute.

B 빈칸에 알맞은 말을 〈보기〉에서 골라 쓰시오. (단, 한 번씩만 사용할 것)

보기	each	all	some	any

1 _____ the windows are open.

2 _____ person has a different opinion.

3 I don't have _____ plans for this weekend.

4 I bought _____ new clothes for the trip.

C 우리말과 일치하도록 괄호 안의 말을 이용하여 문장을 완성하시오.

1 우리 둘 다 라면을 좋아한다. (like, us)

→ _____ _____ _____ _____ instant noodles.

2 이 방의 모든 식물은 햇빛을 필요로 한다. (need)

→ _____ plant in this room _____ sunlight.

3 각 방에는 두 개의 침대와 한 개의 화장실이 있다. (room, have)

→ _____ _____ _____ two beds and one bathroom.

4 가게의 모든 과일은 신선하다. (the fruit)

→ _____ _____ _____ in the store is fresh.

30초 완성 map

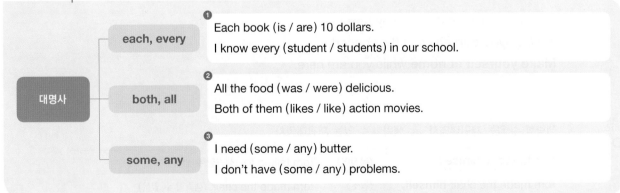

대명사

- **each, every**
  - ❶ Each book (is / are) 10 dollars.
  - I know every (student / students) in our school.

- **both, all**
  - ❷ All the food (was / were) delicious.
  - Both of them (likes / like) action movies.

- **some, any**
  - ❸ I need (some / any) butter.
  - I don't have (some / any) problems.

재귀대명사는 인칭대명사의 소유격이나 목적격에 -self/-selves를 붙인 형태로 '~ 자신'이라는 의미이다.

I → **myself**	you → **yourself**	he → **himself**	she → **herself**
we → **ourselves**	you → **yourselves**	it → **itself**	they → **themselves**

1 목적어로 쓰이는 재귀대명사

주어와 목적어가 동일한 대상일 때, 목적어로 재귀대명사를 쓴다.

Peter	introduced	him.	〈Peter ≠ him〉
Peter	introduced	**himself.**	〈Peter = himself〉

We should learn to respect **ourselves**. 〈We = ourselves〉
Kate is looking at **herself** in the mirror. 〈Kate = herself〉

재귀대명사와 자주 쓰이는 동사

cut oneself	베다	**burn oneself**	데다, 화상을 입다
hurt oneself	다치다	**dress oneself**	옷을 입다

2 강조 용법의 재귀대명사

주어나 목적어를 강조하며, 강조하는 말 바로 뒤나 문장 맨 뒤에 온다. 이때의 재귀대명사는 생략할 수 있다.

Emma **herself** made the cookies.   〈주어 강조〉
= Emma made the cookies **herself**.
I wanted to meet the actor **himself**.   〈목적어 강조〉

3 재귀대명사를 포함한 관용 표현

by oneself	홀로, 혼자서	**enjoy oneself**	즐거운 시간을 보내다
help oneself to	~을 마음껏 먹다	**talk to oneself**	혼잣말하다
make oneself at home	편히 지내다		

Mia decided to go on a trip **by herself**.
We **enjoyed ourselves** at the concert.
Make yourself at home while you are here.

비교 point

생략할 수 없는 재귀대명사 vs. 생략할 수 있는 재귀대명사

Tom talked to **himself**.	〈목적어〉	Tom talked to. (생략할 수 없음)
Tom made the chair **himself**.	〈강조〉	Tom made the chair. (생략할 수 있음)

개념 우선 확인 | 옳은 문장 고르기

1 나는 나 자신을 사랑한다.
- ☐ I love me.
- ☐ I love myself.

2 그는 직접 그 컴퓨터를 고쳤다.
- ☐ He fixed the computer itself.
- ☐ He fixed the computer himself.

A

괄호 안에서 알맞은 것을 고르시오.

1 I wrote a letter to (me / myself).

2 I want to introduce (him / himself) to everyone.

3 Help (you / yourself) to these cookies.

4 I was just talking to (me / myself).

5 We should protect (ourselves / yourselves) from the virus.

B

밑줄 친 부분을 생략할 수 있으면 ○, 생략할 수 없으면 ×를 쓰시오.

1 You <u>yourself</u> should apologize to her.

2 He hurt <u>himself</u> while playing football.

3 Please come in and make <u>yourself</u> at home.

4 My sister made my birthday cake <u>herself</u>.

5 The movie <u>itself</u> was interesting.

C

우리말과 일치하도록 재귀대명사를 이용하여 문장을 완성하시오.

1 너는 혼자서 그곳에 가면 안 된다.

→ You shouldn't go there ＿＿＿＿＿＿ ＿＿＿＿＿＿.

2 그는 난로를 만져서 데였다. (burn)

→ He touched the stove and ＿＿＿＿＿＿ ＿＿＿＿＿.

3 그 아이들은 놀이공원에서 즐거운 시간을 보냈다.

→ The children ＿＿＿＿＿＿ ＿＿＿＿＿＿ at the amusement park.

4 Jane, 우리집에 온 것을 환영합니다. 편하게 지내세요.

→ Welcome to my house, Jane. Please ＿＿＿＿＿ ＿＿＿＿＿ ＿＿＿＿＿ ＿＿＿＿＿.

30초 완성 map

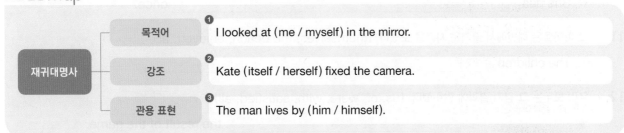

재귀대명사	목적어	❶ I looked at (me / myself) in the mirror.
	강조	❷ Kate (itself / herself) fixed the camera.
	관용 표현	❸ The man lives by (him / himself).

서술형 대비 문장 쓰기

Answers p. 13

□ 빈칸 완성 괄호 안의 말을 이용하여 빈칸 완성하기

01 학교의 모든 학생이 지호를 안다. (student)

→ _____ _____ in the school knows Jiho.

02 Tom, 과일을 마음껏 드세요. (help)

→ Please _____ _____ _____ some fruit, Tom.

03 각각의 색은 다른 의미를 갖는다. (color, have)

→ _____ _____ _____ a different meaning.

04 들어오셔서 편하게 쉬세요. (make, home)

→ Please come in and _____ _____ _____ _____.

✔ 오류 수정 어법에 맞게 문장 고쳐 쓰기

05 My jeans are too small. I need bigger one.

→ My jeans are too small. _____

06 They have two daughters. One is a doctor, and another is a lawyer.

→ They have two daughters. One is a doctor, _____.

07 Some people like sunny days, and other like rainy days.

→ Some people like sunny days, _____.

08 I've been to three countries. One is Japan, the other is Canada, and another is Spain.

→ I've been to three countries. One is Japan, _____.

☰ 배열 영작 괄호 안의 말을 바르게 배열하기

09 나는 시계가 두 개 있다. 두 개 다 한국에서 만든 것이다. (them, of, made, both, were)

→ I have two watches. _____ in Korea.

10 그녀는 혼자 한 번 유럽 여행을 다녀왔다. (by, to, traveled, Europe, herself)

→ She has _____ once.

11 그 아이들은 해변에서 즐거운 시간을 보냈다. (themselves, the beach, enjoyed, at)

→ The children _____.

12 우리 모두는 그 경기 결과에 만족했다. (us, of, were, with, satisfied, all)

→ _____ the result of the game.

시험에 나오는 **출제 포인트**

Answers p. 13

출제 포인트 1 one과 it의 차이를 이해하자!

괄호 안에서 알맞은 것을 고르시오.

(1) I lost my umbrella, so I should buy (it / one).

(2) I read his new book, and I liked (it / one).

> **고득점 POINT** one vs. ones
>
> **어법상 틀린 부분을 찾아 바르게 고쳐 쓰시오.**
>
> Jenny likes black shoes, but I like white one.
>
> _____ → _____

출제 포인트 2 one, another, other의 쓰임을 구분하자!

빈칸에 들어갈 부정대명사를 〈보기〉에서 골라 쓰시오. (중복 사용 가능)

보기	one	another	other	the other

(1) I bought two books. _____ is a novel, and _____ is a comic book.

(2) I watched three movies. _____ was scary, _____ was boring, and _____ was exciting.

출제 포인트 3 each, every, both, all 다음에 오는 동사의 수에 주의하자!

다음 중 어법상 틀린 문장은?

① Every bird has wings.
② All of them are students.
③ Both the twins are healthy.
④ All the food were great.
⑤ Each person here has a nickname.

> **고득점 POINT** 「all / both / each of + 대명사」
>
> **괄호 안의 말을 이용하여 문장을 완성하시오.**
>
> 우리는 각각 다른 관심사를 가지고 있다. (have, each)
> → _____ different interests.

출제 포인트 4 재귀대명사가 강조의 의미일 때는 생략할 수 있다!

밑줄 친 부분을 생략할 수 있는 것은?

> ⓐ I took these photos <u>myself</u>.
> ⓑ We enjoyed <u>ourselves</u> at the party.
> ⓒ Do you love <u>yourself</u>?

① ⓐ   ② ⓑ   ③ ⓒ
④ ⓐ, ⓑ   ⑤ ⓐ, ⓒ

[01-04] 빈칸에 들어갈 말로 알맞은 것을 고르시오.

|8점, 각 2점|

01

_____ student has a different goal.

① All   ② Both
③ Every   ④ Some
⑤ Other

02

Some people like horror movies, but _____ don't.

① ones   ② other
③ the other   ④ others
⑤ another

03

A How about this wallet? It's very popular.
B I don't like this design. Can you show me _____?

① it   ② one
③ other   ④ the other
⑤ another

04

Your new glasses look better than the old _____.

① it   ② one   ③ ones
④ them   ⑤ itself

05 다음 우리말을 영작할 때 빈칸에 알맞은 것은? |3점|

우리 부모님은 두 분 다 여행하기를 좋아하신다.
→ _____ to travel.

① Each my parent like
② Both my parents like
③ All of my parent like
④ Each of my parent likes
⑤ Both of my parents likes

06 밑줄 친 부분을 생략할 수 <u>없는</u> 것은? |3점|

① He <u>himself</u> wrote the letter.
② Be careful not to cut <u>yourself</u>.
③ I want to solve the problem <u>myself</u>.
④ She met the president <u>himself</u>.
⑤ I want to talk with the doctor <u>herself</u>.

최신기출

07 다음 우리말을 영작할 때 필요하지 <u>않은</u> 단어는? |3점|

나는 지갑에 돈이 하나도 없다.

① don't   ② have   ③ any
④ some   ⑤ money

08 밑줄 친 부분이 어법상 틀린 것은? |4점|

① Every dog <u>has</u> its day.
② Each person <u>has</u> a role.
③ All the money <u>is</u> gone.
④ All the people <u>has</u> the right to speak.
⑤ Both of her children <u>are</u> tall.

[09-11] 빈칸에 들어갈 말이 순서대로 바르게 짝지어진 것을 고르시오. |9점, 각 3점|

09

> • My watch is missing. I can't find _____ .
>
> • My computer is too old. I need to buy a new _____ .

① it – one　　② one – ones

③ it – other　　④ one – another

⑤ it – another

10

> • All the files _____ deleted by mistake.
>
> • Each artist _____ a different painting style.

① is – has　　② was – had

③ were – has　　④ was – have

⑤ were – have

11

> There are three girls in the picture. One is playing the violin, _____ is playing the piano, and _____ is singing a song.

① some – others

② some – the other

③ the other – another

④ another – the other

⑤ another – the others

최신기출

12 다음 문장에서 어법상 틀린 부분을 바르게 고친 것은?
|4점|

> Minsu has two sisters. One is a teacher, and other is a soldier. Both of them love him.

① has → have　　② One → Another

③ other → the other　　④ Both of → Both

⑤ love → loves

고난도

13 다음 중 어법상 올바른 문장의 개수는? |5점|

> ⓐ All the work were done yesterday.
>
> ⓑ Some like dogs, and others like cats.
>
> ⓒ Both of the products were made in China.
>
> ⓓ Every students want to pass the test.
>
> ⓔ The queen looked at herself in the mirror.

① 1개　② 2개　③ 3개　④ 4개　⑤ 5개

14 빈칸 ⓐ~ⓒ에 들어갈 말이 순서대로 바르게 짝지어진 것은? |4점|

> A　Would you like __ ⓐ __ cake?
>
> B　Yes, please. I haven't had __ ⓑ __ food today. I'm hungry now.
>
> A　Here you are. Help __ ⓒ __ .

① any – any – you

② some – any – yourself

③ any – some – yourself

④ some – any – you

⑤ some – some – you

15 다음 중 우리말을 영어로 잘못 옮긴 것은? |4점|

① 나에게 종이가 좀 필요해. 네가 좀 갖고 있니?

　→ I need some paper. Do you have any?

② 모든 돈은 옷에 쓰였다.

　→ All the money was spent on clothes.

③ 그들 둘 다 나의 친구들이다.

　→ Both them are my friends.

④ 각각의 소녀는 인형을 가지고 있다.

　→ Each girl has a doll.

⑤ 저는 장미 다섯 송이를 원해요. 붉은 장미 두 송이와 흰 장미 세 송이요.

　→ I want five roses. Two red ones and three white ones.

16 밑줄 친 부분을 바르게 고친 것은? |4점|

① Don't drink <u>any</u> water.
  (→ some)
② There is <u>some</u> milk in the bottle.
  (→ any)
③ I love your cap. I have a similar <u>one</u>.
  (→ ones)
④ I lent Jiho my camera. He still has <u>one</u>.
  (→ it)
⑤ My shoes are too old. I need new <u>ones</u>.
  (→ one)

17 밑줄 친 ⓐ~ⓔ 중 생략할 수 있는 것은? |4점|

My cousin is only six years old, but she can take care of ⓐ <u>herself</u>. She washes ⓑ <u>herself</u> and dresses ⓒ <u>herself</u>. She can even set the table by ⓓ <u>herself</u>. One day, she made sandwiches ⓔ <u>herself</u>.

① ⓐ   ② ⓑ   ③ ⓒ
④ ⓓ   ⑤ ⓔ

고난도

18 어법상 옳은 것을 <u>모두</u> 골라 짝지은 것은? |5점|

ⓐ Some like baseball. Others like soccer.
ⓑ One of the three cups is empty. Others are not.
ⓒ Each worker is wearing a helmet.
ⓓ Every teams have their own flags.
ⓔ All the players did their best.

① ⓐ, ⓑ   ② ⓑ, ⓓ
③ ⓒ, ⓔ   ④ ⓐ, ⓒ, ⓓ
⑤ ⓐ, ⓒ, ⓔ

서술형

19 빈칸에 들어갈 알맞은 대명사를 쓰시오. |3점|

She has two daughters. _____ lives in Seoul, and _____ lives in Daegu.

[20-21] 우리말과 일치하도록 괄호 안의 말을 이용하여 문장을 완성하시오. |6점, 각 3점|

20 Jenny는 자신에게 "난 할 수 있어."라고 말했다. (say to)

→ Jenny _____, "I can do it."

21 저는 영어로 제 소개를 할 수 있습니다. (introduce)

→ I can _____ in English.

최신기출

22 한 학급에서 과목에 대한 선호도를 조사한 결과이다. 표의 내용과 일치하도록 어법상 <u>틀린</u> 부분을 찾아 바르게 고쳐 쓰시오. |4점|

What's your favorite subject?
(Total: 30 students)

Subject	Students
Math	10
English	12
Other subjects	8

Some like math, and the others like English.

_____ → _____

23 글의 내용에 맞게 괄호 안의 말을 바르게 배열하시오.
|4점|

> Jack had to move a heavy box, but there was no one to help him. He decided to (it, by, move, himself).

→ He decided to _____.

24 각 그림과 일치하도록 빈칸에 알맞은 말을 〈보기〉에서 골라 쓰시오.
|4점, 각 2점|

보기	one	some	the other
	others	the others	

(1) (2)

(1) I have two pets. _____ is a dog, and _____ is a cat.

(2) _____ of the students are wearing glasses, and _____ are not.

25 〈조건〉에 맞게 우리말을 영작하시오.
|4점|

> 우리 모두는 특별하다.

조건 1. us, all, we, every, of, is, are, special 중 필요한 단어만을 골라 쓸 것
2. 5단어로 쓸 것

_____

26 괄호 안의 말을 바르게 배열하여 그림을 묘사하는 문장을 완성하시오.
|3점|

> The boy won first place in the contest. He
>
> _____.
>
> (proud, was, himself, of)

27 어법상 틀린 부분을 찾아 바르게 고쳐 쓰시오.
|4점|

> Welcome to our hotel, Mr. Kim. Please make you at home and enjoy your stay.

_____ → _____

28 다음은 Lucy, Tom, Jake가 할 수 있는 일을 나타낸 표이다. 표를 참고하여 〈조건〉에 맞게 문장을 완성하시오.
|8점, 각 4점|

	cooking spaghetti	playing the guitar
Lucy	○	○
Tom	○	○
Jake	×	○

조건 1. Both나 All of로 시작할 것
2. be able to를 이용할 것

(1) _____

cook spaghetti.

(2) _____

play the guitar.

chapter

8

비교

Q. 위 그림을 바르게 표현한 문장은?

☐ The giraffe is as tall as the tree.

☐ The giraffe is taller than the tree.

원급, 비교급, 최상급

1 원급 비교: ~만큼 …한/하게

> 형용사·부사의 기본형

as + 형용사/부사 원급 + as

| Paul is | | **as tall as** | Justin. | Paul은 Justin만큼 키가 크다. |
| Paul is | **not** | **as(so) tall as** | Justin. | Paul은 Justin만큼 키가 크지 않다. |

My bag is **as big as** yours.
He can run **as fast as** I can.
My new shoes are **not as(so) comfortable as** my old ones.

2 비교급 비교: ~보다 더 …한/하게

비교급 + than

| This laptop is | **thinner than** | that one. | 이 노트북은 저것**보다** 더 얇다. |
| She sang | **more beautifully than** | I did. | 그녀는 나**보다** 더 아름답게 노래했다. |

My fingers are **longer than** yours.
New York is **more crowded than** LA.

> 비교급 강조는 비교급 앞에 much, even, far, a lot 등을 써서 나타내며 '훨씬 더 ~한/하게'의 의미이다.
>
> Today is *much* **colder** than yesterday.

3 최상급 비교: 가장 ~한/하게

the + 최상급

| Mt. Everest is | **the highest** | mountain | *in* the world. | 에베레스트산은 세계에서 **가장 높은** 산이다. 〈in + 장소·범위: ~ 안에서〉 |
| This color is | **the most popular** | (one) | *of* the three. | 이 색은 셋 중에서 **가장 인기 있는** 것이다. 〈of + 복수명사: ~ 중에서〉 |

She is **the smartest** student *in* my class.
Which is **the brightest** *of* the stars in the sky?

> **주의** 형용사의 최상급 뒤에 오는 명사는 의미가 반복되는 경우 생략할 수 있다.
> This cup is **the smallest** (one) of the three.

* 불규칙 비교급과 최상급

원급	비교급	최상급
good / well	better	best
bad / ill	worse	worst
many / much	more	most
little	less	least

시험
point

비교급을 강조할 때 주의할 점

형용사·부사의 원급을 강조할 때는 very를 쓸 수 있지만, 형용사·부사의 비교급을 강조할 때는 very를 쓸 수 없다.

1 This car is (very / much) expensive.

2 This car is (very / much) more expensive than that one.

개념 우선 확인 | 옳은 표현 고르기

1 어제만큼 더운	2 너보다 나이가 더 많은	3 가장 쉬운 방법
☐ as hot as yesterday	☐ old than you	☐ the easier way
☐ as hotter as yesterday	☐ older than you	☐ the easiest way

A 괄호 안에서 알맞은 것을 고르시오.

1 This watch is (more / most) expensive than that one.

2 Sally is the (younger / youngest) in our family.

3 I can swim as (well / better) as Peter.

4 Dogs can hear (very / far) better than humans.

5 I'm (interested / more interested) in science than English.

B 밑줄 친 부분을 어법에 맞게 고쳐 쓰시오.

1 The white carpet is <u>softer as</u> the black one.

2 Billy is <u>the quieter</u> student in my class.

3 Today's situation is <u>bad than</u> yesterday's.

4 Victoria is <u>as more brave</u> as her brother.

5 Julia can run <u>very</u> faster than I can.

C 우리말과 일치하도록 괄호 안의 말을 이용하여 문장을 완성하시오.

1 Olivia는 그녀의 언니만큼 마르지 않았다. (thin, as)

   → Olivia is _____ _____ _____ _____ her sister.

2 태양은 달보다 훨씬 더 밝다. (much, bright)

   → The sun is _____ _____ _____ the moon.

3 나는 너보다 더 적은 돈을 썼어. (little, money)

   → I spent _____ _____ _____ you.

4 치즈케이크는 그 식당에서 가장 인기 있는 디저트이다. (popular, dessert)

   → Cheesecake is _____ _____ _____ _____ in the restaurant.

30초 완성 map

비교	원급	❶ 그는 그의 아빠만큼 키가 크다. → He is _____ his father.
	비교급	❷ 그는 그의 아빠보다 키가 더 크다. → He is _____ his father.
		그는 나보다 훨씬 더 빨리 걷는다. → He walks (much / very) faster than I do.
	최상급	❸ 그는 가족 중에서 가장 키가 크다. → He is _____ in his family.

다양한 비교 표현

1 배수 비교 표현: ~보다 몇 배 더 …한/하게

원급이나 비교급 앞에 배수를 표현하는 말을 써서 몇 배 차이가 나는지 나타낼 수 있다.

| My bag is | twice | **as big as** | yours. | 내 가방은 네 것의 **두 배만큼 크다.** |

| This book is | three times | **thicker than** | that one. | 이 책은 저 책보다 **세 배 더 두껍다.** |

Eagles can see **four times as far as** we can. 〈배수사+as+원급+as〉
The sun is almost **100 times bigger than** the earth. 〈배수사+비교급+than〉

▶ '몇 배'를 나타내는 배수사는 three times, 10 times 등으로 나타낸다.

2 비교급+and+비교급: 점점 더 ~한/하게

| Your English | is getting | **better and better.** | 너의 영어는 **점점 더 좋아지고 있다.** |

The weather became **warmer and warmer.**
K-pop stars are getting **more and more popular.**

주의 비교급의 형태가 「more+원급」인 경우 「more and more+원급」으로 쓴다.

3 The+비교급 ~, the+비교급 …: ~하면 할수록 더 …하다

「the+비교급」 다음에는 주어와 동사를 써서 「the+비교급+주어+동사」의 어순으로 쓴다.

| **The sooner** | we leave, | **the earlier** | we'll get there. | 우리가 **더 빨리** 출발할수록, 우리는 **더 일찍** 도착할 것이다. |

The higher we climb, **the colder** the air becomes.
The more you know, **the better** you can understand.

4 one of the+최상급+복수명사: 가장 ~한 …들 중 하나

| Kevin is | **one of the best players** | on our soccer team. | Kevin은 우리 축구팀에서 **가장 뛰어난 선수들 중 하나**이다. |

Niagara Falls is **one of the tallest waterfalls** in the world.
Barcelona is **one of the most beautiful cities** in Europe.

시험 **point**

「one of the+최상급+복수명사」 구문에서 주의할 점

'가장 ~한 …들 중 하나'라는 의미이므로 최상급 다음에는 반드시 복수명사가 와야 한다.

Justin is one of the most popular (singer / singers) in the world.

1 세 배만큼 빠른
- ☐ as three times fast as
- ☐ three times as fast as

2 점점 더 더워지다
- ☐ get hot and hot
- ☐ get hotter and hotter

3 가장 오래된 노래들 중 하나
- ☐ one of the old songs
- ☐ one of the oldest songs

A 괄호 안에서 알맞은 것을 고르시오.

1 The dog is (five / five times) heavier than the cat.

2 The situation is getting (bad / worse) and worse.

3 The less you walk, the (weaker / weakest) your muscles become.

4 Lotte World Tower is one of the (tall / tallest) buildings in the world.

B 밑줄 친 부분을 어법에 맞게 고쳐 쓰시오.

1 The little you sleep, the more tired you feel.

2 Chris is one of the best player on our basketball team.

3 This car is as ten times expensive as my car.

4 Online shopping is getting more and popular these days.

C 우리말과 일치하도록 괄호 안의 말을 이용하여 문장을 완성하시오.

1 나는 점점 더 편안해졌다. (comfortable)

→ I got _____ _____ _____ _____.

2 네가 더 열심히 공부할수록 너의 점수는 더 좋아질 것이다. (hard, good)

→ _____ _____ you study, _____ _____ your score will be.

3 캐나다는 인도의 세 배만큼 크다. (large, as)

→ Canada is _____ _____ _____ _____ _____ India.

4 그는 한국에서 가장 유명한 가수들 중 한 명이다. (famous, singer)

→ He is _____ _____ _____ _____ _____ _____ in Korea.

30초 완성 map

배수 비교 표현
❶ Your room is four times as large as mine.
= Your room is _____ _____ _____ than mine.

비교급 표현
❷ The hole became _____ _____ _____. (big) 그 구멍은 점점 더 커졌다.
_____ _____ you read, the more things you will know. (much)
네가 더 많이 읽을수록, 너는 더 많은 것을 알게 될 것이다.

최상급 표현
❸ It is one of the _____ _____ in the world. (long, cave)
그것은 세계에서 가장 긴 동굴들 중 하나이다.

서술형 대비 문장 쓰기

Answers p. 15

□ 빈칸 완성　괄호 안의 말을 이용하여 빈칸 완성하기

01 나는 Jack만큼 높이 뛸 수 없다. (high)

→ I can't jump ＿＿＿＿＿ ＿＿＿＿＿ ＿＿＿＿＿ Jack can.

02 금은 은보다 훨씬 더 비싸다. (far, expensive)

→ Gold is ＿＿＿＿＿ ＿＿＿＿＿ ＿＿＿＿＿ ＿＿＿＿＿ silver.

03 그녀의 삶은 점점 더 나아지고 있다. (good)

→ Her life is getting ＿＿＿＿＿ ＿＿＿＿＿ ＿＿＿＿＿.

04 오늘은 올해 중 가장 추운 날이다. (cold, day)

→ Today is ＿＿＿＿＿ ＿＿＿＿＿ ＿＿＿＿＿ of the year.

✔ 오류 수정　어법에 맞게 문장 고쳐 쓰기

05 I feel much <u>gooder than</u> yesterday.

→ I feel much ＿＿＿＿＿＿＿＿＿＿＿＿＿＿＿＿＿＿ yesterday.

06 This building is <u>five times as taller as</u> that one.

→ This building is ＿＿＿＿＿＿＿＿＿＿＿＿＿＿＿ that one.

07 His voice became <u>more and more loud</u>.

→ His voice became ＿＿＿＿＿＿＿＿＿＿＿＿＿＿＿.

08 Yesterday was <u>one of the hottest day</u> of the year.

→ Yesterday was ＿＿＿＿＿＿＿＿＿＿＿＿＿＿＿ of the year.

☰ 배열 영작　괄호 안의 말을 바르게 배열하기

09 그 거리는 점점 더 혼잡해졌다. (and, crowded, more, became, more)

→ The street ＿＿＿＿＿＿＿＿＿＿＿＿＿＿＿＿＿＿＿.

10 그는 부는 건강만큼 중요하지 않다고 말한다. (as, not, health, as, important)

→ He says that wealth is ＿＿＿＿＿＿＿＿＿＿＿＿＿＿＿＿＿.

11 네가 더 많이 경험할수록, 너는 더 현명해진다. (the, you, more, wiser, experience, the)

→ ＿＿＿＿＿＿＿＿＿＿＿＿＿＿＿, ＿＿＿＿＿＿＿＿ you become.

12 이 성은 세계에서 가장 오래된 성들 중 하나이다. (of, castles, oldest, the, one)

→ This castle is ＿＿＿＿＿＿＿＿＿＿＿＿＿＿＿＿＿＿ in the world.

시험에 ✓ 나오는 출제 포인트

Answers p. 15

출제 포인트 **원급, 비교급, 최상급의 형태를 잘 구분하여 사용하자!**

괄호 안에서 알맞은 것을 고르시오.

(1) My gradma is as (wise / wiser) as Solomon.

(2) He is (tall / taller) than his father.

(3) Ted is the (funnier / funniest) student in my class.

> **고득점 POINT** 비교 대상의 형태는 동등해야 한다.
>
> **괄호 안에서 알맞은 것을 고르시오.**
>
> (1) Her English score is as high as (me / mine).
>
> (2) For me, skiing is more exciting than (to swim / swimming).

출제 포인트 **비교급을 강조할 때 쓰는 부사를 기억하자!**

빈칸에 들어갈 말로 알맞지 <u>않은</u> 것은?

> K-pop is _____ more popular than J-pop.

① very   ② much   ③ even
④ far   ⑤ a lot

출제 포인트 **비교급을 이용한 표현을 익히자!**

우리말과 일치하도록 밑줄 친 부분을 바르게 고쳐 쓰시오.

(1) 우리 고양이는 점점 더 뚱뚱해졌다.

→ My cat got <u>fat and fat</u>.

(2) 그는 나이가 들수록, 더 활달해졌다.

→ The older he grew, <u>the cheerful he</u> became.

> **고득점 POINT** 「The+비교급 ~, the+비교급 ...」 표현의 어순
>
> **우리말에 맞게 괄호 안의 말을 바르게 배열하시오.**
>
> 네가 더 많이 운동할수록, 너는 더 건강해질 것이다.
>
> (healthier, will, you, the, be)
>
> → The more you exercise, _____.

출제 포인트 **최상급을 이용한 표현을 익히자!**

우리말과 일치하도록 괄호 안의 말을 이용하여 문장을 완성하시오.

그것은 올해 가장 성공적인 영화들 중 하나이다. (successful, movie)

→ It is _____ of the year.

[01-02] 빈칸에 들어갈 말로 알맞은 것을 고르시오.

|4점, 각 2점|

01

I can swim _____ than my sister.

① fast   ② faster
③ fastest   ④ more fast
⑤ the fastest

02

My room is twice as _____ as yours.

① large   ② larger
③ largest   ④ more large
⑤ most large

03 빈칸에 들어갈 말이 순서대로 바르게 짝지어진 것은?

|2점|

• January is as cold _____ December.
• This watch is the most expensive _____ the three.

① as – of   ② as – in
③ than – from   ④ than – of
⑤ in – among

04 다음과 같이 문장을 전환할 때 빈칸에 알맞은 것은? |3점|

India is 33 times bigger than South Korea.
→ India is 33 times _____ South Korea.

① big as   ② as big as
③ bigger as   ④ biggest
⑤ the biggest

[05-06] 빈칸에 들어갈 말로 알맞지 않은 것을 고르시오.

|4점, 각 2점|

05

Seoul is _____ smaller than New York.

① very   ② much   ③ far
④ even   ⑤ a lot

06

Sujin is as _____ as her sister.

① tall   ② kind   ③ smart
④ funny   ⑤ prettier

07 다음 두 문장을 한 문장으로 나타낼 때, 빈칸에 들어갈 말로 알맞은 것은? |3점|

I usually get up at 8 a.m. My brother usually gets up at 7 a.m.
→ My brother usually gets up _____ I do.

① later than   ② earlier than
③ as early as   ④ the earliest
⑤ as late as

08 빈칸에 들어갈 말로 알맞은 것을 <u>모두</u> 고르면? |3점|

Where is the _____ place on earth?

① coldest   ② driest
③ hotter   ④ more crowded
⑤ most beautiful

09 우리말과 일치하도록 할 때, 빈칸에 들어갈 말이 순서대로 바르게 짝지어진 것은? |3점|

> 네가 더 많이 연습할수록, 너는 더 잘 할 것이다.
> → The _____ you practice, the _____ you'll do.

① much – well
② much – better
③ more – better
④ more – best
⑤ most – best

10 다음 중 어법상 틀린 문장은? |4점|

① Jason studies as hard as Kevin does.
② It is the largest desert in the world.
③ Sirius is the brightest star in the sky.
④ Cars are far most expensive than bicycles.
⑤ The more you learn, the more you know.

11 다음 중 〈보기〉와 의미가 통하는 것은? |4점|

> 보기   Today is colder than yesterday.

① Today is as cold as yesterday.
② Today is not as cold as yesterday.
③ Today is not colder than yesterday.
④ Yesterday was not as cold as today.
⑤ Yesterday was colder than today.

12 다음 중 어법상 옳은 문장은? |4점|

① I can jump as higher as Michael Jordan.
② We became more and more bored.
③ The earth is a lot small than the sun.
④ Ice hockey is the more popular in Finland.
⑤ The more slowly you eat, the healthiest you'll be.

13 다음 중 밑줄 친 부분을 바르게 고친 것은? |4점|

① Brian is not as taller as Jack.
　　　　　　　　(→ tallest)
② It is getting warm and warm.
　　　　　　　　(→ more warm and warm)
③ This one is so cheaper than that one.
　　　　　　　　(→ very cheaper)
④ It is one of most exciting movies of the year.
　　　　　　　　(→ the most exciting movie)
⑤ This box is three as heavy as that box.
　　　　　　　　(→ three times as)

14 빈칸 ⓐ~ⓔ에 들어갈 말이 잘못 짝지어진 것은? |4점|

> • Babies usually sleep ___ⓐ___ than adults do.
> • Today is not as hot ___ⓑ___ yesterday.
> • The more you have, ___ⓒ___ more you want.
> • Athens is ___ⓓ___ of the oldest cities in the world.
> • The necklace is the most expensive ___ⓔ___ the shop.

① ⓐ: more
② ⓑ: than
③ ⓒ: the
④ ⓓ: one
⑤ ⓔ: in

15 다음 중 우리말을 영어로 잘못 옮긴 것은? |4점|

① 그 나무는 그 집만큼 오래됐다.
　→ The tree is as old as the house.
② 기말고사가 중간고사보다 훨씬 더 어려웠다.
　→ The final exam was far more difficult than the midterm exam.
③ 진수는 그의 학급에서 가장 빨리 달린다.
　→ Jinsu runs the fastest in his class.
④ 날씨가 점점 더 더워지고 있다.
　→ The weather is getting hot and hot.
⑤ 남극은 세계에서 가장 추운 곳 중 하나이다.
　→ The Antarctic is one of the coldest places in the world.

16 다음 중 어법상 옳은 문장의 개수는? |5점|

> ⓐ Today feels very warmer than yesterday.
> ⓑ This car is far more expensive than his.
> ⓒ My brother is as not tall as me.
> ⓓ I can dance as better as Junsu.
> ⓔ She is one of the greater artists in 20th century.

① 1개 ② 2개 ③ 3개
④ 4개 ⑤ 5개

17 다음 표의 내용과 일치하지 <u>않는</u> 것은? |4점|

	Age	Height	Weight
Mina	14	155	52
Yumi	15	150	50
Jimin	16	160	48

① Mina is not as old as Yumi.
② Jimin is the oldest of the three.
③ Yumi is shorter than Mina.
④ Yumi is not as heavy as Jimin.
⑤ Mina is heavier than Yumi.

18 어법상 옳은 것끼리 짝지어진 것은? |5점|

> ⓐ My hair is not as long as you.
> ⓑ Sora is more diligent than her sister.
> ⓒ He looks badder than you do.
> ⓓ The Nile is the longest river in the world.
> ⓔ The balloon became big and bigger.

① ⓐ, ⓑ ② ⓐ, ⓒ
③ ⓑ, ⓓ ④ ⓒ, ⓔ
⑤ ⓓ, ⓔ

서술형

[19-20] 우리말과 일치하도록 괄호 안의 말을 이용하여 문장을 완성하시오. |6점, 각 3점|

19 우리의 삶은 점점 더 편리해지고 있다. (convenient)

→ Our lives are getting _____

_____ .

20 나는 건강은 돈보다 훨씬 더 중요하다고 생각한다. (important)

→ I think health is _____

_____ than money.

21 주어진 문장을 한 문장으로 나타낼 때, 괄호 안의 말과 비교급을 이용하여 문장을 완성하시오. |4점|

> I'm 13 years old. My grandmother is 65 years old.

→ My grandmother is _____ _____

_____ _____ me. (five, old)

22 주어진 문장과 의미가 통하도록 〈조건〉에 맞게 문장을 완성하시오. |3점|

> Your room is bigger than mine.

> 조건 as와 big을 이용할 것

→ My room is _____

yours.

23 괄호 안의 단어를 이용하여 각 그림을 묘사하는 문장을 완성하시오. |4점, 각 2점|

(1)

(2) $ 1000

$ 1000

(1) The sofa is _____

the chair. (comfortable)

(2) The watch is _____

the ring. (expensive)

[24-26] 우리말과 일치하도록 괄호 안의 말을 바르게 배열하시오. |9점, 각 3점|

24
내 점수는 너의 것보다 훨씬 더 높다.

(yours, a lot, higher, than, is)

→ My score _____

_____.

25
뉴욕은 세계에서 가장 붐비는 도시들 중 하나이다.

(crowded, most, the, one, cities, of)

→ New York is _____

_____ in the world.

26
우리가 동굴 안으로 더 깊이 들어갈수록 더 어두워졌다.

(we, the cave, the deeper, the darker, went into)

→ _____,

_____ it became.

고난도

27 밑줄 친 ⓐ~ⓓ 중 어법상 틀린 것 **두 개**를 찾아 기호를 쓰고 바르게 고쳐 쓰시오. |8점, 각 4점|

Sloths are ⓐ more slow than snails. Their eyesight is ⓑ not very good, and they spend ⓒ most of their time living in trees. This is why they are one of ⓓ the slowest animal in the world. * sloth 나무늘보   snail 달팽이

( ) → _____

( ) → _____

최신기출

28 표의 내용과 일치하도록 괄호 안의 말을 이용하여 지시대로 문장을 완성하시오. |6점, 각 3점|

	Giraffe	Lion	Monkey
Weight	800 kg	200 kg	5 kg
Age	10	8	5

(1) 배수사와 비교급을 사용한 문장

The giraffe is _____
the lion. (heavy, four)

(2) 원급을 사용한 문장

The monkey is _____
the giraffe. (old, not)

chapter

09

동사의 종류

Jenny bought her puppy a new house.

Q. 위 문장으로 보아 Jenny가 산 것은?

☐ 강아지　☐ 새집

감각동사, 수여동사

1 감각동사

'보이다, 들리다, 느끼다' 등 감각을 표현하는 동사이며, 주어를 설명하는 형용사 보어와 함께 쓴다.

주어	동사	주격보어(형용사)	
You	**look**	happy.	너는 행복해 **보인다.**
That	**sounds**	interesting.	그것은 흥미롭게 **들린다.**
The soup	**smells**	good.	그 수프는 좋은 **냄새가 난다.**
It	**tastes**	sweet.	그것은 달콤한 **맛이 난다.**
I	**feel**	tired.	나는 피곤하게 **느낀다.**

주의 보어는 부사처럼 해석하지만, 보어 자리에 부사는 올 수 없으므로 주의한다.

2 수여동사

(1) '~에게 …을 (해) 주다'의 의미를 나타내며, '(누구)에게'와 '(무엇)을'에 해당하는 두 개의 목적어가 온다.

주어	동사	간접목적어(~에게)	직접목적어(…을)	
Lucy	**sent**	*me*	flowers.	Lucy가 *나에게* 꽃을 **보내주었다.**

I **told** *her* my secret.
My uncle **made** *me* a chair.

(2) 두 목적어의 위치를 바꾸어 「주어+동사+직접목적어+전치사(to/for)+간접목적어」 형태의 문장으로도 쓸 수 있다.

Paul	**lent**	*me*	his bike.

Paul	**lent**	his bike	to	*me*.

▶ 동사에 따라 간접목적어 앞에 오는 전치사가 달라진다.

to를 쓰는 동사	give, send, show, tell, teach, lend, bring 등	He **showed** *me* his pictures. → He **showed** his pictures **to** *me*.
for를 쓰는 동사	buy, make, cook, get 등	She **made** *us* cookies. → She **made** cookies **for** *us*.

비교 point

「감각동사+형용사」 vs. 「감각동사+like+명사」

감각동사 뒤에는 명사가 바로 올 수 없지만, 감각동사 뒤에 전치사 like를 쓰면 명사가 올 수 있다.

The cake **looks delicious**.	〈감각동사+형용사〉
The cake **looks like** a Christmas tree.	〈감각동사+like+명사〉

개념 우선 확인 | 옳은 표현 고르기

1 슬퍼 보이다
- ☐ look sad
- ☐ look sadly

2 그에게 사진을 보여주다
- ☐ show him a photo
- ☐ show to him a photo

3 나에게 피자를 만들어 주다
- ☐ make pizza to me
- ☐ make pizza for me

A 괄호 안에서 알맞은 것을 고르시오.

1 The milk smelled (bad / badly).

2 It (tastes / tastes like) chicken.

3 Please give (me some water / some water me).

4 Paul didn't tell the truth (to / for) me.

B 두 문장의 의미가 같도록 알맞은 전치사를 이용하여 문장을 완성하시오.

1 She cooked us spaghetti yesterday.

→ She cooked spaghetti _____ _____ yesterday.

2 Dave lent me his English textbook.

→ Dave lent his English textbook _____ _____.

3 The teacher told us an interesting story.

→ The teacher told an interesting story _____ _____.

C 우리말과 일치하도록 괄호 안의 말을 이용하여 문장을 완성하시오.

1 나는 춥다고 느껴서 코트를 입었다. (cold)

→ I put on the coat as I _____ _____.

2 박 선생님은 우리에게 음악을 가르치신다. (music, teach)

→ Mr. Park _____ _____ _____.

3 그 노래는 나에게 슬프게 들린다. (sad)

→ The song _____ _____ to me.

4 나는 엄마에게 꽃을 좀 사 드렸다. (some flowers, buy)

→ I _____ _____ _____ _____ my mother.

30초 완성 map

동사의 종류	감각동사	❶ She looks (angry / angrily). He looks _____ Santa Claus.	그녀는 화가 나 보인다. 그는 산타클로스처럼 보인다.
	수여동사	❷ Kate gave _____ _____. = Kate gave chocolate _____ _____.	Kate는 나에게 초콜릿을 주었다.

목적격보어가 필요한 동사

1 목적격보어가 필요한 동사

목적어의 성질, 상태, 동작 등을 보충 설명하는 말을 목적격보어라고 하며, 「주어＋동사＋목적어＋목적격보어」의 어순으로 쓴다. 동사에 따라 다양한 형태의 목적격보어가 쓰인다.

주어	동사	목적어	목적격보어	
I	called	the cat	**Coco.** 〈명사〉	나는 그 고양이를 Coco라고 **불렀다.**
She	keeps	her room	**tidy.** 〈형용사〉	그녀는 방을 깔끔하게 **유지한다.**
They	told	me	**to cheer** up. 〈to부정사〉	그들은 나에게 힘내라고 **말했다.**
The rain	made	us	**stay** home. 〈동사원형〉	그 비는 우리를 집에 머물게 **했다.**

▶ 목적격보어의 형태별로 자주 함께 쓰이는 동사가 있다.

> • 명사: make, call, name, elect 등 • 형용사: make, keep, find 등
> • to부정사: want, tell, advise, allow, expect, ask 등
> • 동사원형: 사역동사(make, have, let 등), 지각동사(see, watch, hear, feel 등)

2 사역동사

사역동사(make, have, let 등)는 '~가 …하게 하다[시키다]'의 의미를 나타내며 목적격보어로 동사원형을 쓴다.

The movie	made	him	**cry.**	그 영화는 그를 울게 **했다.**
The teacher	had	us	**solve** the problem.	선생님은 우리에게 그 문제를 풀게 **했다.**
Mom	let	me	**play** games.	엄마는 내가 게임을 하게 **허락했다.**

▶ 사역동사의 의미 차이: make 시키다 / have 하게 하다 / let 허락하다

3 지각동사

지각동사(see, watch, hear, feel 등)는 '~가 …하는 것을 보다/듣다/느끼다'의 의미를 나타내며 목적격보어로 동사원형이나 현재분사를 쓴다.

I	heard	someone	**sing**(**singing**).	나는 누군가가 노래하는 것을 **들었다.**
We	saw	him	**play**(**playing**) football.	우리는 그가 축구하는 것을 **보았다.**

▶ 주로 동작이 진행 중임을 강조할 때 목적격보어로 현재분사를 쓴다.
  He **watched** her **dancing** on the stage.

시험 point

사역동사와 지각동사의 목적격보어 형태

1 Mom made me (study / to study) English.

2 I saw someone (wave / to wave / waving) to me.

개념 우선 확인 | 옳은 표현 고르기

1 그를 Paul이라고 부르다
- ☐ call Paul him
- ☐ call him Paul

2 그녀를 나가게 해 주다
- ☐ let her go out
- ☐ let her to go out

3 그가 노래하는 것을 듣다
- ☐ hear him singing
- ☐ hear him to sing

A 괄호 안에서 알맞은 것을 고르시오.

1 They named their son (Jack / of Jack).

2 My parents want me (be / to be) a pilot.

3 She watched the man (to run / running) away.

4 He allowed me (use / to use) his laptop.

5 Let me (introduce / to introduce) myself to you.

B 밑줄 친 부분을 어법에 맞게 고쳐 쓰시오.

1 They asked her be quiet.

2 You must keep the vegetables freshly.

3 The movie made all of us laughing.

4 I saw her to read a book at the cafe.

C 우리말과 일치하도록 괄호 안의 말을 이용하여 문장을 완성하시오.

1 그 담요가 너를 따뜻하게 해 줄 것이다. (warm, keep)

→ The blanket will _____ _____ _____.

2 우리는 누군가 문을 두드리는 소리를 들었다. (knock, someone)

→ We _____ _____ _____ at the door.

3 아빠는 내가 일찍 잠자리에 들도록 시키셨다. (make, go)

→ Dad _____ _____ _____ to bed early.

4 나는 그가 내 생일 파티에 오기를 기대했다. (come, expect)

→ I _____ _____ _____ _____ to my birthday party.

30초 완성 map

목적격보어가 필요한 동사

❶
We **called** him Spider-Man. 우리는 그를 스파이더맨이라고 불렀다.
You **make** me (happy / happily). 너는 나를 행복하게 한다.
She **told** us (be / to be) quiet. 그녀는 우리에게 조용히 하라고 말했다.

사역동사
❷
He **let** me (use / to use) his smartphone.
그는 내가 그의 스마트폰을 쓰게 허락했다.

지각동사
❸
They **saw** him (play / to play / playing) the piano.
그들은 그가 피아노 연주하는 것을 보았다.

서술형 대비 문장 쓰기

Answers p. 16

↻ 문장 전환 전치사를 이용하여 문장 바꿔 쓰기

01 Dad gave me some advice.

→ Dad _____ _____ _____ _____ me.

02 Mr. Baker made us some cookies.

→ Mr. Baker _____ _____ _____ _____ us.

03 I'll get you some tea.

→ I'll _____ _____ _____ _____ you.

04 My aunt sent me a birthday gift.

→ My aunt _____ _____ _____ _____ _____ me.

✓ 오류 수정 어법에 맞게 문장 고쳐 쓰기

05 They look very happily in this picture.

→ They _____ in this picture.

06 My grandfather told to me a surprising story.

→ My grandfather _____ .

07 The teacher had the students to clean their desks.

→ The teacher had the students _____ .

08 We saw him to run to catch the bus.

→ We saw _____ to catch the bus.

≡ 배열 영작 괄호 안의 말을 바르게 배열하기

09 아빠는 내가 차를 운전하도록 허락하지 않을 것이다. (me, let, drive, won't)

→ Dad _____ a car.

10 나는 네가 내 비밀을 지켜주길 바란다. (you, to, want, keep, my secret)

→ I _____ .

11 누군가가 그에게 러브레터를 보냈다. (to, a love letter, sent, him)

→ Someone _____ .

12 그녀는 무언가가 자신의 다리를 무는 것을 느꼈다. (felt, her leg, something, bite)

→ She _____ .

시험에 ✓ 나오는 출제 포인트

Answers p. 16

출제 포인트 감각동사 뒤에 오는 말의 품사에 주의하자!

괄호 안에서 알맞은 것을 고르시오.

(1) This cake tastes (bad / badly).

(2) Your little sister looks (lovely / nicely).

> **고득점 POINT** 「감각동사+형용사」 vs. 「감각동사+like+명사」
>
> **괄호 안의 말을 이용하여 문장을 완성하시오. (필요시 단어를 추가할 것)**
>
> (1) That sounds _____ . (interesting)
>
> (2) That sounds _____ . (a funny movie)

출제 포인트 수여동사 뒤에 오는 두 개의 목적어의 순서에 주의하자!

우리말과 일치하도록 괄호 안의 말을 바르게 배열하시오.

(1) 산타클로스가 그 아이들에게 선물을 주었다.

  (the children, presents, gave)

  → Santa Claus _____ .

(2) Julie는 나에게 그녀의 비밀을 말해 주었다.

  (me, her secret, told)

  → Julie _____ .

> **고득점 POINT** 수여동사가 있는 문장의 전환
>
> **두 문장의 의미가 같도록 빈칸에 알맞은 말을 쓰시오.**
>
> (1) My dad made us sandwiches.
>
>   → My dad made sandwiches _____ .
>
> (2) He gave me some medicine.
>
>   → He gave some medicine _____ .

출제 포인트 동사에 따라 알맞은 목적격보어의 형태를 기억하자!

어법상 틀린 문장을 모두 고르면?

① That will keep you warmly.

② Mom wants me to study harder.

③ I heard someone playing the violin.

④ He told me get some rest.

⑤ She let me use her new smartphone.

출제 포인트 **4** 사역동사와 지각동사의 목적격보어 형태를 기억하자!

빈칸에 들어갈 말이 순서대로 바르게 짝지어진 것은?

> • I _____ him running in the park.
>
> • Mom didn't _____ me go there alone.

① saw – let ② made – let ③ saw – allow

④ made – have ⑤ heard – want

[01-02] 빈칸에 들어갈 말로 알맞지 <u>않은</u> 것을 고르시오.

|4점, 각 2점|

01

Emily looks _____ today.

① busy   ② tired
③ happy   ④ angrily
⑤ lovely

02

Mom _____ me play the piano.

① made   ② let
③ had   ④ saw
⑤ allowed

03 밑줄 친 부분의 쓰임이 나머지와 <u>다른</u> 것은? |3점|

① People call him <u>a genius</u>.
② The movie made her <u>a superstar</u>.
③ My uncle bought me <u>a bike</u>.
④ We elected Jane <u>team captain</u>.
⑤ She named her daughter <u>Lala</u>.

최신기출

04 다음 우리말을 영작할 때 어법상 틀린 것은? |3점|

엄마는 내가 캠핑 가는 것을 허락하지 않으셨다.
→ Mom <u>didn't</u> <u>let</u> <u>me</u> <u>going</u> <u>camping</u>.
        ①   ②   ③   ④   ⑤

[05-06] 빈칸에 들어갈 말로 알맞은 것을 고르시오.

|4점, 각 2점|

05

I saw Jack _____ something behind his back.

① hides   ② hiding
③ to hide   ④ hidden
⑤ was hiding

06

The doctor advised me _____ some exercise.

① get   ② got
③ to get   ④ getting
⑤ gotten

07 빈칸에 들어갈 말이 나머지와 <u>다른</u> 것은? |3점|

① He sent a gift _____ her.
② I bought shoes _____ my mom.
③ Ben gave his toy robot _____ his brother.
④ Ms. Kim told a story _____ her students.
⑤ Paul showed his new camera _____ me.

08 빈칸에 알맞은 말을 <u>모두</u> 고르면? |3점|

I heard her _____.

① sang   ② crying
③ call my name   ④ plays the flute
⑤ to open the door

09 〈보기〉에서 빈칸에 들어갈 수 있는 것의 개수는? |4점|

| 보기 | ⓐ let | ⓑ had | ⓒ wanted |
| | ⓓ told | ⓔ made | ⓕ advised |

The teacher _____ the students to read the book.

① 1개　　　② 2개　　　③ 3개
④ 4개　　　⑤ 5개

10 〈보기〉의 밑줄 친 부분과 쓰임이 같은 것은? |3점|

보기　He told me his name.

① She named her baby Tom.
② I told you to listen to me.
③ Did you see the children fight?
④ The waiter brought me the dessert.
⑤ The gloves will keep your hands warm.

11 우리말을 영어로 바르게 옮긴 것을 모두 고르면? |3점|

그는 부모님께 저녁 식사를 요리해 드렸다.

① He cooked his parents dinner.
② He cooked dinner to his parents.
③ He cooked dinner for his parents.
④ He cooked for his parents dinner.
⑤ He cooked to his parents dinner.

12 다음 중 어법상 틀린 문장은? |4점|

① The blanket felt soft.
② She taught English to us.
③ I asked him carrying the box.
④ We found the movie boring.
⑤ People watched the sun rising.

13 빈칸에 들어갈 말이 순서대로 바르게 짝지어진 것은?|4점|

• He always makes me _____.
• I felt someone _____ my arm.

① laugh – touch
② laugh – to touch
③ laughing – touch
④ laughing – touching
⑤ to laugh – touching

14 다음 중 어법상 옳은 문장의 개수는? |5점|

ⓐ I expected him to be home.
ⓑ You should keep your room clean.
ⓒ Jason felt someone looking at him.
ⓓ I had Jack to fix my computer.
ⓔ My aunt made a teddy bear to me.

① 1개　② 2개　③ 3개　④ 4개　⑤ 5개

15 밑줄 친 made의 쓰임이 같은 것끼리 짝지어진 것은?
|4점|

ⓐ She made us lemonade.
ⓑ The music made me comfortable.
ⓒ I made some paper flowers for you.
ⓓ The news made people surprised.

① ⓐ, ⓑ　　　　② ⓐ, ⓓ
③ ⓑ, ⓒ　　　　④ ⓑ, ⓓ
⑤ ⓒ, ⓓ

16 다음 중 밑줄 친 부분을 <u>잘못</u> 고친 것은? |5점|

① His voice sounds <u>sweetly</u>.
　　　　　　　　　(→ sweet)
② He told <u>a funny story me</u>.
　　　　　　　　　(→ me a funny story)
③ The baby <u>looks</u> an angel.
　　　　　　　　　(→ looks like)
④ I heard someone <u>knocked</u> at the door.
　　　　　　　　　(→ to knock)
⑤ My dog always makes me <u>to smile</u>.
　　　　　　　　　(→ smile)

17 빈칸 ⓐ~ⓔ에 들어갈 말이 <u>잘못</u> 짝지어진 것은? |4점|

- Please show your passport ___ⓐ___ me.
- His dad made a toy car ___ⓑ___ him.
- Jisu gave her doll ___ⓒ___ her sister.
- I lent my bike ___ⓓ___ my friend.
- They bought a cake ___ⓔ___ their parents.

① ⓐ: to　　② ⓑ: for　　③ ⓒ: for
④ ⓓ: to　　⑤ ⓔ: for

18 밑줄 친 ⓐ~ⓔ 중 어법상 <u>틀린</u> 것은? |4점|

A　ⓐ <u>You look different.</u> What did you do?
B　ⓑ <u>I cut my hair a little.</u>
A　ⓒ <u>Did you do it yourself?</u>
B　No, ⓓ <u>I asked my sister do it.</u>
A　I see. Anyway, ⓔ <u>your new hairstyle</u>
　　makes you look better.

① ⓐ　　② ⓑ　　③ ⓒ　　④ ⓓ　　⑤ ⓔ

서술형

19 두 문장의 의미가 같도록 빈칸에 알맞은 말을 쓰시오. |2점|

I made my friends Christmas cards.

→ I made Christmas cards _____
_____ _____.

[20-21] 우리말과 일치하도록 괄호 안의 말을 이용하여 문장을 완성하시오. |6점, 각 3점|

20 그 이야기는 이상하게 들렸다. (strange)
→ The story _____.

21 우리는 땅이 흔들리는 것을 느꼈다.
(the ground, shake)
→ We _____.

22 어법상 <u>틀린</u> 부분을 <u>두 곳</u> 찾아 바르게 고쳐 쓰시오. |8점, 각 4점|

　Mom told me water the flowers. While watering them, I heard someone to call my name. When I turned around, I saw Peter waving to me.

(1) _____ → _____
(2) _____ → _____

23 우리말과 일치하도록 괄호 안의 말을 바르게 배열하시오.

|3점|

> 나는 그에게 컴퓨터 기술을 배우라고 조언했다.
> (I, him, learn, advised, to, computer skills)

→ _____

24 그림의 내용과 일치하도록 괄호 안의 말을 바르게 배열하여 문장을 완성하시오.

|3점|

→ I watched _____.

(a boy, running behind, a dog)

25 밑줄 친 ⓐ~ⓔ 중 어법상 틀린 것을 두 개 찾아 기호를 쓰고, 바르게 고쳐 쓰시오.

|6점, 각 3점|

> Last Saturday, I hung out with my friends until late at night. The next morning, I felt ⓐ cold and sick. Mom wanted me ⓑ get up early, but I couldn't. She saw me ⓒ lying in bed and made ⓓ chicken soup me. The hot soup made me ⓔ feel much better.

(   ) → _____

(   ) → _____

[26-27] 우리말을 〈조건〉에 맞게 영작하시오.

|8점, 각 4점|

26

> Anna는 내가 그녀의 컴퓨터를 사용하게 허락했다.

> 조건   1. 과거시제로 쓸 것
>   2. allow, use, computer를 이용하여 6단어로 쓸 것

→ Anna _____

_____.

27

> 나는 네가 너의 마음을 바꾸게 할 것이다.

> 조건   1. 미래시제로 쓸 것
>   2. make, change, mind를 이용하여 6단어로 쓸 것

→ I _____

_____.

28 각 그림의 내용과 일치하도록 괄호 안의 말을 사용해서 과거시제 문장을 완성하시오.

|4점, 각 2점|

(1)    (2)

(1) The boy _____.

(look, sad)

(2) They _____.

(name, the cat)

chapter

10

접속사

We played a board game **after** we had dinner.

①

②

Q. 위 문장으로 보아 먼저 일어난 일은?

☐ ①　　☐ ②

시간·이유·조건의 접속사

1 시간을 나타내는 접속사

when	~할 때	**When** I looked outside, it was snowing.
while	~하는 동안	He called me **while** I was taking a nap.
until	~할 때까지	Let's wait **until** the rain stops.
before	~하기 전에	Look both ways **before** you cross the street.
after	~한 후에	**After** we have lunch, let's take a walk.
as	~할 때, ~하면서	**As** he grew older, he became more careful.

2 이유·결과를 나타내는 접속사

because since as	~이기 때문에, ~이므로	I like Jack **because** he is kind. **Since** he failed the test, he felt depressed. I went to the doctor **as** I had a cold.
so	그래서	I lost my umbrella, **so** I had to buy a new one.
so ~ that ...	매우(너무) ~해서 …하다	He was **so** nervous **that** he couldn't eat anything.

cf. All flights were canceled **because of** *the hurricane.*   〈because of + 명사(구)〉

3 조건·양보를 나타내는 접속사

if	(만약) ~하면	**If** you need more information, visit our website.
unless	(만약) ~하지 않으면 (= if ~ not)	**Unless** you get up now, you'll be late for school. = **If** you **don't** get up now, you'll be late for school.
though although even though	~에도 불구하고, 비록 ~이지만	**Though** he was sick, he went to school. **Although** it was raining, we played soccer. Ella is really thin **even though** she eats a lot.

주의 unless에는 부정의 의미가 포함되어 있으므로 not을 함께 쓰지 않는다.
Unless you ~~don't~~ have a ticket, you can't get in. (×)

시험 point

시간·조건 부사절의 시제

시간이나 조건을 나타내는 부사절에서는 미래시제 대신 현재시제를 써서 미래의 일을 나타낸다.

1 When I (come / will come) back, I will call you.   〈시간 부사절〉

2 If it (rains / will rain) tomorrow, the event will be canceled.   〈조건 부사절〉

1 Please wait here <u>until I come back</u>.

☐ 내가 돌아오기 때문에
☐ 내가 돌아올 때까지

2 <u>If it stops raining</u>, let's go on a picnic.

☐ 비오는 것이 멈추면
☐ 비오는 것이 멈추지 않으면

A 괄호 안에서 알맞은 것을 고르시오.

1 I set the table (while / unless) Dad was cooking pasta.

2 Emily couldn't call you (until / because) she was very busy.

3 It was so hot (as / that) I couldn't do anything.

4 Steve got good grades (if / even though) he didn't study hard.

B 밑줄 친 부분을 어법에 맞게 고쳐 쓰시오.

1 If you <u>will call</u> her, she will be pleased.

2 Jack didn't come <u>because of</u> he was sick.

3 Unless you <u>don't leave</u> now, you'll be late for the meeting.

4 She'll study abroad after she <u>will graduate</u> from high school.

C 〈보기〉에서 알맞은 접속사를 골라 괄호 안의 말을 이용하여 문장을 완성하시오. (단, 한 번씩만 쓸 것)

보기	since	although	unless	when

1 두통이 있을 때 이 약을 먹어. (have)

→ Take this medicine _____ _____ _____ a headache.

2 비밀번호를 잊어버려서 나는 그 파일을 열 수 없었다. (forget)

→ I couldn't open the file _____ _____ _____ the password.

3 비록 나는 피곤했지만 잠을 잘 수 없었다. (tired)

→ _____ _____ _____ _____, I couldn't sleep.

4 네가 바쁘지 않으면 쇼핑하러 가자. (busy)

→ _____ _____ _____ _____, let's go shopping.

30초 완성 map

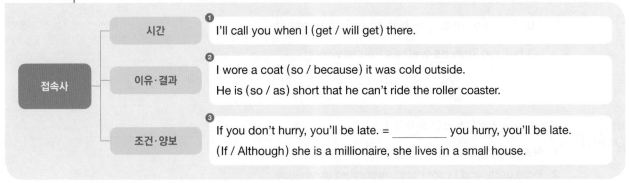

접속사

시간
❶ I'll call you when I (get / will get) there.

이유·결과
❷ I wore a coat (so / because) it was cold outside.
He is (so / as) short that he can't ride the roller coaster.

조건·양보
❸ If you don't hurry, you'll be late. = _____ you hurry, you'll be late.
(If / Although) she is a millionaire, she lives in a small house.

명령문＋and / or, 짝을 이루는 접속사

1　명령문, and / or ~

명령문, and ~	…해라, 그러면 ~	**Hurry up, and** you'll get there on time. = **If** you hurry up, you'll get there on time.
명령문, or ~	…해라, 그러지 않으면 ~	**Be careful, or** you might get hurt. = **If** you are **not** careful, you might get hurt. = **Unless** you are careful, you might get hurt.

Exercise regularly, and you'll be healthier.

= **If** you exercise regularly, you'll be healthier.

Get up early, or you'll have no time for breakfast.

= **If** you don't get up early, you'll have no time for breakfast.

= **Unless** you get up early, you'll have no time for breakfast.

2　짝을 이루는 접속사 (상관접속사)

두 대상을 연결해 주는 접속사로, 연결되는 두 대상은 문법적으로 같은 형태여야 한다.

both *A* and *B*	A와 B 둘 다	My uncle likes **both** cooking **and** baking. **Both** her father **and** her mother enjoy tennis.
either *A* or *B*	A나 B 둘 중 하나	I'll have **either** pasta **or** pizza. You can get there **either** by train **or** by ship.
neither *A* nor *B*	A도 B도 아닌	He looked neither **bored** nor **interested**. **Neither** he **nor** his wife can speak French.
not only *A* but (also) *B*	A뿐만 아니라 B도 (=*B* as well as *A*)	She likes **not only** singing **but also** dancing. (= She likes dancing **as well as** singing.)

▶ 짝을 이루는 접속사로 연결되는 대상이 문장의 주어일 때, both A and B는 항상 복수 취급하고 나머지는 B에 동사의 수를 일치시킨다.

Both <u>learning</u> **and** <u>playing</u> **are** important.
주어

Either <u>you</u> **or** <u>Harry</u> **has** to cook dinner.
주어

I believe **not only** <u>you</u> **but also** <u>Tom</u> **is** wrong.
주어

= I believe <u>Tom</u> **as well as** <u>you</u> **is** wrong.
주어

시험
point

짝을 이루는 접속사가 쓰인 문장의 수 일치

1　Neither Paul nor I (am / is) good at sports.

2　Both Judy and I (am / are) interested in science.

1 택시를 타, 그러면 늦지 않을 거야.

☐ Take a taxi, or you won't be late.
☐ Take a taxi, and you won't be late.

2 나는 여름도 겨울도 좋아하지 않는다.

☐ I like either summer or winter.
☐ I like neither summer nor winter.

A 괄호 안에서 알맞은 것을 고르시오.

1 Put on your coat, (and / or) you'll be cold.

2 I have been to (either / both) Spain and France.

3 Either Jack (or / nor) you have to clean the window.

4 Neither Sally nor her brother (like / likes) baseball.

B 두 문장의 의미가 같도록 빈칸에 알맞은 말을 쓰시오.

1 Jenny is good at not only running but also swimming.

  → Jenny is good at swimming _____ _____ _____ running.

2 Go straight, and you'll find the restroom.

  → _____ _____ _____ straight, you'll find the restroom.

3 Take this medicine, or you won't get better.

  → _____ _____ _____ this medicine, you won't get better.

C 우리말과 일치하도록 괄호 안의 말과 접속사를 이용하여 문장을 완성하시오.

1 나는 행복하지도 슬프지도 않았다. (feel)

  → I _____ _____ happy _____ sad.

2 언니와 나는 둘 다 뮤지컬 보는 것을 즐긴다. (enjoy)

  → _____ my sister _____ I _____ watching musicals.

3 너는 점심으로 햄버거나 샌드위치 중 하나를 먹을 수 있다. (have)

  → You can _____ _____ a hamburger _____ a sandwich for lunch.

4 너뿐만 아니라 Chris도 연극부에 가입하고 싶어 한다. (want)

  → _____ _____ you _____ _____ Chris _____ to join the drama club.

30초 완성 map

접속사	명령문, and / or	❶ Go straight, (and / or) you'll find the bank. Go to bed early, (and / or) you'll be tired tomorrow.
	짝을 이루는 접속사	❷ Both Yuna and I (am / are) very hungry. Either you or I (am / are) wrong. I'm good at neither math (or / nor) English.

✔ 오류 수정 어법에 맞게 문장 고쳐 쓰기

01 Unless Jack <u>doesn't come</u>, I won't go to the party.

→ _____, I won't go to the party.

02 Emily brought her umbrella <u>because of it was cloudy</u>.

→ Emily brought her umbrella _____.

03 I'll call you back <u>when the meeting will be over</u>.

→ I'll call you back _____.

04 Henry as well as you <u>are responsible for the problem</u>.

→ Henry as well as you _____.

↻ 문장 전환 같은 의미의 문장으로 바꿔 쓰기

05 Speak loudly, or I won't be able to hear you.

→ Unless _____, I won't be able to hear you.

06 Judy hates insects, and her sister also hates insects.

→ Both _____.

07 Chris doesn't know the answer. James doesn't know the answer, either.

→ Neither _____.

08 Unless you are an adult, you can't watch this movie.

→ If _____, you can't watch this movie.

☐ 빈칸 완성 괄호 안의 말을 이용하여 빈칸 완성하기

09 지하철을 타, 그러면 제시간에 그곳에 도착할 거야. (get there)

→ Take the subway, _____ on time.

10 그는 너무 피곤해서 빨리 잠들었다. (tired, fall asleep)

→ He was _____ quickly.

11 비록 우리는 그 경기에서 졌지만, 우리는 실망하지 않았다. (lose the game)

→ _____, we weren't disappointed.

12 Tom이나 Mia 둘 중 한 명이 저녁을 준비해야 한다. (have to)

→ _____ prepare dinner.

시험에 ✓ 꼭 나오는 출제 포인트

Answers p. 18

출제 포인트 1   시간·조건의 부사절에서 시제에 주의하자!

괄호 안의 말을 이용하여 대화를 완성하시오.

A   Jack, how about going to the park tomorrow?

B   If the weather _____ good, I'll go with you. (be)

> **고득점 POINT**   unless의 의미
>
> 두 문장의 의미가 같도록 빈칸에 알맞은 말을 쓰시오.
>
> I can't finish the work today unless you help me.
>
> → I can't finish the work today if you _____ me.

출제 포인트 2   이유, 결과, 양보를 나타내는 접속사의 의미를 기억하자!

밑줄 친 부분의 쓰임이 어색한 것은?

① I like animals, <u>so</u> I often go to the zoo.

② <u>Though</u> she is young, she is very smart.

③ <u>Because</u> it was so hot, I turned on the fan.

④ <u>Since</u> Mike wasn't invited, he couldn't come to the party.

⑤ <u>Although</u> I was tired, I went to bed early last night.

출제 포인트 3   「명령문, and / or ~」 구문의 의미를 이해하자!

두 문장의 의미가 같도록 빈칸에 알맞은 말을 쓰시오.

(1) Do your homework first, and I'll let you play games.

   → _____ _____ _____ your homework first, I'll let you play games.

(2) Study hard, or you'll fail the test.

   → _____ _____ _____ _____ hard, you'll fail the test.

출제 포인트 4   짝을 이루는 접속사의 형태를 기억하자!

우리말과 일치하도록 빈칸에 알맞은 말을 쓰시오.

(1) 나는 수학과 영어를 둘 다 좋아한다.

   → I like _____ math _____ English.

(2) 그는 커피도 차도 마시지 않았다.

   → He drank _____ coffee _____ tea.

> **고득점 POINT**   짝을 이루는 접속사의 수 일치
>
> 빈칸에 like를 알맞은 형태로 쓰시오. (현재형으로 쓸 것)
>
> (1) Neither Roy nor Ben _____ Chinese food.
>
> (2) Both Roy and Ben _____ Korean food.

유형	문항수	배점	점수
객관식	18	60	
서술형	10	40	

[01-04] 빈칸에 들어갈 말로 알맞은 것을 고르시오.

|8점, 각 2점|

01

I listened to music _____ I was taking a shower.

① after　　② if　　③ while
④ until　　⑤ so

02

Jack couldn't go to the movies _____ he had a bad cold.

① so　　② before　　③ unless
④ though　　⑤ since

03

_____ we did our best, our team lost the game.

① If　　② When　　③ Because
④ Although　　⑤ Unless

04

Mark is _____ handsome nor rich, but he is smart and funny.

① so　　② both　　③ either
④ neither　　⑤ not only

05 빈칸에 들어갈 말이 순서대로 바르게 짝지어진 것은? |3점|

If you don't take the taxi, you'll be late.
= _____ you take the taxi, you'll be late.
= Take the taxi, _____ you'll be late.

① Though – and　　② Unless – so
③ Though – so　　④ Unless – or
⑤ Unless – and

06 빈칸에 들어갈 말이 나머지와 다른 것은? |3점|

① It was too late, _____ I couldn't call you.
② The box is _____ heavy that I can't carry it.
③ I was thirsty, _____ I drank a bottle of water.
④ She was tired _____ she worked all day.
⑤ He was _____ hungry that he couldn't sleep.

[07-08] 빈칸에 공통으로 들어갈 말로 알맞은 것을 고르시오.

|6점, 각 3점|

07

• _____ I was tired, I got some rest.
• _____ we arrived at the station, the train was leaving.

① As　　② If　　③ Until
④ Since　　⑤ While

08

• It was cold, _____ I wore a winter coat.
• Mike went to bed _____ late that he couldn't get up early the next morning.

① so　　② as　　③ if
④ when　　⑤ until

[09-10] 빈칸에 들어갈 말이 순서대로 바르게 짝지어진 것을 고르시오. |6점, 각 3점|

09

> • I have been to both Italy _____ Mexico.
> • They are neither rich _____ poor.

① or – but ② and – nor

③ and – but ④ but – nor

⑤ or – nor

10

> • _____ it was too cold, I stayed home.
> • I couldn't sleep _____ the noise outside.

① As – because ② So – since

③ As – since ④ As – because of

⑤ So – because of

11 주어진 문장과 바꿔 쓸 수 있는 것을 <u>모두</u> 고르면? |4점|

> Take an umbrella with you, or you will get wet.

① If you take an umbrella with you, you will get wet.

② If you don't take an umbrella with you, you will get wet.

③ Unless you take an umbrella with you, you will get wet.

④ Unless you take an umbrella with you, you won't get wet.

⑤ Unless you don't take an umbrella with you, you will get wet.

12 빈칸 ⓐ~ⓔ에 들어갈 접속사가 <u>잘못</u> 짝지어진 것은? |4점|

> • He set the table ⓐ I was cooking.
> • Brush your teeth ⓑ you go to bed.
> • He ate a whole pizza ⓒ he was very hungry.
> • I'd like to sit here, ⓓ you don't mind.
> • The flower will die ⓔ you take care of it.

① ⓐ: while ② ⓑ: before ③ ⓒ: since

④ ⓓ: if ⑤ ⓔ: because

[13-14] 밑줄 친 부분이 어법상 틀린 것을 고르시오.
|8점, 각 4점|

13 ① After the rain <u>will stop</u>, we will go out.

② If we <u>don't leave</u> now, we'll miss the train.

③ I can bake you cookies if you <u>want</u> some.

④ I'll call you when I <u>arrive</u> at the airport.

⑤ If it <u>is</u> sunny tomorrow, let's go on a picnic.

14 ① Both Tom and Joe <u>were</u> late for school.

② Neither her father nor her mother <u>is</u> tall.

③ Not only Seoul but also Busan <u>is</u> a big city.

④ Either we or Jane <u>have</u> to go there.

⑤ Paul, as well as you, <u>is</u> important to me.

15 다음 중 밑줄 친 부분을 바르게 고친 것은? |4점|

① I was late, <u>but</u> I took a taxi.
　　　　(→ because)

② I felt worse <u>after</u> I took the medicine.
　　　　(→ if)

③ <u>Before</u> I was watching a movie, I fell asleep.
　　　　(→ While)

④ He was hungry <u>unless</u> he didn't have lunch.
　　　　(→ though)

⑤ Exercise more, <u>or</u> you'll be healthy.
　　　　(→ so)

16 (A)~(C)에 들어갈 말이 바르게 짝지어진 것은? |4점|

> • Both Mina (A) |or / and| I have cats.
> • I am neither tired (B) |or / nor| sleepy.
> • My English teacher is not only intelligent
> (C) |and / but| also kind.

	(A)		(B)		(C)
①	or	·····	or	·····	and
②	or	·····	nor	·····	but
③	and	·····	or	·····	and
④	and	·····	nor	·····	but
⑤	and	·····	nor	·····	and

고난도

17 밑줄 친 ⓐ~ⓔ 중 대화의 흐름상 어색한 것은? |5점|

> **A** I'm so worried about the English speaking test.
> **B** ⓐ Don't worry. ⓑ You'll do well.
> **A** ⓒ You are a good English speaker.
> ⓓ Please tell me how I can speak English well like you.
> **B** ⓔ Practice a lot, or you will be good at speaking English.

① ⓐ ② ⓑ ③ ⓒ ④ ⓓ ⑤ ⓔ

고난도

18 짝지어진 두 문장의 의미가 서로 다른 것은? |5점|

① When he drives, my father listens to the radio.
  = My father listens to the radio as he drives.
② I don't like pork. I don't like beef, either.
  = I like neither pork nor beef.
③ Since she lost the key, she couldn't open it.
  = She lost the key, so she couldn't open it.
④ He is not only an actor but also a singer.
  = He is either an actor or a singer.
⑤ If you get some rest, you will feel better.
  = Get some rest, and you will feel better.

서 술 형

19 우리말과 일치하도록 빈칸에 알맞은 말을 쓰시오. |2점|

> 그 영화가 너무 슬퍼서 모든 사람들이 울었다.

→ The movie was _____ sad _____ everyone cried.

[20-21] 〈보기〉에서 알맞은 접속사를 골라 괄호 안의 말을 이용하여 문장을 완성하시오. |6점, 각 3점|

보기	unless	though	since

20 흡연을 그만두지 않으면 너는 건강 문제가 생길 것이다. (stop smoking)

→ _____,
you'll have health problems.

21 내 차는 오래되었음에도 불구하고 여전히 아주 잘 달린다. (my car, old)

→ _____,
it still runs very well.

[22-23] 〈조건〉에 맞게 우리말을 영작하시오. |8점, 각 4점|

22 나는 중국어를 읽지도 말하지도 못한다.

> 조건 1. read, speak, Chinese를 이용할 것
> 2. 접속사를 사용하여 5단어로 쓸 것

→ I can _____.

23

Chris와 Helen은 둘 다 캐나다에서 태어났다.

> 조건 1. be born을 이용할 것
>   2. 접속사를 사용하여 6단어로 쓸 것

→ _____ in

Canada.

---

24 〈보기〉에서 알맞은 부사절을 골라 문장을 완성하시오. (단, 한 번씩만 사용할 것) |6점, 각 2점|

> 보기 • because it snowed a lot
>   • even though it was raining
>   • until the movie ended

(1) They played soccer outside _____

_____ .

(2) I didn't turn on my smartphone _____

_____ .

(3) We decided not to go out _____

_____ .

---

25 다음 그림을 보고 〈조건〉에 맞게 그림을 묘사하는 **두 개의** 문장을 완성하시오. |4점, 각 2점|

5:00 p.m.   7:00 p.m.

> 조건 do one's homework와 watch TV를 이용할 것

(1) After I _____ ,

I _____ .

(2) I _____ before

I _____ .

---

26 두 문장의 의미가 같도록 빈칸에 알맞은 말을 쓰시오.
|2점|

She is not only a scientist but also a writer.

→ She is a writer _____ _____

_____ a scientist.

---

27 다음 글을 읽고 우리말과 일치하도록 괄호 안의 말을 바르게 배열하시오. |4점, 각 2점|

Last Sunday, I was home alone. My parents went out early. (1) <u>나는 너무 배가 고파서 기다릴 수 없었다</u> until they came home. I made a salad myself. (2) <u>그것은 신선할 뿐만 아니라 맛있었다</u>.

(1) (that, couldn't, hungry, so, I, wait)

→ I was _____

_____ until they came home.

(2) (only, also, delicious, not, but, fresh)

→ It was _____

_____ .

---

28 밑줄 친 부분이 어법상 틀린 문장 **두 개**를 찾아 기호를 쓰고, 바르게 고쳐 쓰시오. |8점, 각 4점|

ⓐ The picnic will be canceled <u>if it will rain</u>.

ⓑ My friend called me several times <u>while I was sleeping</u>.

ⓒ Turn left, <u>and you will see a bank</u>.

ⓓ <u>Unless you don't show your ID</u>, you can't go inside.

(   ) → _____

(   ) → _____

chapter

11

관계사

I have a friend who lives in Paris.

Q. 위 문장을 통해서 알 수 있는 것은?

☐ 나는 파리에 산다.　　☐ 내 친구는 파리에 산다.

unit 1 관계대명사의 개념

1 관계대명사란?

(1) 관계대명사는 절을 이용하여 명사를 꾸며 줄 때 쓰며, 관계대명사가 있는 문장은 명사 뒤에 위치한다.

| I saw a **scary** movie. | 나는 **무서운** 영화를 봤어. | 〈형용사＋명사〉 |
| I saw the movie **that you talked about**.
관계대명사 | 나는 **네가 말했던** 영화를 봤어. | 〈명사＋관계대명사절〉 |

(2) 관계대명사는 두 문장을 연결해 주며, 관계대명사가 이끄는 절은 앞에 있는 명사(선행사)를 수식한다.

| I have **a friend**. | ＋ | **He** loves animals. | 나는 한 친구가 있다.
＋ 그는 동물을 사랑한다. |
| I have **a friend**
선행사
(관계대명사 앞에 오는 명사) | **who**
관계대명사
(두 문장을 연결) | *loves animals.* | 나는 동물을 사랑하는 **한 친구**가 있다. |

2 관계대명사의 종류

관계대명사는 선행사와 관계대명사의 역할(주격, 목적격, 소유격)에 따라 다르게 사용된다.

	주격	목적격	소유격	
사람	who/that	who(m)/that	whose	구어체에서는 주로 목적격으로 whom 대신에 who를 쓴다.
동물, 사물	which/that			
사람＋동물/사물	that		-	

A vegetarian is someone **who** doesn't eat meat.
　선행사(사람)

Joe lives in a house **which** has a beautiful garden.
　선행사(사물)

❯ 관계대명사 that은 선행사의 종류와 관계없이 쓸 수 있으며, 특히 선행사가 동물 또는 사물인 경우 주로 that을 쓴다.

Do you remember the photos **that**〔**which**〕 I showed you?

비교 **point**

의문사 who vs. 관계대명사 who

의문사 who는 주로 의문문에 쓰여 '누가, 누구'의 의미를 나타내고, 관계대명사 who는 선행사를 수식하는 절을 이끈다.

| 의문사 | **Who** broke the window? | **누가** 그 창문을 깼니? |
| 관계대명사 | I have an aunt **who** lives in London. | 나는 런던에 사는 고모가 있다. |

개념 우선 확인 | 옳은 해석 고르기

1 the girl who is reading a book
- ☐ 소녀는 책을 읽고 있다
- ☐ 책을 읽고 있는 소녀

2 the boy who I met
- ☐ 내가 만난 소년
- ☐ 나와 소년을 만난 사람

3 the shoes that I want to buy
- ☐ 내가 사고 싶은 신발
- ☐ 내가 원하는 신발을 사다

A 선행사에 밑줄을 긋고, 관계대명사에 동그라미 하시오.

1 They are the people who visited us last week.

2 We found the bike that Peter lost a few days ago.

3 I opened the package that arrived yesterday.

4 Do you know the girl whom Daniel helped on the street?

5 He talked about a man whose son is a soccer player.

B 괄호 안에서 알맞은 것을 고르시오.

1 This is a book (who / which) is about the Korean War.

2 I invited the man (who / which) I met in France.

3 I don't like movies (who / that) have sad endings.

4 Susan interviewed the director (who / which) made the movie.

5 Do you remember the dress (whom / that) I wore for the party?

C 밑줄 친 부분을 어법에 맞게 고쳐 쓰시오.

1 That is the tree <u>who</u> my grandfather planted.

2 Did you see a boy <u>which</u> is wearing a backpack?

3 I like the watch <u>whom</u> my father bought for me.

4 A vet is someone <u>which</u> treats sick animals.

5 Julia showed me the pictures <u>whom</u> she took in Japan.

30초 완성 map

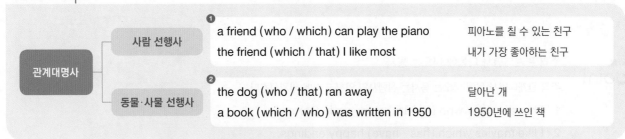

관계대명사

사람 선행사
- ❶ a friend (who / which) can play the piano — 피아노를 칠 수 있는 친구
- the friend (which / that) I like most — 내가 가장 좋아하는 친구

동물·사물 선행사
- ❷ the dog (who / that) ran away — 달아난 개
- a book (which / who) was written in 1950 — 1950년에 쓰인 책

unit 2 관계대명사의 역할

1 주격 관계대명사

관계대명사절에서 주어 역할을 하며 선행사에 따라 who, which, that을 쓴다.

I saw	**a man**.		나는 **한 남자**를 보았다.
	He	was sleeping on a bench.	그는 벤치에서 자고 있었다.
→ I saw	**a man** who	☒ was sleeping on a bench.	나는 벤치에서 자고 있는 **한 남자**를 보았다.

▶ 관계대명사가 주어 역할을 하므로 주격 관계대명사 뒤에 나오는 동사는 선행사의 인칭과 수에 일치시킨다.
　He is <u>an actor</u> who **appears** in a lot of popular movies.
　　　　　↘ 선행사(an actor)의 인칭과 수에 일치

2 목적격 관계대명사

관계대명사절에서 목적어 역할을 하며 선행사에 따라 who(m), which, that을 쓴다.

She lost	**the ring**.		그녀는 **반지**를 잃어버렸다.
Dave gave	**the ring**	to her.	Dave는 **그 반지**를 그녀에게 주었다.
→ She lost	**the ring** which	Dave gave ☒ to her.	그녀는 Dave가 그녀에게 준 **반지**를 잃어버렸다.

주의 관계대명사가 목적어 역할을 하므로 관계대명사절에 목적어를 또 쓰지 않도록 주의한다.
　This is the cell phone that I bought ~~it~~ yesterday. (×)

3 소유격 관계대명사

관계대명사절에서 소유격 역할을 하며 선행사에 관계없이 whose를 쓴다.

I have	**a dog**.		나는 **개 한 마리**가 있다.
	His	legs are short.	**그것의** 다리는 짧다.
→ I have	**a dog** whose	☒ legs are short.	나는 다리가 짧은 **개 한 마리**가 있다.

주의 whose 뒤에는 항상 명사가 온다.

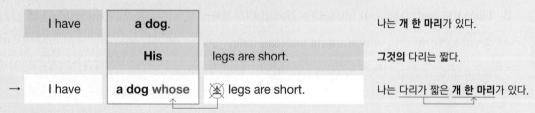

시험 point

주격 관계대명사 다음에 나오는 동사

주격 관계대명사 뒤에 나오는 동사는 선행사의 인칭과 수에 일치시킨다.

1 I have a sister who (is / are) studying in Germany.

2 I like movies which (has / have) happy endings.

1 내가 좋아하는 책
- ☐ the book that I like
- ☐ the book that I like it

2 아버지가 의사인 어떤 남자
- ☐ a man whose father is a doctor
- ☐ a man whose his father is a doctor

3 도움이 필요한 사람들
- ☐ people who need help
- ☐ people who needs help

A 괄호 안에서 알맞은 것을 고르시오.

1 I have a brother (who / whom) is 10 years old.

2 My dad helped a woman (who / whose) car broke down.

3 I have an aunt who (live / lives) in London.

4 Look at the children who (is / are) playing football.

B 빈칸에 알맞은 관계대명사를 〈보기〉에서 골라 문장을 완성하시오. (단. 한 번씩만 사용할 것)

보기　　who　　whom　　whose　　which

1 The girl ＿＿＿＿＿ called me yesterday was Sophia.

2 I have a cat ＿＿＿＿＿ eyes are blue.

3 He made a salad with the tomatoes ＿＿＿＿＿ he grew.

4 The man ＿＿＿＿＿ I met this morning was my uncle.

C 우리말과 일치하도록 괄호 안의 말과 관계대명사를 이용하여 문장을 완성하시오.

1 너는 이 기계를 발명한 사람을 아니? (invent)

→ Do you know the person ＿＿＿＿＿＿＿＿＿＿＿＿ this machine?

2 나는 꿈이 우주비행사가 되는 것인 한 소년을 만났다. (a boy, dream)

→ I met ＿＿＿＿＿＿＿＿＿＿＿＿ is to be an astronaut.

3 나는 우리가 어젯밤에 봤던 영화가 정말 좋았어. (see)

→ I really liked the movie ＿＿＿＿＿＿＿＿＿＿＿＿ last night.

4 표지가 빨간색인 책이 있다. (a book, cover)

→ There is ＿＿＿＿＿＿＿＿＿＿＿＿ is red.

30초 완성 map

관계대명사

주격
| ❶ I know a man (who / which) can speak French.
나는 ＿＿＿＿＿＿＿＿＿＿＿＿ 안다.

목적격
| ❷ I found the pen (whom / that) I lost yesterday.
나는 어제 ＿＿＿＿＿＿＿＿＿＿＿＿ 찾았다.

소유격
| ❸ I know a boy (who / whose) mother is a famous actress.
나는 ＿＿＿＿＿＿＿＿＿＿＿＿ 안다.

관계대명사 what, 관계대명사의 생략

1 관계대명사 what

(1) 관계대명사 what은 선행사를 포함하고 있으며 '~하는 것'으로 해석한다.

| This is | the bag | **that** | I want. | 이것이 내가 원하는 가방이다. |
| | **what** | | | 이것이 내가 원하는 **것**이다. (what = the thing that(which)) |

주의 what은 선행사를 포함하고 있으므로 what 앞에는 선행사를 쓰지 않는다.
Swimming is the thing what I enjoy most. (×)
→ Swimming is **what** I enjoy most.
→ Swimming is **the thing that(which)** I enjoy most.

(2) 관계대명사 what이 이끄는 명사절은 문장에서 주어, 목적어, 보어로 쓰인다.

What I need	is	this book.	내가 필요한 <u>것</u>은 이 책이다. 〈주어〉
I	didn't hear	**what** he said.	나는 <u>그가 말한 것</u>을 듣지 못했다. 〈목적어〉
This	is	**what** we did.	이것이 <u>우리가 한 것</u>이다. 〈보어〉

2 관계대명사의 생략

(1) 목적격 관계대명사 who(m), which, that은 생략할 수 있다.

| I'm wearing the hat | **that(which)** | I bought yesterday. |
→ | I'm wearing the hat I bought yesterday. |

| I saw the actor | **who(m)(that)** | I like most. |
→ | I saw the actor I like most. |

(2) 「주격 관계대명사＋be동사」는 뒤에 분사(구)가 오는 경우 생략할 수 있다.

| The woman | **(who is)** waiting | for me is my mom. |
→ | The woman waiting for me is my mom. |

| I'm reading a novel | **(which was)** written | in English. |
→ | I'm reading a novel written in English. |

비교 point

what과 that의 여러 가지 쓰임

what	That is not **what** I did.	그것은 내가 한 것이 아니다.	〈관계대명사〉
	What are you doing?	너는 무엇을 하고 있니?	〈의문사〉
that	I carried a box **that** had books in it.	나는 책이 들어 있는 상자를 옮겼다.	〈관계대명사〉
	I know **that** he lied to me.	나는 그가 나에게 거짓말한 것을 안다.	〈접속사〉

개념 우선 확인 | 밑줄 친 부분의 옳은 해석 고르기

1 I like the story that I read on the Internet.

☐ 내가 읽은 것
☐ 내가 읽은 그 이야기

2 That's exactly what I want.

☐ 내가 원하는 것
☐ 내가 무엇을 원하는지

A 괄호 안에서 알맞은 것을 고르시오.

1 (That / What) you heard is not true.

2 The earrings (that / what) she is wearing are mine.

3 He gave me some lotion (that / what) is good for dry skin.

4 I want to know (that / what) he said about me.

5 Look at the couple (who / what) are walking down the street.

B 생략 가능한 부분에 동그라미하고, 없는 경우 ×를 쓰시오.

1 This is what I'm interested in.

2 She really liked the present that I made for her.

3 Billy has a friend who lives in New York.

4 I'm reading the magazine which I bought yesterday.

5 The boy who is playing the drums is my brother.

C 우리말과 일치하도록 괄호 안의 말을 바르게 배열하시오.

1 검은색 재킷을 입고 있는 여자아이가 내 여동생이야. (wearing, is, a black jacket, the girl)

→ _____ my sister.

2 Paul은 이탈리아에서 산 지갑을 잃어버렸다. (the wallet, bought, he, lost)

→ Paul _____ in Italy.

3 나는 프랑스어로 쓰인 오래된 책을 한 권 발견했다. (an old book, found, I, written)

→ _____ in French.

4 내가 먹고 싶은 것은 피자 한 조각이다. (is, I, to, what, eat, want)

→ _____ a piece of pizza.

30초 완성 map

관계대명사	what	❶ This is the car (that / what) I want to buy.	이것이 내가 사고 싶은 차이다.
		This is (that / what) I want to buy.	이것이 내가 사고 싶은 것이다.
	생략	❷ Do you know the girl who is talking with Paul?	(생략 가능한 부분: _____)
		The movie that we saw last night was boring.	(생략 가능한 부분: _____)

unit 04 관계부사

1 관계부사란?

관계부사는 「접속사+부사」의 역할을 하며, 관계부사가 이끄는 문장은 앞에 있는 명사(선행사)를 수식한다.

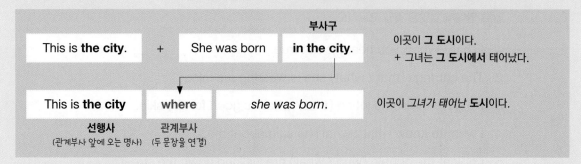

| This is **the city**. | + | She was born | **부사구**
in the city. | 이곳이 **그 도시**이다.
+ 그녀는 **그 도시에서** 태어났다. |

| This is **the city**
선행사
(관계부사 앞에 오는 명사) | where
관계부사
(두 문장을 연결) | *she was born*. | 이곳이 *그녀가 태어난* **도시**이다. |

2 관계부사의 종류

(1) when : 시간을 나타내는 관계부사로 the time, the day, the year 등이 선행사로 쓰인다.

I remember	**the day**		my brother was born.
I will never forget	**the summer**	when	I went to Jeju-do.

(2) where : 장소를 나타내는 관계부사로 the place, the city, the house 등이 선행사로 쓰인다.

New York is	**the city**		I want to live.
This is	**the school**	where	he studied music.

(3) why : 이유를 나타내는 관계부사로 the reason이 선행사로 쓰인다.

She told me	**the reason**		she was angry.
I didn't know		why	he called me.

(4) how : 방법을 나타내는 관계부사로 the way가 선행사로 쓰이나, how와 the way는 함께 쓰지 않는다.

I'll tell you	how	I study Chinese.
	the way	

주의 I'll tell you **the way how** I study Chinese. (×)

비교 point

관계대명사 vs. 관계부사

관계사절 내에서 관계사가 하는 역할에 따라 관계대명사와 관계부사로 구분할 수 있다.

관계대명사	I like *the city* **which** has the Eiffel Tower. → **The city** has the Eiffel Tower. 〈주어: 명사〉
관계부사	I like *the city* **where** I live. → I live **in the city**. 〈부사구〉

1 the day _____
- ☐ when ☐ where

2 the reason _____
- ☐ how ☐ why

3 the house _____
- ☐ how ☐ where

A 괄호 안에서 알맞은 것을 고르시오.

1 Do you know the hotel (when / where) he is staying?

2 He never told us the reason (where / why) he had to leave.

3 We remember the day (when / how) we won the game.

B 우리말과 일치하도록 빈칸에 알맞은 관계부사를 쓰시오.

1 너는 나에게 네가 결석한 이유를 말해야만 한다.

→ You should tell me the reason _____ you were absent.

2 나는 내가 은하수를 봤던 밤을 잊을 수 없을 것이다.

→ I will never forget the night _____ I saw the Milky Way.

3 그의 고향은 내가 자란 마을에서 멀지 않다.

→ His hometown is not far from the town _____ I grew up.

4 너에게 내가 이 수학 문제를 푼 방법을 가르쳐 줄게.

→ I will teach you _____ I solved this math problem.

C 우리말과 일치하도록 괄호 안의 말을 바르게 배열하시오.

1 나는 그가 나에게 말하는 방식을 좋아하지 않는다. (talks to, he, me, how)

→ I don't like _____.

2 나는 우리가 자전거를 타곤 했던 그 공원을 좋아한다. (we, ride our bikes, where, used to)

→ I like the park _____.

3 그는 한국이 월드컵을 개최했던 해에 태어났다. (hosted, when, Korea, the World Cup)

→ He was born in the year _____.

30초 완성 map

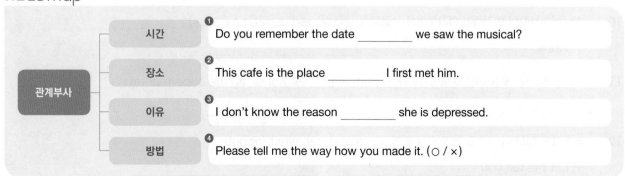

관계부사

시간	❶ Do you remember the date _____ we saw the musical?
장소	❷ This cafe is the place _____ I first met him.
이유	❸ I don't know the reason _____ she is depressed.
방법	❹ Please tell me the way how you made it. (○ / ×)

서술형 대비 문장 쓰기

Answers p. 20

☐ **빈칸 완성** 괄호 안의 말을 이용하여 빈칸 완성하기

01 그가 그리는 만화는 매우 재미있다. (draw)

→ The cartoon ＿＿＿＿＿ ＿＿＿＿＿ ＿＿＿＿＿ is very funny.

02 네가 저녁 식사로 먹고 싶은 것을 알려줘. (want)

→ Let me know ＿＿＿＿＿ ＿＿＿＿＿ ＿＿＿＿＿ to eat for dinner.

03 나는 학교 축제에서 노래를 불렀던 그 남자아이를 안다. (sing)

→ I know the boy ＿＿＿＿＿ ＿＿＿＿＿ at the school festival.

04 나는 그 영화가 인기 있는 이유를 모르겠다. (the movie, popular)

→ I don't know the reason ＿＿＿＿＿ ＿＿＿＿＿ ＿＿＿＿＿ ＿＿＿＿＿ ＿＿＿＿＿.

✔ **오류 수정** 어법에 맞게 문장 고쳐 쓰기

05 That's the restaurant that owner is a famous actor.

→ That's the restaurant ＿＿＿＿＿＿＿＿＿＿＿＿＿＿＿＿.

06 Justin finally found his wallet that he had lost it.

→ Justin finally found his wallet ＿＿＿＿＿＿＿＿＿＿＿＿＿＿＿＿.

07 This is the way how I made the cheesecake.

→ This is ＿＿＿＿＿＿＿＿＿＿＿＿＿＿＿＿.

08 She can't remember the place when she parked her car.

→ She can't remember the place ＿＿＿＿＿＿＿＿＿＿＿＿＿＿＿＿.

☰ **배열 영작** 괄호 안의 말을 바르게 배열하기

09 내가 어제 산 바지는 나에게 잘 맞지 않는다. (I, that, the pants, yesterday, bought)

→ ＿＿＿＿＿＿＿＿＿＿＿＿＿＿＿＿ don't fit me well.

10 나는 머리카락이 빨간색인 여자아이를 보았다. (whose, red, a girl, hair, was)

→ I saw ＿＿＿＿＿＿＿＿＿＿＿＿＿＿＿＿.

11 이곳은 24시간 문을 여는 슈퍼마켓이다. (open, which, 24 hours, is, the supermarket)

→ This is ＿＿＿＿＿＿＿＿＿＿＿＿＿＿＿＿.

12 내가 그에 대해 아는 것을 네게 말해 줄게. (I, him, know, what, about)

→ Let me tell you ＿＿＿＿＿＿＿＿＿＿＿＿＿＿＿＿.

시험에 ✓ 나오는 출제 포인트

Answers p. 20

출제 포인트 1 관계대명사 what 앞에는 선행사가 없음에 주의하자!

괄호 안에서 적절한 것을 고르시오.

(1) (That / What) he has done is amazing.

(2) Do you know (which / what) she was talking to David?

출제 포인트 2 관계대명사 that과 접속사 that을 구분하자!

밑줄 친 that의 쓰임이 나머지와 다른 것은?

① I didn't know that he liked me.
② She is the one that knows the answer.
③ He lost the hat that I gave to him.
④ They are the doctors that helped me last night.
⑤ These are the gloves that my mom made for me.

출제 포인트 3 관계대명사가 생략되는 경우를 기억하자!

다음 문장에서 생략 가능한 부분을 찾아 괄호로 표시하시오.

(1) I like the jeans that you are wearing today.

(2) They are watching a man who is dancing on the stage.

출제 포인트 4 관계부사 how의 쓰임에 주의하자!

어법상 틀린 부분을 찾아 바르게 고쳐 문장을 다시 쓰시오.

This is the way how I brush my teeth.

→ _____

> **고득점 POINT** 관계대명사 vs. 관계부사
>
> **괄호 안에서 알맞은 것을 고르시오.**
>
> (1) Can you tell me the place (which / where) you had dinner yesterday?
>
> (2) I know a restaurant (which / where) is not far from here.

유형	문항수	배점	점수
객관식	18	60	
서술형	10	40	

[01-04] 빈칸에 들어갈 말로 알맞은 것을 고르시오.
|8점, 각 2점|

01
Ben is watching a documentary _____ is about global warming. * global warming 지구 온난화

① who   ② what
③ that   ④ whom
⑤ whose

02
That's _____ I am interested in.

① who   ② what
③ which   ④ whom
⑤ whose

03
I have a dog _____ tail is short.

① its   ② that
③ which   ④ what
⑤ whose

04
You can choose the place _____ you want to study.

① why   ② how
③ that   ④ when
⑤ where

05 ①~⑤ 중 생략된 관계대명사가 들어갈 위치로 알맞은 곳은?
|2점|

The dream (①) I (②) had (③) last night (④) was (⑤) very scary.

06 다음 두 문장을 한 문장으로 나타낼 때 빈칸에 알맞은 것은?
|2점|

I have a friend. His dream is to be a violinist.
→ I have a friend _____ dream is to be a violinist.

① that   ② who   ③ what
④ whose   ⑤ whom

07 밑줄 친 who(Who)의 쓰임이 〈보기〉와 같은 것을 모두 고르면?
|4점|

> 보기   I have a friend who dances very well.

① Who is that tall man?
② I can't tell you who broke the window.
③ The girl who is wearing a cap is Susan.
④ I have no idea who you're talking about.
⑤ I have someone who can help me.

08 밑줄 친 what(What)의 쓰임이 나머지와 다른 것은?
|4점|

① I know what you did.
② I can't understand what he said.
③ What happened to her yesterday?
④ That's what I want to say.
⑤ What I like most is playing the piano.

09 빈칸에 들어갈 말이 순서대로 바르게 짝지어진 것은? |3점|

> • I don't know the reason _____ she is surprised.
> • This is _____ I cooked the pasta.

① why – what
② which – how
③ how – what
④ why – how
⑤ how – which

10 밑줄 친 that의 쓰임이 나머지와 다른 것은? |4점|

① I believe that he told me the truth.
② I lost the wallet that I bought in France.
③ Is that the man that you saw in the park?
④ Picasso is the artist that I like most.
⑤ The city that I visited last summer has a beautiful beach.

11 다음 문장에서 생략할 수 있는 것은? |3점|

> The man who is cooking in the kitchen is
> ①   ②   ③   ④   ⑤
> my uncle.

12 빈칸에 who가 들어갈 수 없는 것은? |4점|

① I have a cousin _____ lives in London.
② Look at the boy _____ is playing with a ball.
③ I know the girl _____ bike was stolen.
④ We're looking for someone _____ can speak French.
⑤ The woman _____ we saw at the park was an actress.

13 밑줄 친 부분이 어법상 틀린 것은? |4점|

① Technology changes how we live.
② 2010 is the year when I was born.
③ Justin is a singer that has many fans.
④ I know a boy whose nickname is AlphaGo.
⑤ I don't believe which you said.

14 다음 중 밑줄 친 부분을 생략할 수 없는 것은? |4점|

① He is a man who I can trust.
② The girl who is wearing glasses is my sister.
③ I read a novel which was written in English.
④ I like boys who are good at singing.
⑤ The movie which I watched yesterday was boring.

15 (A)~(C)에 들어갈 말이 바르게 짝지어진 것은? |4점|

> **A** Do you know the man and the dog _____(A)_____ are walking over there?
> **B** Do you mean the dog _____(B)_____ fur is brown?
> **A** Yes, I do.
> **B** He is my neighbor. I told you about the man _____(C)_____ moved next door to me. He is that guy.

	(A)		(B)		(C)
①	who	……	which	……	that
②	who	……	whose	……	that
③	that	……	which	……	who
④	that	……	whose	……	who
⑤	which	……	whose	……	who

16 어법상 옳은 문장의 개수는? |4점|

> ⓐ I like the way how he talks.
> ⓑ That I want is a glass of water.
> ⓒ Busan is the city where I was born.
> ⓓ The boy who is holding balloons is Ted.
> ⓔ This is the laptop that I bought it yesterday.

① 1개   ② 2개   ③ 3개
④ 4개   ⑤ 5개

최신기출   고난도
17 빈칸 ⓐ~ⓔ에 들어갈 말이 잘못 짝지어진 것은? |5점|

> • I have an uncle ___ⓐ___ is living in Canada.
> • This is not ___ⓑ___ I want.
> • That's ___ⓒ___ I made the cookies.
> • New York is a city ___ⓓ___ you must visit.
> • A man ___ⓔ___ name was Jack lived there.

① ⓐ: who   ② ⓑ: what   ③ ⓒ: how
④ ⓓ: where   ⑤ ⓔ: whose

고난도
18 우리말을 영어로 잘못 옮긴 것은? |5점|

① 네가 그 문제를 푼 방법을 알려줘.
   → Let me know the way you solved the problem.
② 2002년은 나의 부모님이 결혼한 해이다.
   → 2002 is the year when my parents got married.
③ 이 집은 내가 살았던 곳이다.
   → This house is the place where I used to live in.
④ 너는 그녀가 오늘 결석한 이유를 아니?
   → Do you know the reason why she was absent today?
⑤ 나는 지금 내가 읽고 있는 것에 집중할 수가 없다.
   → I can't focus on what I am reading now.

[19-20] 빈칸에 알맞은 관계사를 쓰시오. |4점, 각 2점|

19
> Do you know the reason _____ they fought yesterday?

20
> This music is _____ he played at the concert.

[21-22] 다음 두 문장을 관계사를 이용하여 한 문장으로 쓰시오. |8점, 각 4점|

21
> I know a nice restaurant. The restaurant is open late at night.

→ I know _____
   late at night.

22
> Christmas is a day. People exchange gifts on that day.

→ Christmas is _____
_____.

23 그림의 내용과 일치하도록 괄호 안의 말을 바르게 배열하여 문장을 완성하시오.　|8점, 각 4점|

(1)

(2)

(1) (in Paris, was, which, a photo, taken)

　→ She showed me _____

　_____.

(2) (born, where, I, the hospital, was)

　→ This is _____

　_____.

24 다음 문장에서 생략 가능한 부분을 생략하여 문장을 다시 쓰시오.　|3점|

I am watching a movie which was made in the 1980s.

→ _____

_____

25 어법상 틀린 부분을 찾아 바르게 고쳐 쓰시오.　|4점|

I remember the day which I rode a roller coaster for the first time. It was really exciting.

_____ → _____

[26-27] 우리말과 일치하도록 〈조건〉에 맞게 영작하시오.　|8점, 각 4점|

26 우리는 드럼을 칠 수 있는 누군가가 필요해.

> 조건　1. need, someone, can, play the drums을 이용할 것
> 　　　2. 관계대명사를 포함하여 8단어로 쓸 것

→ _____

_____

27 바구니 안에 있는 그 사과들은 맛있다.

> 조건　1. the apples, in the basket, be, delicious 를 이용할 것
> 　　　2. 관계대명사를 포함하여 9단어로 쓸 것

→ _____

_____

28 다음 포스터를 보고 〈보기〉의 단어와 관계대명사를 이용하여 문장을 완성하시오.　|5점|

보기	them	the beach	clean up
	will	volunteers	with

→ They're looking for _____

_____.

chapter

12

가정법

If I had a ticket, I could go to the concert.

Q. 위 문장으로 보아 알 수 있는 것은?

☐ 나는 콘서트에 갈 수 있다.　　☐ 나는 콘서트에 갈 수 없다.

가정법 과거

1 if가 쓰이는 상황

조건문은 실제로 일어날 수 있는 일을 말하는 반면, 가정법은 실현 불가능한 일을 가정하여 말할 때 쓴다.

조건문	**If** you **go** to Paris,	you **can see** the Eiffel Tower.
가정법	**If** you **went** to Paris,	you **could see** the Eiffel Tower.

네가 파리에 **가면**, 에펠탑을 **볼 수 있어.** (파리에 갈 수 있는 상황)

만약 네가 파리에 **간다면**, 에펠탑을 **볼 수 있을 텐데.** (파리에 갈 수 없는 상황)

2 가정법 과거

가정법 과거는 현재 사실에 반대되는 상황이나 실현 가능성이 낮은 일을 가정할 때 쓴다.

If + 주어	**were** ~,	주어	**would**	동사원형 ...
	동사의 과거형 ~,		**could**	
			might	

(만약) ~**한다면**, …할 텐데.

(만약) ~**한다면**, …할 수 있을 텐데.

(만약) ~**한다면**, …할지도 모를 텐데.

If I **knew** the answer, I **would tell** you. 내가 답을 **안다면**, 너에게 **말해줄 텐데.**
If he **were** not busy, he **could go** with us. 그가 바쁘지 않**으면**, 우리와 함께 **갈 수 있을 텐데.**
If the news **were** true, people **might get** upset. 그 뉴스가 사실**이면**, 사람들이 화낼 **수도 있을 텐데.**

주의 가정법 과거에서 if절의 be동사는 주어의 인칭과 수에 관계없이 were를 쓴다.

3 가정법 과거의 직설법 전환

가정법 과거는 '현재 사실에 대한 반대나 이룰 수 없는 소망'을 나타내므로 반대 의미의 직설법 현재로 바꿔 쓸 수 있다.

If I **were not** sick, I **could go** on the school trip today.
(→ As I **am** sick, I **can't go** on the school trip today.)
If he **visited** us, we **would be** happy.
(→ As he **doesn't visit** us, we **aren't** happy.)

시험 point

가정법을 직설법으로 전환할 때 주의할 점

① 가정법 과거가 '긍정'일 때 직설법은 '부정'으로, 가정법 과거가 '부정'일 때 직설법은 '긍정'으로 바뀐다.
② 가정법 과거는 동사의 과거형을 쓰지만 현재에 대한 이야기이므로 직설법에서는 현재시제를 쓴다.

가정법	If I **had** time, I **could help** you.
직설법	As I (have / don't have) time, I (couldn't / can't) help you.

1 If he were tall, he would be a basketball player.

☐ 그는 지금 농구 선수이다.

☐ 그는 지금 농구 선수가 아니다.

2 If I knew her phone number, I could call her.

☐ 나는 그녀의 전화번호를 안다.

☐ 나는 그녀의 전화번호를 모른다.

A

괄호 안에서 알맞은 것을 고르시오.

1 If I (am / were) you, I would stop playing games.

2 If the weather is nice tomorrow, we (will go / would go) hiking.

3 If you (goes / went) to the concert, you would be so happy.

4 If it (rains / rained), we'll have lunch inside.

5 If I lived in Korea, I (can / could) visit Gyeongju.

B

주어진 문장을 가정법으로 바꿔 쓸 때, 빈칸에 알맞은 말을 쓰시오.

1 As it is cold, we can't go swimming.

→ If it _____ cold, we _____ _____ swimming.

2 As he doesn't have a car, he can't give me a ride home.

→ If he _____ a car, he _____ _____ me a ride home.

3 As she is shy, she doesn't start a conversation.

→ If she _____ shy, she _____ _____ a conversation.

C

우리말과 일치하도록 괄호 안의 말을 이용하여 문장을 완성하시오.

1 내가 용감하다면, 그에게 도전할 텐데. (be, will, challenge)

→ If I _____ brave, I _____ _____ him.

2 네가 그녀에게 부탁하면, 그녀가 우리를 도와줄지도 모를텐데. (ask, may, help)

→ If you _____ her, she _____ _____ us.

3 우리에게 열쇠가 있다면, 그 사물함을 열 수 있을 텐데. (have, can, open)

→ If we _____ the key, we _____ _____ the locker.

30초 완성 map

가정법 과거

형태와 의미

❶
If it (was / were) sunny, we would go on a picnic.
날씨가 _____, 우리는 소풍을 _____.

직설법 전환

❷
If he knew Kate, he could introduce her to us.
→ As he _____ Kate, he _____ her to us.

가정법 과거완료

1 가정법 과거완료

가정법 과거완료는 과거 사실에 반대되는 상황을 가정할 때 쓴다.

If+주어	had+p.p. ~,	주어	would	have+p.p. ...	(만약) ~**했다면**, …**했을 텐데**.
			could		(만약) ~**했다면**, …**할 수 있었을 텐데**.
			might		(만약) ~**했다면**, …**했을지도 모를 텐데**.

If I **had had** an umbrella, I **wouldn't have gotten** wet. 내가 우산이 **있었다면**, (비에) 젖지 **않았을 텐데**.

If you **had gotten** up earlier, you **could have seen** the sunrise.
네가 더 일찍 **일어났다면**, 일출을 **볼 수 있었을 텐데**.

If he **had known** your phone number, he **might have called** you.
그가 너의 전화번호를 **알았다면**, 너에게 **전화했을지도 모를 텐데**.

2 가정법 과거완료의 직설법 전환

가정법 과거완료는 '과거 사실에 대한 반대나 이루지 못한 소망'을 나타내므로 반대 의미의 직설법 과거로 바꿔 쓸 수 있다.

If I **had taken** a taxi, I **would have arrived** on time.
(→ As I **didn't take** a taxi, I **didn't arrive** on time.)

If you **had gone** there, you **could have seen** the actor.
(→ As you **didn't go** there, you **couldn't see** the actor.)

3 가정법 과거와 가정법 과거완료 비교

가정법 과거는 if절에 동사의 과거형을 쓰고 현재 사실에 반대되는 상황을 가정하는 반면, 가정법 과거완료는 if절에 동사의 과거완료형을 쓰고 과거 사실에 반대되는 상황을 가정한다.

If I	had	a camera,	I	could take	pictures.	(현재) 카메라가 **있다면**, 사진을 **찍을 수 있을 텐데**.
	had had			could have taken		(과거에) 카메라가 **있었다면**, 사진을 **찍을 수 있었을 텐데**.

비교 point

가정법 과거 vs. 가정법 과거완료

가정법 과거와 가정법 과거완료 문장에서 if절과 주절에 쓰이는 시제에 주의한다.

	if절	주절
가정법 과거	If+주어+**were**/동사의 과거형 ~,	주어+**would**/**could**/**might**+동사원형 ...
가정법 과거완료	If+주어+**had**+p.p. ~,	주어+**would**/**could**/**might**+have+p.p. ...

개념 우선 확인 | 옳은 가정법 시제 고르기

1 If he had asked me, I would have helped him.

☐ 가정법 과거
☐ 가정법 과거완료

2 If he were rich, he could buy the car.

☐ 가정법 과거
☐ 가정법 과거완료

A 괄호 안에서 알맞은 것을 고르시오.

1 If you had been there, you (might see / might have seen) her.

2 If I (were / had been) a doctor, I would help children in poor countries.

3 If I (had / had had) time, I could have gone to the movies.

4 If he had seen her, he (would say / would have said) hello to her.

B 주어진 문장을 가정법으로 바꿔 쓸 때, 빈칸에 알맞은 말을 쓰시오.

1 As you helped me, I didn't fail the test.

→ If you _____ _____ me, I _____ _____ _____ the test.

2 As the bus didn't arrive on time, he was late for school.

→ If the bus _____ _____ on time, he _____ _____ _____ late for school.

3 As you told a lie, I couldn't trust you.

→ If you _____ _____ a lie, I _____ _____ _____ you.

C 우리말과 일치하도록 괄호 안의 말을 이용하여 문장을 완성하시오.

1 우리 할머니가 살아 계신다면, 그 소식을 듣고 기뻐하실 텐데. (be, will, be)

→ If my grandmother _____ alive, she _____ happy to hear the news.

2 눈이 많이 왔다면, 우리는 눈사람을 만들 수 있었을 텐데. (snow, can, make)

→ If it _____ a lot, we _____ a snowman.

3 내가 지갑을 잃어버리지 않았다면, 나는 햄버거를 샀을 텐데. (lose, will, get)

→ If I _____ my wallet, I _____ a hamburger.

30초 완성 map

가정법
과거완료

형태와 의미

❶
If I (arrived / had arrived) earlier, I could have met Julia.
내가 더 일찍 _____, Julia를 _____.

직설법 전환

❷
If I had been careful, I wouldn't have made a mistake.
→ As I _____ careful, I _____ a mistake.

I wish 가정법, as if 가정법

1 I wish 가정법

(1) I wish + 가정법 과거

'~한다면 좋을 텐데'의 의미로, 현재 상황에 대한 아쉬움이나 이룰 수 없는 소망을 나타낼 때 쓴다.

주어+**동사의 과거형**

| I wish | I **were** good at English. | 내가 영어를 잘**하면 좋을 텐데.** |
| I wish | he **didn't have** a girlfriend. | 그가 여자친구가 **없다면 좋을 텐데.** |

I wish I **were** a lawyer. (→ I'm sorry that I **am not** a lawyer.)
I wish you **believed** me. (→ I'm sorry that you **don't believe** me.)

(2) I wish + 가정법 과거완료

'~했다면 좋을 텐데'의 의미로, 과거 일에 대한 아쉬움이나 유감을 나타낼 때 쓴다.

주어+**had+p.p.**

| I wish | it **had snowed** last night. | 어젯밤에 **눈이 왔다면 좋을 텐데.** |
| I wish | I **hadn't lost** my cell phone. | 내가 휴대전화를 잃어버리지 않았다면 좋을 텐데. |

I wish you **hadn't lied** to me. (→ I'm sorry that you **lied** to me.)
I wish I **had finished** the work yesterday. (→ I'm sorry that I **didn't finish** the work yesterday.)

2 as if 가정법

(1) as if + 가정법 과거

'마치 ~한 것처럼'의 의미로, 실제로는 아니지만 주절과 같은 시점에 마치 그런 것처럼 가정할 때 쓴다.

as if+주어+**동사의 과거형**

| She acts | **as if** she **were** a queen. | 그녀는 **마치 여왕인 것처럼** 행동한다. |
| He talks | **as if** he **knew** everything. | 그는 **마치 모든 것을 아는 것처럼** 말한다. |

She talks **as if** she **had** a boyfriend. (→ In fact, she **doesn't have** a boyfriend.)
He acts **as if** he **could carry** it alone. (→ In fact, he **can't carry** it alone.)

(2) as if + 가정법 과거완료

'마치 ~했던 것처럼'의 의미로, 실제로는 아니지만 주절보다 앞선 시점에 마치 그랬던 것처럼 가정할 때 쓴다.

as if+주어+**had+p.p.**

| She looks | **as if** she **had seen** a ghost. | 그녀는 **마치 유령을 보았던 것처럼** 보인다. |
| He talks | **as if** he **had lived** in Australia. | 그는 **마치 호주에 살았던 것처럼** 말한다. |

He acts **as if** he **had met** her. (→ In fact, he **didn't meet** her.)
She talks **as if** she **had watched** the movie. (→ In fact, she **didn't watch** the movie.)

개념 우선 확인 | **옳은 의미 고르기**

1 I wish I had a lot of friends.

☐ 나는 친구가 많다.

☐ 나는 친구가 많지 않다.

2 He talks as if he had lived in London.

☐ 그는 런던에 산 적이 없다.

☐ 그는 런던에 산 적이 있다.

A 괄호 안에서 알맞은 것을 고르시오.

1 I wish I (am / were) the class president.

2 My aunt treats me as if I (am / were) her son.

3 Lucy acts as if she (didn't meet / hadn't met) me before.

4 I wish it (were / had been) sunny yesterday.

5 I wish I (had / had had) a cell phone. I can't send text messages now.

B 우리말과 일치하도록 괄호 안의 말을 이용하여 문장을 완성하시오.

1 나에게 강아지가 있으면 좋을 텐데. (have)

→ I wish I _____ a puppy.

2 그녀가 내 비밀을 친구들에게 말하지 않았다면 좋을 텐데. (tell)

→ I wish she _____ my secret to my friends.

3 그녀는 마치 전에 부자였던 것처럼 행동한다. (be)

→ She acts as if she _____ rich before.

4 그는 마치 모든 답을 알고 있는 것처럼 말한다. (know)

→ He talks as if he _____ all the answers.

C 우리말과 일치하도록 괄호 안의 말을 바르게 배열하시오.

1 내가 노래를 잘하면 좋을 텐데. (were, singing, good, I, at)

→ I wish _____.

2 그녀는 마치 어젯밤에 잠을 잘 못 잤던 것처럼 보였다. (slept, as, hadn't, she, if)

→ She looked _____ well last night.

3 네가 그 영화를 봤다면 좋을 텐데. (wish, watched, I, had, you)

→ _____ that movie.

30초 완성 map

I wish 가정법	❶ I wish I _____ taller. (be)	내가 더 키가 크다면 좋을 텐데.
	I wish I _____ well last night. (sleep)	내가 어젯밤에 잘 잤다면 좋을 텐데.
as if 가정법	❷ He talks as if he _____ a teacher. (be)	그는 마치 자신이 교사인 것처럼 말한다.
	He talks as if he _____ the book. (read)	그는 마치 자신이 그 책을 읽었던 것처럼 말한다.

서술형 대비 문장 쓰기

□ 빈칸 완성 괄호 안의 말을 이용하여 빈칸 완성하기

01 내가 너라면, 더 열심히 공부할 텐데. (be, study)

→ If I _____ you, I _____ harder.

02 내가 Jeff를 잘 알았다면, 나는 그에게 도움을 요청할 수 있었을 텐데. (know, ask)

→ If I _____ Jeff well, I _____ him for help.

03 Mike는 마치 그가 유명한 배우인 것처럼 행동한다. (be)

→ Mike acts _____ he _____ a famous actor.

04 내가 어렸을 때 수영하는 방법을 배웠다면 좋을 텐데. (learn)

→ I wish I _____ how to swim when I was young.

↻ 문장 전환 의미가 통하는 문장으로 바꿔 쓰기

05 As he doesn't have a driver's license, he can't drive the car. * driver's license 운전면허증

→ If he _____ , he _____ the car.

06 If it had snowed, we would have gone snowboarding.

→ As it _____ , we _____ snowboarding.

07 He talks as if he had been to Russia.

→ In fact, he _____ to Russia.

08 I'm sorry that I can't go to the concert.

→ I wish I _____ to the concert.

☰ 영작 완성 괄호 안의 말을 이용하여 영작하기

09 그는 마치 그가 나를 이해하는 것처럼 말한다. (understand)

→ He talks _____ .

10 내가 어젯밤에 아이스크림을 먹지 않았다면 좋을 텐데. (eat, ice cream)

→ I wish _____ last night.

11 그녀의 아버지가 아직 살아 계시면, 그녀를 자랑스러워하실 텐데. (be, will, be proud of)

→ If her dad _____ still alive, he _____ .

12 내가 긴장하지 않았다면, 나는 실수를 하지 않았을 텐데. (be, will, make a mistake)

→ If I _____ nervous, I _____ .

시험에 꼭 나오는 출제 포인트

Answers p. 22

출제 포인트 ❶ 가정법 과거 문장의 형태에 주의하자!

괄호 안에서 알맞은 것을 고르시오.

(1) If I (have / had) a car, I could go there.

(2) If I were you, I (didn't / wouldn't) do that.

> **고득점 POINT 가정법 과거의 직설법 전환**
>
> **두 문장의 의미가 같도록 빈칸에 알맞은 말을 쓰시오.**
>
> If I knew your number, I could call you.
>
> → As I _____ your number,
>   I _____ you.

출제 포인트 ❷ 가정법 과거완료 문장의 형태에 주의하자!

괄호 안의 말을 이용하여 문장을 완성하시오.

(1) If you hadn't helped me yesterday, I
  _____ the work.
  (can, finish, not)

(2) If you _____ to her,
  she would have forgiven you. (apologize)

> **고득점 POINT 가정법 과거완료의 직설법 전환**
>
> **두 문장의 의미가 같도록 빈칸에 알맞은 말을 쓰시오.**
>
> As I didn't save money, I couldn't buy a smartwatch.
>
> → If I _____ money,
>   I _____ a smartwatch.

출제 포인트 ❸ 「I wish + 가정법」의 형태와 의미를 파악하자!

두 문장의 의미가 같을 때, 빈칸에 들어갈 말로 알맞은 것은?

> I'm sorry that you didn't come to my birthday party.
> → I wish you _____ to my birthday party.

① come   ② came   ③ will come
④ have come   ⑤ had come

출제 포인트 ❹ 「as if + 가정법」의 형태와 의미를 파악하자!

주어진 문장과 의미가 같도록 빈칸에 알맞은 말을 쓰시오.

(1) He acts as if he were a famous singer.

  → In fact, he _____ a famous singer.

(2) She talks as if she had not eaten the cake.

  → In fact, she _____ the cake.

[01-04] 빈칸에 들어갈 말로 알맞은 것을 고르시오.

|8점, 각 2점|

01

If I had enough money, I _____ a new car.

① bought
② can buy
③ could buy
④ had bought
⑤ could have bought

02

I wish I _____ a good dancer.

① am
② be
③ were
④ been
⑤ would be

03

If I _____ his phone number, I would have called him yesterday.

① know
② knew
③ have known
④ had known
⑤ haven't known

04

She talks as if she _____ his face, but she didn't actually see anything.

① sees
② saw
③ has seen
④ had seen
⑤ hadn't seen

최신기출

05 다음 우리말을 영작할 때 어법상 틀린 것은? |3점|

내가 그 콘서트에 갔다면, 내가 가장 좋아하는 가수를 볼 수 있었을 텐데.

→ If I have gone to the concert, I could
　　①　　② ③ ④
have seen my favorite singer.
　　⑤

06 다음 가정법 질문에 대한 대답으로 가장 적절한 것은? |3점|

What would you do if you were a billionaire?

① I help poor people.
② I can help poor people.
③ I will help poor people.
④ I would help poor people.
⑤ I would have helped poor people.

07 빈칸에 공통으로 들어갈 말로 알맞은 것은? |3점|

- I wish I _____ a famous singer.
- She acts as if she _____ a doctor, but she is not.

① be
② has been
③ were
④ have been
⑤ had been

08 밑줄 친 부분이 어법상 틀린 것은? |3점|

① I wish I <u>could speak</u> French.

② If it <u>didn't rain</u>, we could go on a picnic.

③ If the shoes <u>were</u> cheaper, I would buy them.

④ If I <u>had</u> a ticket, I could go to the concert.

⑤ If it <u>snowed</u>, we would have gone skiing.

09 다음 문장의 의미로 알맞은 것은? |3점|

I wish he had come to the party.

① I'm sorry that he comes to the party.

② I'm sorry that he didn't come to the party.

③ I'm sorry that he doesn't come to the party.

④ I'm sorry that he came to the party.

⑤ I'm sorry that he won't come to the party.

10 다음 문장을 가정법으로 바르게 바꾼 것은? |3점|

Because I don't have a tent, I can't go camping.

① If I have a tent, I can go camping.

② If I had a tent, I can go camping.

③ If I have a tent, I could go camping.

④ If I had a tent, I could go camping.

⑤ If I didn't have a tent, I couldn't go camping.

11 빈칸에 들어갈 말이 순서대로 바르게 짝지어진 것은? |4점|

• If I _____ wings, I would fly to you.

• If you _____ more careful, you could have avoided the accident.

① have – are   ② had – were

③ have – were   ④ had – had been

⑤ have – had been

12 다음 문장을 가정법으로 바꿔 쓸 때, 빈칸에 알맞은 것은? |3점|

As he lied to me, I didn't trust him.

→ If he _____ to me, I would have trusted him.

① didn't lie   ② has lied

③ had lied   ④ hasn't lied

⑤ hadn't lied

[13-14] 우리말을 영어로 바르게 옮긴 것을 고르시오. |8점, 각 4점|

13 Alex는 자신이 마치 왕인 것처럼 행동한다.

① Alex acts as if he is a king.

② Alex acts as if he isn't a king.

③ Alex acts as if he wasn't a king.

④ Alex acts as if he were a king.

⑤ Alex acts as if he weren't a king.

14 내가 너의 충고를 따랐다면 좋을 텐데.

① I wish I followed your advice.

② I wish I don't follow your advice.

③ I wish I had followed your advice.

④ I wish I didn't follow your advice.

⑤ I wish I hadn't followed your advice.

고난도

15 어법상 옳은 것끼리 짝지어진 것은? |5점|

ⓐ If I was you, I would apologize to her.

ⓑ If I knew her email address, I would send her an email.

ⓒ I wish I were 20 years old.

ⓓ I wish Harry didn't lie to me then.

ⓔ You talk as if you are my mom.

① ⓐ, ⓒ   ② ⓐ, ⓓ   ③ ⓑ, ⓒ

④ ⓑ, ⓔ   ⑤ ⓓ, ⓔ

16 짝지어진 두 문장의 의미가 서로 <u>다른</u> 것은? |4점|

① He acts as if he were from China.
   → In fact, he is not from China.
② You act as if you hadn't eaten lunch.
   → In fact, you ate lunch.
③ I wish I were good at cooking.
   → I'm sorry that I am good at cooking.
④ If he were healthy, he could play soccer.
   → As he isn't healthy, he can't play soccer.
⑤ If I had been there, I would have met Jamie.
   → As I wasn't there, I didn't meet Jamie.

고난도
17 밑줄 친 ⓐ~ⓔ 중 어법상 <u>틀린</u> 것은? |5점|

> A What's up? ⓐ <u>You look upset.</u>
> B ⓑ <u>I fought with Emily.</u>
> A What happened?
> B ⓒ <u>She laughed at me.</u> ⓓ <u>If she hasn't</u>
>   <u>laughed, I wouldn't have gotten angry.</u>
> A I see. ⓔ <u>If I were you, I would talk to her</u>
>   <u>about it.</u>

① ⓐ   ② ⓑ   ③ ⓒ   ④ ⓓ   ⑤ ⓔ

고난도
18 다음 중 우리말을 영어로 <u>잘못</u> 옮긴 것은? |5점|

① 아빠가 담배를 끊으시면 좋을 텐데.
   → I wish my dad had stopped smoking.
② 그녀는 마치 어제 그곳에서 나를 봤던 것처럼 말한다.
   → She talks as if she had seen me there
     yesterday.
③ 내가 휴식을 취한다면, 나는 기분이 더 나아질 텐데.
   → If I got some rest, I would feel better.
④ 네가 이곳에 나와 함께 있다면 좋을 텐데.
   → I wish you were here with me.
⑤ 그가 진실을 알았다면, 너를 용서했을 텐데.
   → If he had known the truth, he would have
     forgiven you.

19 다음 문장을 가정법으로 바꿔 쓸 때, 빈칸에 알맞은 말을 쓰시오. |3점|

> As I am busy, I can't help you.

→ If I _____ busy, I _____ _____
  you.

20 다음 문장을 I wish 가정법으로 바꿔 쓰시오. |3점|

> I don't have a skateboard. I want one.

→ I wish _____.

[21-22] 우리말과 일치하도록 괄호 안의 말을 이용하여 문장을 완성하시오. |8점, 각 4점|

21
> 내가 차가 있다면 너를 공항까지 태워다 줄 텐데.
> (have, give)

→ If I _____ a car,
  I _____ you a ride
  to the airport.

22
> 내가 더 일찍 일어났다면 아침을 먹을 수 있었을 텐데.
> (get up, have)

→ If I _____ earlier,
  I _____ breakfast.

23 그림을 보고 주어진 우리말과 일치하도록 문장을 완성하시오. |4점|

그 소년은 마치 의사인 것처럼 행동한다.

→ The boy acts _____.

24 다음 글을 읽고, 괄호 안의 말을 이용하여 상황에 맞는 문장을 완성하시오. |5점|

Yesterday my family went to a popular restaurant for dinner. We didn't make a reservation, so we had to wait for an hour.
* reservation 예약

→ I wish we _____
_____. (make a reservation)

고난도

25 우리말과 일치하도록 〈조건〉에 맞게 문장을 완성하시오. |5점|

Emily는 마치 그녀가 아프지 않았던 것처럼 보인다.

조건 sick을 포함한 6단어로 쓸 것

→ Emily looks _____
_____.

26 그림의 내용과 일치하도록 괄호 안의 말을 이용하여 글을 완성하시오. |4점|

Emma wants to ride the roller coaster, but she can't. If she _____ taller, she _____ _____ the roller coaster.

[27-28] 다음 글을 읽고, 밑줄 친 부분을 어법에 맞게 고쳐 쓰시오. |8점, 각 4점|

27
I have a friend from Russia. He has lived in Seoul for 10 years, and speaks Korean fluently. He can speak Korean as if it is his native language.
* fluently 유창하게 native language 모국어

→ _____

28
Yesterday was my birthday. I invited my friends to the party, but I forgot to invite Jason by mistake. He would have come to the party if I invited him.

→ _____

**동사의
불규칙 변화형**

• A-B-B형

동사원형	과거형	과거분사형(p.p.)	
bring	brought	brought	가져오다
build	built	built	짓다
buy	bought	bought	사다
catch	caught	caught	잡다
feel	felt	felt	느끼다
find	found	found	찾다
hang	hung	hung	걸다
have	had	had	가지다
hear	heard	heard	듣다
hold	held	held	잡다
keep	kept	kept	유지하다
leave	left	left	떠나다
lose	lost	lost	잃어버리다
make	made	made	만들다
meet	met	met	만나다
pay	paid	paid	지불하다
say	said	said	말하다
sell	sold	sold	팔다
send	sent	sent	보내다
sit	sat	sat	앉다
sleep	slept	slept	자다
spend	spent	spent	소비하다
stand	stood	stood	서다
teach	taught	taught	가르치다
tell	told	told	말하다
think	thought	thought	생각하다
understand	understood	understood	이해하다
win	won	won	이기다

• A-B-A형

동사원형	과거형	과거분사형(p.p.)	
become	became	become	~이 되다
come	came	come	오다
run	ran	run	달리다

• A-B-C형

동사원형	과거형	과거분사형(p.p.)	
be (am / are / is)	was / were	been	~이다, 있다
begin	began	begun	시작하다
break	broke	broken	부수다
choose	chose	chosen	선택하다
do	did	done	하다
draw	drew	drawn	그리다
drink	drank	drunk	마시다
drive	drove	driven	운전하다
eat	ate	eaten	먹다
fall	fell	fallen	떨어지다
fly	flew	flown	날다
forget	forgot	forgotten	잊어버리다
get	got	gotten	얻다
give	gave	given	주다
go	went	gone	가다
grow	grew	grown	자라다
hide	hid	hidden	숨다
know	knew	known	알다
ride	rode	ridden	타다
see	saw	seen	보다
sing	sang	sung	노래하다
speak	spoke	spoken	말하다
steal	stole	stolen	훔치다
swim	swam	swum	수영하다
take	took	taken	가져가다
throw	threw	thrown	던지다
write	wrote	written	쓰다

• A-A-A형

동사원형	과거형	과거분사형(p.p.)	
cut	cut	cut	자르다
hit	hit	hit	치다
put	put	put	놓다
read	read [red]	read [red]	읽다
set	set	set	세우다

부록

비교급·최상급

• 규칙 변화 (-er, -est)

원급	비교급	최상급	
friendly	friendlier	friendliest	친근한
hungry	hungrier	hungriest	배고픈
lazy	lazier	laziest	게으른
lonely	lonelier	loneliest	외로운
nice	nicer	nicest	멋진
noisy	noisier	noisiest	시끄러운
poor	poorer	poorest	가난한
scary	scarier	scariest	무서운
ugly	uglier	ugliest	못생긴
wet	wetter	wettest	젖은
wide	wider	widest	넓은

• 규칙 변화 (more, most)

원급	비교급	최상급	
afraid	more afraid	most afraid	두려운
boring	more boring	most boring	지루하게 하는
curious	more curious	most curious	궁금한
foolish	more foolish	most foolish	어리석은
helpful	more helpful	most helpful	도움이 되는
nervous	more nervous	most nervous	초조한
slowly	more slowly	most slowly	느리게
tired	more tired	most tired	피곤한
useful	more useful	most useful	유용한

• 불규칙 변화

원급	비교급	최상급	
ill	worse	worst	아픈
little	less	least	적은
late	latter	last	(순서가) 늦은
far	further	furthest	먼

중학 영문법

클리어.

Level 2

ANSWERS

CHAPTER 1 시제

Q. 여자아이는 고양이를 찾았을까요?
→ 못 찾았다

UNIT 01 현재시제, 과거시제, 미래시제

p. 13

개념 우선 확인 1 물은 100도에서 끓는다. 2 그 버스는 8시에 도착할 것이다. 3 나는 그녀를 만날 것이다.

A 1 plays 2 went 3 rises 4 to have
   5 will buy
B 1 reserved 2 will be 또는 is going to be
   3 wears
C 1 works 2 will eat 또는 am going to eat
   3 went

30초 완성 map

① works, is ② visited, ended ③ going to

UNIT 02 현재진행형, 과거진행형

p. 15

개념 우선 확인 1 비가 오는 중이었다. 2 나는 지금 공원에 가는 중이다. 3 그는 피자를 먹고 있다.

A 1 believe 2 are taking 3 checks 4 hates
   5 was doing
B 1 have 2 are 3 understand 4 snows
   5 was sleeping
C 1 are going 2 were dancing 3 am reading
   4 was swimming

30초 완성 map

① ride, am riding ② watched, was watching
③ have

UNIT 03 현재완료의 개념

p. 17

개념 우선 확인 1 I watched the movie last year.

2 It has rained for three days.

A 1 built 2 known 3 has 4 met
   5 did you go
B 1 won 2 has used 3 ○ 4 Have
   5 has never eaten
C 1 visited 2 has written 3 has not called

30초 완성 map

① have / has, not (never), Have / Has
② played, have played

UNIT 04 현재완료의 쓰임

p. 19

개념 우선 확인 1 2년 동안 중국어를 배워 왔다
2 반지를 잃어버려서 지금 없다

A 1 완 2 경 3 계 4 결
B 1 for 2 yet 3 been
C 1 has gone 2 has worked 3 have watched

30초 완성 map

① for ② 본 적이 없다 ③ has, heard
④ 런던으로 가 버렸다, has been

W 서술형 대비 문장 쓰기

p. 20

01 wears
02 is going to open
03 were waiting
04 has never been
05 haven't (have not) seen
06 was sleeping
07 has
08 did you take
09 will be a middle school student next year
10 have you had a headache
11 has never written a letter
12 am going to the airport

시험에 꼭 나오는 출제포인트

p. 21

1 ①
2 (1) love (2) is fixing (3) knows
3 ④ **고득점 POINT** (1) since (2) for
4 ③ **고득점 POINT** (1) been (2) gone

01 ③	**02** ②	**03** ⑤	**04** ④	**05** ③
06 ③,⑤	**07** ④	**08** ①	**09** ①	**10** ③
11 ②	**12** ①,④	**13** ④	**14** ⑤	
15 ③	**16** ②	**17** ④,⑤	**18** ⑤	

19 am baking
20 have never seen
21 were cooking
22 No, I haven't
23 I am going to learn Chinese
24 has been sick since
25 traveled, is, was
26 did you return
27 hasn't finished
28 (1) got up (2) has watched a movie
　　(3) will(is going to) do his homework

01 now는 지금 현재를 나타내므로 현재진행형이 알맞다.

02 yesterday가 있으므로 과거시제가 알맞다.

03 기간을 나타내는 말이 쓰였으므로 계속을 나타내는 현재완료로 써야 하고, 주어가 They이므로 have worked가 알맞다.

04 과거의 특정 시점에 진행 중이었던 일을 나타내므로 과거진행형이 알맞다.

05 ③ 현재완료는 have(has) 다음에 과거분사형을 써야 하므로 have known이 되어야 한다.

06 tomorrow가 있으므로 미래를 나타내는 말이 와야 한다.

07 과거시제 문장이므로 '~부터'라는 의미의 since는 적절하지 않다.

08 '한 시간 후에'라는 표현이 있으므로 미래시제가 알맞다. 현재시제나 현재진행형은 가까운 미래의 일정을 나타낼 수 있다.

09 ① 상태를 나타내는 know는 진행형으로 쓰지 않는 동사이다.

10 ③ 현재완료는 특정 과거 시점을 나타내는 표현(last year)과 함께 쓸 수 없다.

11 ②는 동작이나 상태가 시작된 과거 시점을 나타내는 since가 알맞고, 나머지는 기간을 나타내는 for가 적절하다.

12 ② 소유를 나타내는 have는 진행형으로 쓸 수 없다. ③, ⑤ 현재완료는 특정 과거 시점을 나타내는 표현(yesterday)이나 when과 함께 쓸 수 없다.

13 첫 번째 문장은 last weekend가 있으므로 과거시제로 써야 하고, 두 번째 문장은 경험을 나타내는 현재완료가 알맞다.

14 현재완료 의문문은 「Have / Has + 주어 + p.p. ~?」형태

이므로 Did가 아닌 Have를 써야 한다.

15 ③은 가까운 미래를 나타내고, 나머지는 현재 진행 중인 동작이나 상황을 나타내는 현재진행형이다.

16 ⓑ 과거를 나타내는 부사구가 있으므로 과거시제로 써야 한다. ⓓ believe는 진행형으로 쓸 수 없는 동사이다. ⓔ have gone to는 '~에 가 버렸다'는 뜻이므로 경험을 나타내는 have been to로 써야 한다.

17 〈보기〉와 같이 완료의 의미로 쓰인 것은 ④, ⑤이다. ①, ②는 경험, ③은 결과를 나타낸다.

18 해석 A 너는 이번 주말에 계획이 있니?
　　B 응, 나는 가족들이랑 캠핑을 갈 거야. 난 캠핑이 정말 좋아. 너는 캠핑을 좋아하니?
　　A 사실 나는 전에 캠핑을 가 본 적이 없어.
　　B 우리와 같이 갈래? 이번 주말에 우린 캠핑장에 갈 거야.
　　A 좋아. 재밌을 것 같아.
　　→ ⑤ 이번 주말의 계획을 말하는 것이므로 미래시제로 써야 한다. be going to 또는 will을 쓰거나 현재진행형을 써서 가까운 미래의 계획을 나타낼 수 있다.

19 현재진행형으로 물었으므로 현재진행형으로 답하는 것이 자연스럽다.

20 과거부터 현재까지의 경험은 현재완료를 써서 나타내며, 현재완료의 부정문은 「have/has + never + p.p.」형태로 쓴다.

21 과거 특정 시점에 진행 중이었던 동작을 나타내므로 과거진행형으로 쓴다.

22 대화의 흐름상 부정의 대답이 들어가야 한다. 현재완료로 물었으므로 have동사를 이용하여 답한다.

23 「be going to + 동사원형」을 써서 미래에 예정된 일이나 계획에 대해 말할 수 있다.

24 과거에 시작된 동작이나 상태가 현재까지 지속되고 있으므로 현재완료(have/has + p.p.)를 쓰고 어제부터 아팠다는 것은 since를 이용해서 나타낼 수 있다.

25 해석 지난달에 우리 가족은 만리장성을 보기 위해 중국으로 여행을 갔다. 만리장성은 세계에서 가장 긴 벽이다. 그것은 대단히 멋진 경험이었다.
　　→ 첫 번째 문장과 세 번째 문장은 과거 특정 시점(last month)의 일을 설명하므로 과거시제로 쓰고, 두 번째 문장은 일반적인 사실에 대한 설명이므로 현재시제로 쓴다.

26 When과 함께 쓰여 과거의 특정 시점에 한 일에 대해 묻고 있으므로 과거시제를 쓴다.

27 현재완료 부정문은 「have/has + not + p.p.」로 쓰며, yet은 현재완료 부정문에 주로 쓰여 '아직 (~하지 않았다)'의 의미를 나타낸다.

28 (1) 과거의 특정 시점에 일어난 일이므로 과거시제로 쓴다.
　　(2) 과거에 시작된 일이 현재까지 지속되고 있음을 나타내므로 현재완료로 쓴다.
　　(3) 앞으로의 계획이므로 will이나 be going to를 이용해서 쓴다.

UNIT 01   can, may, will

pp. 28~29

시험 point   will be able to

개념 우선 확인   **1** 그는 기타를 칠 수 있다.   **2** 그것은 사실일지도 모른다.   **3** 나를 도와줄래?

A   **1** 능력   **2** 예정   **3** 허가   **4** 요청
B   **1** Will   **2** Can   **3** may not
C   **1** Can(May) I use   **2** won't forget
     3 was able to solve

30초 완성 map

① able to, Can(Could) you, be able to
② may, May   ③ will

UNIT 02   must, should, had better, used to

pp. 30~31

비교 point   **1** must not   **2** don't have to

개념 우선 확인   **1** 그는 천재임에 틀림없다.   **2** 너는 거짓말을 해서는 안 된다.   **3** 너는 지금 떠나는 게 좋겠다.

A   **1** had to   **2** should   **3** must not   **4** must
B   **1** had better   **2** used to   **3** should
C   **1** had better not call   **2** doesn't have to
     worry   **3** must not talk loudly

30초 완성 map

① has to, must be, don't have to   ② 공부해야
한다   ③ had better not   ④ used to

 서술형 대비 문장 쓰기

p. 32

01 May(Can) I come
02 had better not go

03 doesn't have to answer
04 used to live
05 He must be
06 You will be able to speak
07 You had better not tell
08 There used to be a theater
09 Could you speak
10 had to borrow some money
11 You should take care of
12 will not be able to call

시험에 꼭 나오는 출제포인트

p. 33

1   (1) am able to carry   (2) has to get
     고득점 POINT ③
2   ①, ③   고득점 POINT used to
3   (1) must not   (2) don't have to
4   You had better not go home now.

실전 Test

pp. 34~37

01 ②	**02** ⑤	**03** ④	**04** ④	**05** ①
06 ①	**07** ①, ③	**08** ③	**09** ③	**10** ①
11 ②, ⑤	**12** ②	**13** ⑤	**14** ①	**15** ③
16 ⑤	**17** ④	**18** ⑤		

19 used to live
20 must be busy
21 has to take care of his cat
22 (1) had not better → had better not
     (2) will able to → will be able to
23 used to be a swing
24 (1) will be able to enjoy
     (2) had to
25 You should go to bed.
26 were not able to
27 (1) don't have to take   (2) must not cross
28 (1) should not eat or drink
     (2) should not talk on the phone
     (3) should read books quietly

01 문맥상 충고를 나타내는 should가 알맞다.
02 문맥상 '~할 필요가 없다'의 의미인 don't have to가 알맞다.
03 과거의 상태를 나타낼 때에는 used to를 쓴다.
04 의무를 나타내는 must는 have to로 바꿔 쓸 수 있다.
05 '~해서는 안 된다'는 must not을 써서 나타낸다.

06 ①은 better를 써서 had better not(~하지 않는 게 좋겠다)으로 나타낸다. 나머지는 to가 적절하다.

07 '~해 주시겠어요?'라는 뜻으로 상대방에게 요청하는 표현은 Can(Could) you~? 또는 Will(Would) you ~?이다.

08 ③은 '허가'를 나타내고, 나머지는 '능력'을 나타낸다.

09 used to가 과거의 상태(~가 있었다)를 나타내는 의미로 쓰일 때는 would로 바꿔 쓸 수 없다.

10 had better: ~하는 게 좋겠다
had to: ~했어야 했다 (have to의 과거형)

11 ② will be going to → will 또는 is going to
⑤ have to → had to

12 우리말을 영작하면 You had better not travel alone.이다.

13 ⓐ, ⓓ는 '~임에 틀림없다'는 강한 추측을 나타내고, ⓑ, ⓒ, ⓔ는 '~해야 한다'는 의미로 의무를 나타낸다.

14 〈보기〉와 같이 '~해도 좋다'는 허가의 뜻을 나타내는 것은 ①이다. 나머지는 '~일지도 모른다'는 뜻의 불확실한 추측을 나타낸다.

15 ③ '~해서는 안 된다'는 must not으로 쓴다. (don't have to → must not)

16 '~할 수 있다'의 미래시제이므로 will 다음에 be able to를 써서 나타낸다. 조동사 두 개는 연달아 쓰지 않는다.

17 must not은 '~해서는 안 된다'는 뜻이고 don't have to는 '~할 필요가 없다'는 뜻이다.

18 [해석] 학생 여러분, 안녕하세요. 동물원에 오신 것을 환영합니다. 관람하는 동안, 여러분은 많은 종류의 동물들을 볼 수 있을 겁니다. 그 동물들은 귀여워 보이지만 그 중 일부는 위험합니다. 그러니 조심해야 합니다. 여러분은 그들을 만지거나 그들에게 먹이를 주어서는 안 됩니다. 여러분이 관람을 즐기기를 바랍니다.
→ 내용상 '~해서는 안 된다'는 금지의 표현이 들어가야 한다.

19 과거의 지속적인 습관이나 상태를 나타낼 때는 「used to+동사원형」을 쓴다.

20 '~임에 틀림없다'는 의미의 강한 추측을 나타낼 때는 must를 쓴다.

21 '~해야 한다'는 「have/has to+동사원형」으로 나타내며, '~을 돌보다'라는 의미의 숙어는 take care of이다.

22 (1) had better의 부정형은 had better not으로 쓴다.
(2) be able to의 미래는 will be able to로 쓴다.

23 과거의 상태를 나타낼 때는 used to를 쓴다.

24 (1) 조동사는 두 개 연달아 쓸 수 없으므로 will be able to로 나타낸다.
(2) must의 과거형은 had to를 쓴다.

25 충고의 의미를 가진 조동사는 should와 had better이며, 5단어로 써야 하므로 should를 써서 나타낸다.

26 능력의 의미를 나타내는 can의 과거는 could이고, 이것은 was/were able to로 바꿔 쓸 수 있다.

27 (1) '~할 필요가 없다'는 don't/doesn't have to로 쓴다.
(2) '~해서는 안 된다'는 must not으로 쓴다.

28 해야 하는 일은 should를, 하지 말아야 할 일은 should not을 써서 나타낸다.

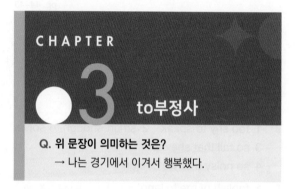

CHAPTER
3
to부정사

Q. 위 문장이 의미하는 것은?
→ 나는 경기에서 이겨서 행복했다.

UNIT 01   to부정사의 명사적 용법

p. 41

[개념 우선 확인] **1** I want to go with you.
2 My job is to teach English.   **3** I don't know what to do.

A **1** ㉠ **2** ㉡ **3** ㉢ **4** ㉠

B **1** It, to watch **2** It, to live **3** what to buy
4 how to fix

C **1** is to travel **2** choose where to live
3 decided not to miss

30초 완성 map

① 게임을 하는 것은, 새 신발을 사기를, 가수가 되는 것
② how to do

UNIT 02   to부정사의 형용사적·부사적 용법

p. 43

[개념 우선 확인] **1** I bought something to drink.
2 He ran to catch the bus.

A **1** to eat **2** to be **3** to see **4** to hear
5 to buy

B **1** to write with　**2** anything fun to do
　　3 to sit on

C **1** happy to go　**2** someone to talk to〔with〕
　　3 (in order) to celebrate her birthday
　　4 to be a great soccer player

30초 완성 map

① work to do, to live in
② 의사가 되기 위해, 그 소식을 들어서, 나를 도와주다니

UNIT 03　to부정사의 의미상 주어, to부정사 구문

pp. 44~45

시험 point　strong enough

개념 우선 확인　**1** Jack은 일찍 일어나는 것이 힘들다.
2 그 상자는 너무 무거워서 옮길 수 없다.

A **1** for　**2** too　**3** long enough　**4** of

B **1** too shy to speak　**2** smart enough to solve
　　3 so tall that she can
　　4 so noisy that we couldn't

C **1** foolish of me to lend
　　2 too busy to have lunch
　　3 interesting enough to watch

30초 완성 map

① for, of　② too, to, enough to

W　서술형 대비 문장 쓰기

p. 46

01 It, to exercise
02 when to leave
03 too busy to help
04 so rich that, can buy
05 old enough to sleep
06 a pen to write with
07 of you to admit
08 something interesting to tell
09 is to train dogs
10 agreed not to eat fast food
11 pleased to hear from you
12 too difficult for me to read

시험에 꼭 나오는 출제포인트

p. 47

1 ④　고득점 POINT is hard to get

---

2 ①　고득점 POINT anything warm to wear
3 (1) of you　(2) for her
4 (1) so, couldn't do　(2) so strong that, can
　　고득점 POINT she can't buy

실전 Test

pp. 48~51

01 ③　**02** ④　**03** ③　**04** ⑤　**05** ⑤
06 ②　**07** ②　**08** ①　**09** ④
10 ③,⑤　**11** ②　**12** ②,⑤　**13** ②　**14** ④
15 ③　**16** ④　**17** ②　**18** ②

19 where we should stay
20 so, that he could
21 for → of
22 to say important → important to say
23 is difficult for me to express myself
24 It is too cold for us to go out.
25 to not answer → not to answer
26 (1) large enough for us to share
　　(2) someone wise to talk to
27 I can't decide what to wear.
28 It is dangerous to swim here.

01 It은 가주어이며 진주어는 to부정사로 나타낸다.

02 to부정사의 의미상 주어는 「for+목적격」으로 쓴다.

03 의미상 '너무 ~해서 …할 수 없다'가 되어야 하므로 too tired가 알맞다.

04 ⑤는 부사적 용법(목적)의 to부정사이고, 나머지는 형용사적 용법의 to부정사이다.

05 to부정사의 의미상 주어는 보통 「for+목적격」으로 나타내며, 사람의 성격이나 성향을 나타내는 형용사 다음에는 「of+목적격」으로 쓴다.

06 〈보기〉와 ②는 부사적 용법(목적)으로 쓰였다.
　　①, ⑤ 형용사적 용법 ③, ④ 명사적 용법

07 '(같이) 놀 친구들'의 의미가 되어야 하므로 to play with가 any friends를 수식해야 한다.

08 ① '~할 만큼 충분히 …한'은 「형용사+enough+to부정사」의 어순으로 쓴다. (→ warm enough to eat)

09 우리말을 영작하면 To walk on water is impossible. 또는 It is impossible to walk on water.이다.

10 〈보기〉와 같이 it이 가주어로 쓰인 것은 ③, ⑤이다.
　　①과 ④는 비인칭 주어이고, ②는 대명사이다.

11 to부정사의 의미상 주어는 보통 「for+목적격」으로 나타내지만, 사람의 성격이나 성향을 나타내는 형용사 다음에는 for 대신 of를 쓰므로 ②에는 of가 들어간다.

12 '무엇을 해야 할지'는 「what+to부정사」 또는 「what+주

어+should+동사원형」으로 나타낼 수 있다.

13 ⓐ, ⓓ 부사적 용법(목적)　ⓑ. ⓔ 부사적 용법(판단의 근거)　ⓒ 부사적 용법(감정의 원인)

14 '너무 ~해서 …할 수 없는'은 「too+형용사/부사(+의미상 주어)+to부정사」의 어순으로 쓴다.

15 to부정사의 부정형은 「not+to부정사」로 쓴다.

16 ④ 「too+형용사/부사(+의미상 주어)+to부정사」는 「so+형용사/부사+주어+can't+동사원형」으로 바꿔 쓸 수 있으므로 can이 아닌 can't로 써야 한다.

17 **해석** A 무슨 일 있어?
B 수학 숙제를 하려고 하는 중인데, 그것은 내가 혼자 하기에 너무 어려워.
A 걱정 마. 내가 널 도와줄 수 있어.
B 고마워!
→ 문맥상 '그것(숙제)은 내가 혼자 하기에 너무 어렵다'는 말이 와야 자연스러우므로 「too+형용사/부사+to부정사」 구문을 써서 it's too difficult for me to do ~ 로 나타낸다.

18 ⓐ 「-thing+형용사+to부정사」의 어순으로 써야 한다.
ⓒ to talk는 someone을 수식하므로 뒤에 전치사 to(with)가 필요하다.
ⓓ enough는 형용사 뒤에 와야 한다.

19 「의문사+to부정사」는 「의문사+주어+should+동사원형」으로 바꿔쓸 수 있다.

20 「형용사/부사+enough+to부정사」 구문은 「so+형용사/부사+that+주어+can/could+동사원형」 구문으로 바꿔 쓸 수 있다.

21 사람의 성격이나 성향을 나타내는 형용사(foolish) 다음에 오는 to부정사의 의미상 주어는 「of+목적격」으로 쓴다.

22 -thing으로 끝나는 대명사를 수식하는 형용사와 to부정사가 같이 오면 「대명사+형용사+to부정사」의 형태로 쓴다.

23 가주어 it으로 시작하므로 진주어인 to부정사구는 문장 뒤에 쓴다. to부정사의 의미상 주어는 「for+목적격」으로 쓴다

24 「too+형용사/부사+to부정사」 구문을 이용하여 '너무 추워서 나갈 수 없다'는 의미를 나타낸다. to부정사의 의미상 주어는 to부정사 앞에 「for+목적격」으로 나타낸다.

25 to부정사의 부정형은 「not+to부정사」의 형태로 쓴다.

26 (1) '~할 만큼 충분히 …한'은 「형용사+enough +to부정사」 구문으로 나타낼 수 있다.
(2) -one으로 끝나는 대명사를 수식하는 형용사와 to부정사가 같이 오면 「대명사+형용사+to부정사」의 형태로 쓴다.

27 '무엇을 ~해야 할지'이므로 「what+to부정사」로 쓴다.

28 가주어 it으로 시작하므로 진주어인 to부정사구는 문장의 뒤에 와야 한다.

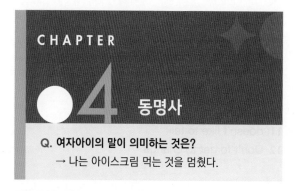

CHAPTER 04 동명사

Q. 여자아이의 말이 의미하는 것은?
→ 나는 아이스크림 먹는 것을 멈췄다.

UNIT 01　동명사의 역할

pp. 54~55

시험 point　seeing

개념 우선 확인　1 그 책을 읽는 것을　2 영화를 보는 것

A 1 ㉧　2 ㉵　3 ㉧　4 ㉦　5 ㉵

B 1 invite → inviting　2 are → is　3 to take → taking　4 hear → hearing

C 1 spent two hours fixing　2 am used to meeting　3 is worth reading　4 kept knocking

30초 완성 map

① is, watching, flying　② going, falling

UNIT 02　동명사와 to부정사

p. 57

개념 우선 확인　1 practice dancing　2 promise to help　3 remember visiting

A 1 baking　2 to quit　3 cleaning　4 to meet

B 1 to go　2 crying(to cry)　3 waiting　4 playing(to play)　5 swimming

C 1 forgot to water　2 tried to open　3 remember living　4 stopped eating

30초 완성 map

① doing, to read　② to turn, meeting

 서술형 대비 문장 쓰기

p. 58

01 enjoy reading
02 Thanks for explaining
03 decided to tell
04 remember going

05 is good for your health

06 doing anything today

07 looking forward to seeing us

08 to do this weekend

09 tries to understand me

10 spent three hours chatting with

11 doesn't like to talk

12 Don't forget to change

시험에 꼭 나오는 출제포인트　　　p. 59

1 ①, ④ 　고득점 POINT　 are → is

2 (1) is busy cooking
　(2) couldn't help laughing 　고득점 POINT　 going

3 ②

4 remember seeing

실전 Test　　　pp. 60~63

01 ⑤	02 ④	03 ③	04 ⑤	05 ②
06 ⑤	07 ④	08 ③	09 ②	10 ③
11 ①,③,⑤		12 ①	13 ①	14 ②
15 ⑤	16 ③	17 ④	18 ③	

19 writing

20 spent an hour cleaning his room

21 trying to understand my situation

22 It is worth watching many times.

23 are → is

24 is busy doing her homework

25 decided to quit smoking

26 turning off the computer

27 ⓒ → I gave up trying to persuade my parents.
　ⓔ → He doesn't mind working on weekends.

28 to bring his textbook

01 stop은 목적어로 동명사를 취하는 동사이다.

02 agree는 목적어로 to부정사를 취하는 동사이다.

03 「feel like -ing」는 '~하고 싶다'는 의미를 나타낸다.

04 ⑤는 보어로 쓰인 동명사이고, 나머지는 목적어로 쓰인 동명사이다.

05 expect는 to부정사만 목적어로 취할 수 있다. 나머지는 to부정사와 동명사를 둘 다 목적어로 취할 수 있는 동사이다.

06 ⑤ look forward to 다음에는 동명사가 와야 한다.
　(see → seeing)

07 ④ promise는 to부정사를 목적어로 취한다.
　(coming → to come)

08 avoid는 동명사를 목적어로 취한다. 나머지는 to부정사를 목적어로 취하는 동사이다.

09 ⓐ 동명사 주어는 단수 취급한다. (are → is)
　ⓒ '(앞으로) ~할 것을 잊지 마'라는 의미이므로 forget 다음에 to부정사를 써야 한다. (saving → to save)
　ⓓ avoid는 목적어로 동명사를 취하는 동사이다. (to eat → eating)

10 decide는 to부정사를 목적어로 취하고, practice는 동명사를 목적어로 취한다.

11 동명사를 목적어로 취할 수 있는 동사는 like, enjoy, stop이다. want와 expect는 to부정사를 목적어로 취한다.

12 ① agree는 목적어로 to부정사를 취한다.

13 ① 앞으로 할 일을 기억하라는 의미이므로 Remember 다음에 to부정사를 써야 한다. (locking → to lock)

14 stop 뒤에 동명사가 목적어로 쓰여 '~하는 것을 멈추다'의 의미를 나타낸다.

15 　해석　 수민이의 취미는 사진을 찍는 것이다. 그녀는 아름다운 사진을 찍는 것을 잘한다. 그런데 그녀는 지난주에 카메라를 망가뜨렸다. 그녀는 사진 찍는 것을 계속할 수 없었다. 다행히 그녀의 아버지가 생일에 새 카메라를 사주셨다. 그녀는 다시 사진 찍기를 시작할 수 있었다. 그녀는 아버지의 사진을 가장 먼저 찍어드리기로 계획했다.
　→ ⑤ plan은 목적어로 to부정사를 취한다.

16 '~하는 데 익숙하다'는 「be used to -ing」로 나타낼 수 있으며, 부정형은 be동사 다음에 not을 쓴다.

17 '~하려고 노력하다'는 「try+to부정사」로 나타낸다. to부정사의 부정은 to 앞에 not을 쓴다.

18 (A) 동명사 주어는 항상 단수 취급한다.
　(B) hope는 목적어로 to부정사를 취한다.
　(C) '~하지 않을 수 없다'는 「can't help -ing」이다.

19 finish는 동명사를 목적어로 취하는 동사이다.

20 '~하는 데 (시간)을 쓰다'는 「spend+시간+-ing」로 나타낸다.

21 전치사의 목적어로는 동명사가 와야 하며, '~하려고 노력하다'는 「try+to부정사」로 쓴다

22 '~할 가치가 있다'는 「be worth -ing」이다.

23 동명사 주어는 항상 단수 취급한다.

24 「be busy -ing」를 써서 '~하느라 바쁘다'의 의미를 나타낼 수 있다. '숙제를 하다'는 do one's homework이고 right now가 있으므로 현재시제로 쓴다.

25 decide는 목적어로 to부정사를 취하며, quit은 목적어로 동명사를 취한다.

26 '(과거에) ~한 것을 기억하다'는 「remember -ing」이다.

27 give up(포기하다)과 mind(꺼리다)는 목적어로 동명사만을 취한다.

28 '(앞으로) ~할 것을 잊다'는 「forget+to부정사」이다.

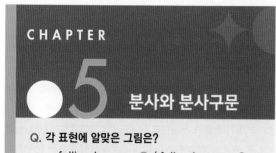

CHAPTER
05 분사와 분사구문

Q. 각 표현에 알맞은 그림은?
→ falling leaves - ① / fallen leaves - ②

UNIT 01 현재분사와 과거분사

p. 67

개념 우선 확인 **1** broken glass **2** a boy talking with Amy **3** a shocking event

A **1** fried **2** crying **3** pleased **4** satisfying
5 found

B **1** amazing **2** made **3** shocked **4** drawn
5 sleeping

C **1** his lost puppy **2** a letter written
3 the man playing

30초 완성 map

① 노래하고 있는 ② 잡힌 ③ excited, exciting

UNIT 02 분사구문

p. 69

개념 우선 확인 **1** 시간이 없었기 때문에
2 숙제를 끝낸 후에

A **1** Walking **2** Having **3** Being
B **1** ⓒ **2** ⓓ **3** ⓑ **4** ⓐ
C **1** she washed her hands
2 he is rich
3 he was playing the piano

30초 완성 map

① Seeing a rat ② 들었을 때, 일어나서

 서술형 대비 문장 쓰기

p. 70

01 broken
02 interesting
03 talking

04 shocked
05 Leaving early
06 Eating popcorn
07 Arriving in Busan
08 Playing soccer
09 the balloon flying over your head
10 is reading a book written
11 Getting off the bus, he dropped
12 Having little time, we have to

시험에 꼭 나오는 출제포인트

p. 71

1 (1) dancing (2) stolen 고득점 POINT The birds sitting in the tree are singing.
2 ③
3 (1) interested (2) boring
고득점 POINT surprised, shocking
4 (1) Being tired (2) (After) Having dinner

실전 Test

pp. 72~75

01 ④ **02** ④ **03** ③ **04** ② **05** ③
06 ① **07** ①,③,⑤ **08** ⑤ **09** ②
10 ④ **11** ⑤ **12** ⑤ **13** ② **14** ③
15 ③ **16** ② **17** ② **18** ②
19 shocking **20** fallen
21 Traveling abroad **22** Being angry
23 wearing a cap
24 Since I knew a shortcut
25 ⓓ → left **26** Making spaghetti
27 We were pleased to hear the news.
28 After having lunch, Sumin(she) rode her bicycle.

01 '춤추고 있는' 소년이라는 의미가 되어야 하므로 능동·진행을 나타내는 현재분사 dancing이 적절하다.
02 소설책이 '쓰여진' 것이므로 수동을 나타내는 과거분사 written이 알맞다.
03 부사절 Because I was sleepy를 분사구문으로 나타낸 문장으로, 부사절의 동사가 be동사일 때는 Being을 써서 분사구문을 나타낸다.
04 '시간이 없었기 때문에 아침을 먹지 못했다'라는 의미가 되어야 자연스러우므로 이유의 부사절과 의미가 통한다.
05 부사절을 분사구문으로 전환할 때 접속사와 주어를 생략하고, 부사절의 동사를 현재분사(동사원형+-ing)로 바꾼다. 부사절의 동사가 진행형일 때 be동사는 삭제한다.

06 주어진 두 문장을 한 문장으로 바꾸면 Look at the woman playing the guitar.가 된다.

07 부사절은 분사구문으로 나타낼 수 있으며, 분사구문의 의미를 명확히 나타내기 위해 접속사와 함께 쓰기도 한다.

08 ① 주어가 지루한 감정을 일으키는 것이므로 boring
② '날고 있는' 새라는 의미가 되어야 하므로 flying
③ 주어가 신나는 감정을 느끼는 것이므로 excited
④ 진행형을 분사구문으로 만들 때는 be동사를 생략하고 현재분사로 시작하므로 Crying

09 주어가 어떤 감정을 일으키는 경우에는 현재분사를 쓰고, 어떤 감정을 느끼는 경우에는 과거분사를 쓴다.

10 ④ 연설은 지루한 감정을 일으키는 것이므로 현재분사 boring을 써야 한다.

11 ⑤ '밝게 웃으면서'라는 의미를 나타내는 분사구문이 와야 하므로 Smiling으로 써야 한다.

12 ③ '떨어지고 있는 비'라는 의미가 되어야 하므로 진행의 의미를 가진 현재분사 falling으로 고쳐야 한다.

13 〈보기〉와 ①, ③, ④, ⑤는 명사를 수식하는 현재분사이다. ②는 주격보어로 쓰인 동명사이다.

14 ⓑ는 주어가 지루한 감정을 일으키는 것이므로 bored를 boring으로, ⓔ는 주어가 충격을 느끼는 것이므로 shocking을 shocked로 고쳐야 한다.

15 '통화하고 있는'의 의미이므로 현재분사 talking이 the man을 수식하며, 분사 뒤에 수식어구가 있으므로 명사 뒤에 위치한다.

16 〈보기〉와 같이 현재분사로 쓰인 것은 ⓑ, ⓒ이고, 나머지는 동명사이다.

17 ② 음악을 들으면서 청소를 한 것이므로 As나 While 등을 사용하여 동시 동작의 부사절로 바꿔야 한다.

18 ⓑ '깨진 유리'이므로 broken이 맞다.
ⓒ 지루한 감정을 느끼게 하는 것이므로 boring이 맞다.
ⓔ 주어가 놀라운 감정을 느끼는 것이므로 amazed가 맞다.

19 '충격적인' 감정을 일으킨 것이므로 현재분사를 쓴다.

20 '떨어진' 것이므로 완료의 의미를 나타내는 과거분사를 쓴다.

21 부사절의 접속사와 주어를 생략하고 동사를 현재분사로 쓴다.

22 부사절의 동사가 be동사일 때는 Being을 써서 분사구문을 만든다.

23 '모자를 쓰고 있는'의 의미를 나타내는 분사구가 들어가야 한다.

24 문맥상 이유를 나타내는 부사절이 와야 의미가 통하므로 since를 써야 한다.

25 〔해석〕 어젯밤에 나는 숲 근처를 걷고 있었다. 갑자기 누군가가 "불이야! 불이야!"하며 비명을 질렀다. 숲속에는 불타고 있는 오두막집이 있었다. 화재를 보고 나는 119에 전

화를 했다. 곧 소방관들이 도착했다. 그 화재 후에 오두막집 안에는 아무것도 남겨져 있지 않았다.
→ ⓓ '남겨진'의 의미가 되어야 하므로 과거분사로 써야 한다.

26 부사절의 동사가 진행형이므로 being을 생략하고 현재분사로 시작하는 분사구문을 만든다.

27 주어가 기뻐한 것이므로 please의 과거분사인 pleased로 쓰고, 감정의 원인을 나타내는 부사적 용법의 to부정사를 뒤에 써서 나타낸다.

28 After Sumin had lunch, she rode her bicycle.에서 시간의 부사절을 분사구문으로 바꿀 수 있다.

CHAPTER

06 수동태

Q. 위 문장의 내용과 일치하는 그림은?
→ ②

UNIT 01   수동태의 기본 개념

p. 79

〔개념 우선 확인〕   1 사랑받는다   2 잡혔다

A 1 were baked   2 was taken   3 visit
4 will be held

B 1 is used   2 was respected by   3 are eaten by   4 will be translated by him

C 1 was built   2 will be released   3 is sung by

30초 완성 map

① was stolen by
② is loved, were written, will be finished

UNIT 02   수동태의 여러 가지 형태

pp. 80~81

시험 point   can be recycled

〔개념 우선 확인〕   1 The game was not canceled.

2 Promises should be kept.

A 1 was 2 Was 3 should be cleaned
4 wasn't

B 1 wasn't made 2 Was the report written
3 shouldn't be broken

C 1 can be fixed 2 Was, caught by 3 must be washed 4 When was, invented

30초 완성 map

① was not broken ② Was the window broken
③ should be kept

UNIT 03 주의해야 할 수동태

pp. 82~83

시험 point was taken care of by

개념 우선 확인 **1** He was laughed at by his friends. **2** The garden is filled with flowers.

A 1 in 2 at 3 of 4 with

B 1 was run over by 2 was brought up by
3 appeared 4 happen

C 1 is worried about 2 was covered with
3 will be put off 4 was taken care of by

30초 완성 map

① was looked up to ② appeared, don't resemble
③ of, with

서술형 대비 문장 쓰기

p. 84

01 was decorated by
02 was not written by
03 was covered with
04 can be used
05 The flowers are watered by Lucy
06 Many patients were looked after
07 Buildings and roads were destroyed
08 A new smartwatch will be introduced
09 wasn't(was not) broken by me
10 were computers invented
11 shouldn't(should not) be changed
12 is satisfied with her current job

---

1 (1) was invented by (2) were carried by him
2 ④
3 must be changed
고득점 POINT should not be broken
4 (1) with (2) about
고득점 POINT was turned off by

실전 Test

pp. 86~89

01 ③	02 ⑤	03 ③	04 ②	05 ④
06 ①	07 ③	08 ③	09 ①	10 ②
11 ①	12 ④	13 ⑤	14 ④	
15 ②,④	16 ②	17 ③	18 ④	

19 was saved by
20 is looked up to by
21 When was the Internet invented
22 should not be sold to children
23 (1) was taken by (2) was written by
24 will be held
25 (1) was designed by (2) was built
26 (1) are not satisfied with (2) will be refunded
27 A lot of people were killed in the war.
28 ⓓ → will be caught

---

01 미술관이 관광객들에 의해 '방문되는' 것이므로 수동태로 써야 한다.

02 수동태의 부정문은 「be동사+not+p.p.」로 쓴다.

03 사진은 '찍히는' 것이므로 수동태로 써야 하며 작년에 있었던 일이므로 과거시제로 쓴다.

04 행위자가 막연한 일반인이거나 분명하지 않을 때는 생략할 수 있다.

05 수동태의 형태는 「be동사+p.p.」이다. 주어가 3인칭 단수이고 과거시제이므로 be동사는 was가 맞다.

06 수동태 문장에서 행위자 앞에는 일반적으로 by를 쓰며, '~에 싫증이 나다'라는 의미는 수동태 표현 be tired of로 쓴다.

07 ① 수동태의 의문문: 의문사+be동사+주어+p.p. ~? (the plan was → was the plan)
② ~에 관심이 있다: be interested in
④ resemble은 수동태로 쓰지 않는 동사이다. (are resembled → resemble)
⑤ take care of의 수동태이므로 be taken care of로 써야 한다.

08 ① 수동태의 의문문: Be동사+주어+p.p. ~?

(Did → Was)

② 수동태의 부정문: be동사+not+p.p.

(doesn't → isn't)

④ happen은 수동태로 쓰지 않는 자동사이다.

(be happened → happen)

⑤ 주어가 복수이므로 was가 아니라 were를 써야 한다.

09 ① 소유를 나타내는 동사(have, belong 등)는 수동태로 쓰지 않는다.

10 조동사가 있는 수동태의 형태는 「조동사+be+p.p.」이다.

11 우리말을 영작하면 When will the film be released? 이다.

12 ④에는 about을 써야 하며, 나머지에는 with가 적절하다.

13 동사구 turn off의 수동태이므로 「be동사+turned off+by+행위자」의 어순으로 써야 한다.

14 '~에 관심이〔흥미가〕 있다'는 be interested in으로 나타낸다. 수동태의 의문문은 「Be동사+주어+p.p. ~?」로 쓴다.

15 arrive와 같이 목적어가 없는 자동사나 have와 같이 소유를 나타내는 타동사는 수동태로 쓸 수 없다.

16 ⓐ be tired of(~에 싫증이 나다)

ⓑ be worried about(~에 대해 걱정하다)

ⓒ be satisfied with(~에 만족하다)

ⓓ be surprised at〔by〕(~에 놀라다)

17 ③ 방은 '칠해지는' 것이므로 수동태를 써야 하고 조동사 will이 있으므로 「will be+p.p.」형태로 써야 한다.

(→ will be painted)

18 ⓐ는 The tickets가 주어이므로 수동태로 써야 하고, ⓑ 는 many people이 주어이므로 능동태로 써야 한다.

19 수동태의 형태는 「be동사+p.p.」이고, 주어가 3인칭 단수이고 과거시제이므로 be동사는 was로 쓴다. 행위자는 by를 써서 나타낸다.

20 동사구의 수동태는 동사를 「be동사+p.p.」로 쓰고 나머지 부분을 그대로 쓴다.

21 의문사가 있는 의문문의 수동태는 「의문사+be동사+주어+p.p. ~?」의 어순으로 쓴다.

22 조동사가 있는 수동태 문장의 부정문은 「조동사+not+be+p.p.」의 어순으로 쓴다.

23 (1) '(사진을) 찍다'의 의미인 take를 이용해 수동태로 써야 한다.

(2) '쓰다'의 의미인 write를 이용해 수동태로 써야 한다.

24 미래시제 수동태는 「will+be+p.p.」의 어순으로 쓴다.

25 둘 다 과거에 건축된 것이므로 「was+p.p.」를 이용하여 나타낸다.

26 (1) '~에 만족하지 않다'는 「be동사+not satisfied with」로 나타낸다.

(2) '환불 받을 것이다'는 조동사 will 다음에 be refunded를 써서 나타낼 수 있다.

27 kill(죽이다)을 이용해야 하므로 수동태로 쓴다.

28 해석 어제 우리 동네의 보석 상점이 털렸다. 도둑들은 CCTV 카메라에 찍히지 않았지만 경찰은 그곳에서 지문 몇 개를 발견했다. 그 도둑들은 곧 잡힐 것이다.

→ ⓓ 조동사가 있는 수동태는 조동사 뒤에 「be+p.p.」로 쓴다.

CHAPTER

07 대명사

Q. 위 문장이 나타내는 해변은?

→ ①

UNIT 01 부정대명사 I

pp. 92~93

비교 point **1** the other **2** another

개념 우선 확인 **1** one **2** the other

A **1** ones **2** it **3** others **4** the other

　 5 another

B **1** another **2** one **3** the other **4** others

C **1** made another movie **2** a new one

　 3 the others are novels

30초 완성 map

① ones ② the other, one, another, the other

③ others, some, the others

UNIT 02 부정대명사 II

pp. 94~95

비교 point **1** wears **2** wear

개념 우선 확인 **1** every person **2** both my

brothers **3** all of us

A **1** sentence **2** some **3** were **4** Both

B **1** All **2** Each **3** any **4** some

C 1 Both of us like 2 Every, needs
　 3 Each room has 4 All the fruit

① is, student ② was, like ③ some, any

UNIT 03 재귀대명사

p. 97

개념 우선 확인 1 I love myself. 2 He fixed the computer himself.

A 1 myself 2 him 3 yourself 4 myself
　 5 ourselves
B 1 ○ 2 × 3 × 4 ○ 5 ○
C 1 by yourself 2 burned himself 3 enjoyed themselves 4 make yourself at home

① myself ② herself ③ himself

W 서술형 대비 문장 쓰기

p. 98

01 Every student
02 help yourself to
03 Each color has
04 make yourself(yourselves) at home
05 I need bigger ones.
06 and the other is a lawyer
07 and others like rainy days
08 another is Canada, and the other is Spain
09 Both of them were made
10 traveled to Europe by herself
11 enjoyed themselves at the beach
12 All of us were satisfied with

시험에 꼭 나오는 출제포인트

p. 99

1 (1) one (2) it 고득점 POINT one → ones
2 (1) One, the other (2) One, another, the other
3 ④ 고득점 POINT Each of us has
4 ①

실전 Test

pp. 100~103

01 ③	02 ④	03 ⑤	04 ③	05 ②
06 ②	07 ④	08 ④	09 ①	10 ③
11 ④	12 ③	13 ③	14 ②	15 ③
16 ④	17 ⑤	18 ⑤		

19 One, the other
20 said to herself
21 introduce myself
22 the others → others
23 move it by himself
24 (1) One, the other (2) Some, the others
25 All of us are special.
26 was proud of himself
27 you → yourself
28 (1) Both Lucy and Tom are able to
　 (2) All of them are able to

01 뒤에 단수명사와 단수동사가 쓰였으므로 every가 알맞다.
02 정해지지 않은 범위 내에서 '다른 몇몇'을 나타낼 때는 others를 쓴다.
03 '또 다른 하나'를 나타낼 때는 another를 쓴다.
04 앞에 언급한 명사(glasses)와 동일한 종류의 다른 것을 가리키며, glasses는 복수명사이므로 ones가 알맞다.
05 '~ 둘 다'라는 의미는 「both (of)+복수명사」로 나타낼 수 있으며, 복수 취급하므로 뒤에는 복수동사를 쓴다.
06 ②의 yourself는 목적어이므로 생략할 수 없다.
07 우리말을 영작하면 I don't have any money in my wallet.이다. some은 주로 긍정문이나 권유의 의문문에 쓴다.
08 all은 뒤에 나오는 명사가 단수면 단수 취급하고, 복수면 복수 취급하므로 all the people 뒤에는 have가 와야 한다.
09 앞에서 언급한 것과 동일한 대상을 가리킬 때는 it을 쓰고, 동일한 종류일 때는 one을 쓴다.
10 all은 다음에 나오는 명사에 따라 단수 또는 복수 취급하고, each는 단수 취급한다.
11 셋 중에서 하나씩 가리킬 때는 차례로 one, another, the other를 쓴다.
12 둘 중에서 '하나, 나머지 하나'는 one, the other이다.
13 ⓐ all 다음에 단수명사가 오면 단수 취급하므로 were를 was로 고쳐야 한다.
　 ⓓ every 다음에는 단수명사가 오고 단수 취급하므로 Every student wants ~가 되어야 한다.
14 ⓐ 음식을 권유하는 의문문이므로 some이 알맞다.

ⓑ 부정문이므로 any가 알맞다.

ⓒ '마음껏 먹다'는 help oneself이다.

15 ③ both나 all 뒤에 대명사가 올 때는 「both/all+of+대명사」 형태로 쓴다. (Both them → Both of them)

16 ④ 앞에 언급한 것과 동일한 것을 가리킬 때는 it을 써야 한다.

17 [해석] 나의 사촌은 고작 여섯 살이지만, 자신을 돌볼 수 있다. 그녀는 스스로 씻고 옷을 입는다. 그녀는 심지어 혼자서 식탁을 차릴 수 있다. 어느 날, 그녀는 직접 샌드위치를 만들었다.

→ ⓔ의 재귀대명사는 강조 용법이므로 생략 가능하다.

18 ⓑ '나머지 모두'는 The others이다. (Others → The others)

ⓓ every는 단수 취급하므로 뒤에 단수명사와 단수동사를 써야 한다. (→ Every team has its own flag.)

19 둘 중에서 하나씩 가리킬 때는 one, the other를 쓴다.

20 주어가 she에 해당하고, 주어와 목적어가 같으므로 said to herself가 적절하다.

21 '내가 나를 소개하다'라는 의미이고 주어와 목적어가 같으므로 introduce myself가 적절하다.

22 수학을 좋아하는 학생 외에 몇몇이 영어를 좋아하므로 others가 적절하다.

23 도와줄 사람이 없어서 혼자 옮기기로 결심했다는 의미이므로 move it 다음에 '혼자서'의 의미인 by himself를 쓴다.

24 (1) 둘 중에서 '하나, 나머지 하나'는 one, the other이다.

(2) 범위가 정해진 사물이나 사람들 중 '몇몇, 나머지 모두'는 some, the others이다

25 '우리 모두'는 all of us이고 복수 취급한다.

26 '~을 자랑스러워하다'는 be proud of이고, 주어와 목적어가 동일한 대상이므로 전치사의 목적어 자리에 재귀대명사가 와야 한다.

27 make oneself at home은 '편히 지내다'라는 의미이며, 명령문은 주어 you가 생략된 형태이므로 make yourself at home이 알맞다.

28 both는 항상 복수 취급하고, all은 뒤에 복수명사가 오면 복수 취급한다. all 뒤에 대명사가 올 때는 「all of+대명사」 형태로 쓴다.

CHAPTER 08 비교

Q. 위 그림을 바르게 표현한 문장은?
→ The giraffe is as tall as the tree.

UNIT 01 원급, 비교급, 최상급

pp. 106~107

시험 point **1** very **2** much

개념 우선 확인 **1** as hot as yesterday
2 older than you **3** the easiest way

A **1** more **2** youngest **3** well **4** far
5 more interested

B **1** softer than 또는 as soft as **2** the quietest
3 worse than 또는 as bad as **4** as brave
5 much(even, far, a lot)

C **1** not as thin as **2** much brighter than
3 less money than
4 the most popular dessert

30초 완성 map

① as tall as ② taller than, much ③ the tallest

UNIT 02 다양한 비교 표현

pp. 108~109

시험 point singers

개념 우선 확인 **1** three times as fast as **2** get hotter and hotter **3** one of the oldest songs

A **1** five times **2** worse **3** weaker **4** tallest

B **1** The less **2** the best players
3 ten times as expensive **4** more popular

C **1** more and more comfortable
2 The harder, the better
3 three times as large as
4 one of the most famous singers

30초 완성 map

① four times larger ② bigger and bigger
③ The more ④ longest caves

01 as high as
02 far more expensive than
03 better and better
04 the coldest day
05 better than
06 five times as tall as 또는 five times taller than
07 louder and louder
08 one of the hottest days
09 became more and more crowded
10 not as important as health
11 The more you experience, the wiser
12 one of the oldest castles

시험에 꼭 나오는 출제포인트   p. 111

1 (1) wise (2) taller (3) funniest
    고득점 POINT (1) mine (2) swimming
2 ①
3 (1) fatter and fatter (2) the more cheerful
    고득점 POINT the healthier you will be
4 one of the most successful movies

실전 Test   pp. 112~115

01 ②	02 ①	03 ①	04 ②	05 ①
06 ⑤	07 ②	08 ①, ②, ⑤		09 ③
10 ④	11 ④	12 ②	13 ⑤	14 ②
15 ④	16 ①	17 ④	18 ③	

19 more and more convenient
20 much(even, far, a lot) more important
21 five times older than
22 not as(so) big as
23 (1) more comfortable than
    (2) as expensive as
24 is a lot higher than yours
25 one of the most crowded cities
26 The deeper we went into the cave, the
    darker
27 ⓐ → slower
    ⓓ → the slowest animals
28 (1) four times heavier than
    (2) not as(so) old as

01 than 앞에는 비교급을 써야 하며 fast의 비교급은

faster이다.
02 「as ~ as」구문에는 형용사나 부사의 원급을 써야 한다.
03 as+원급+as: ~만큼 …한 / of+복수명사: ~ 중에서
04 배수 비교 표현은 「배수사+비교급+than」 또는 「배수사
+as+원급+as」이다.
05 very는 비교급을 수식할 수 없다.
06 「as ~ as」원급 비교 구문이므로 빈칸에는 형용사의 원급
이 들어가야 한다.
07 '나보다 더 일찍 일어난다'라는 의미가 되어야 하므로 「비
교급(earlier)+than」으로 쓴다.
08 앞에 the가 있고 명사 앞이므로 형용사의 최상급이 들어
가야 한다.
09 '~하면 할수록 더 …하다'는 「the+비교급 ~, the+비교
급 …」으로 나타낸다.
10 ④ 자동차와 자전거를 비교하는 문장으로 뒤에 than이 있
으므로 비교급 more expensive가 되어야 한다.
11 ①은 오늘이 어제만큼 춥다는 의미이고, ②, ③, ⑤는 어제
가 더 추웠다는 의미이다. 〈보기〉와 ④는 오늘이 어제보다
더 춥다는 의미이다.
12 ① higher → high ③ small → smaller
④ more → most ⑤ healthiest → healthier
13 ⑤ '몇 배'인지를 나타낼 때 사용하는 배수사는 3배 이상
일 때 「서수+times」로 쓴다.
14 ② 원급 비교이므로 than이 아닌 as를 써야 한다.
15 ④ '점점 더 ~한'은 「비교급+and+비교급」으로 나타낸
다. (hot and hot → hotter and hotter)
16 ⓐ very → much(even, far, a lot) ⓒ as not →
not as ⓓ better → well ⓔ greater → greatest
17 Yumi가 Jimin보다 더 무거우므로 ④는 Jimin is not
as heavy as Yumi.가 되어야 한다.
18 ⓐ you → yours ⓒ badder → worse ⓔ big →
bigger
19 '점점 더 ~한/하게'라는 의미일 때 앞에 more가 붙어서
비교급이 되는 경우에는 「more and more+원급」으로
쓴다.
20 '훨씬 더 ~한'의 의미를 표현하려면 비교급 앞에 much,
even, far, a lot 등을 쓴다.
21 '나보다 나이가 5배 더 많은'을 비교급으로 표현하려면 배
수사 five times 다음에 older than을 쓴다.
22 '네 방은 내 방보다 더 크다'는 원급 비교 표현을 이용해서
'내 방은 네 방만큼 크지 않다'로 바꿔 쓸 수 있다.
23 두 대상 중 한쪽이 다른 한쪽보다 정도가 더 높은 것은 비
교급 비교 표현을 이용해서 나타내고, 정도가 같은 것은
원급 비교 표현으로 나타낸다.
24 비교급 강조 부사인 a lot을 비교급 앞에 써서 '훨씬 더 ~
한'의 의미를 나타낸다.

25 가장 ~한 …들 중 하나: one of the+최상급+복수명사

26 '~하면 할수록 더 …하다'는 「The+비교급+주어+동사 ~, the+비교급+주어+동사 …」로 쓴다.

27 해석 나무늘보는 달팽이보다 더 느리다. 그들의 시력은 아주 좋지 않고, 그들은 대부분의 시간을 나무 위에서 보낸다. 이것이 그들이 세상에서 가장 느린 동물들 중 하나인 이유이다.
(1) slow의 비교급은 slower 이다.
(2) '가장 ~한 …들 중 하나'는 「one of the+최상급+복수명사」로 쓴다.

28 (1) 기린이 사자보다 4배 더 무거우므로 four times 다음에 비교급을 써서 나타낸다.
(2) 원숭이는 기린만큼 나이가 많지 않으므로 「not as (so)+원급+as」를 써서 나타낸다.

CHAPTER 09 동사의 종류

Q. 위 문장으로 보아 Jenny가 산 것은?
→ 새집

UNIT 01 감각동사, 수여동사

p. 119

개념 우선 확인 **1** look sad **2** show him a photo
3 make pizza for me

A 1 bad **2** tastes like **3** me some water
4 to

B 1 for us **2** to me **3** to us

C 1 felt cold **2** teaches us music
3 sounds sad **4** bought some flowers for

30초 완성 map

① angry, like ② me chocolate, to me

UNIT 02 목적격보어가 필요한 동사

pp. 120~121

시험 point **1** study **2** wave, waving

개념 우선 확인 **1** call him Paul **2** let her go out
3 hear him singing

A 1 Jack **2** to be **3** running **4** to use
5 introduce

B 1 to be **2** fresh **3** laugh **4** read(reading)

C 1 keep you warm
2 heard someone knock(knocking)
3 made me go
4 expected him to come

30초 완성 map

① happy, to be ② use ③ play, playing

W 서술형 대비 문장 쓰기

p. 122

01 gave some advice to
02 made some cookies for
03 get some tea for
04 sent a birthday gift to
05 look very happy
06 told me a surprising story 또는 told a surprising story to me
07 clean their desks
08 him run(running)
09 won't let me drive
10 want you to keep my secret
11 sent a love letter to him
12 felt something bite her leg

시험에 꼭 나오는 출제포인트

p. 123

1 (1) bad (2) lovely
고득점 POINT (1) interesting (2) like a funny movie

2 (1) gave the children presents
(2) told me her secret
고득점 POINT (1) for us (2) to me

3 ①, ④

4 ①

01 ④ **02** ⑤ **03** ③ **04** ④ **05** ②
06 ③ **07** ② **08** ②,③ **09** ③ **10** ④
11 ①,③ **12** ② **13** ① **14** ③ **15** ④
16 ④ **17** ③ **18** ④
19 for my friends
20 sounded strange
21 felt the ground shake(shaking)
22 (1) water → to water
　　 (2) to call → call(calling)
23 I advised him to learn computer skills.
24 a dog running behind a boy
25 ⓑ → to get up
　　 ⓓ → chicken soup for me 또는 me chicken soup
26 allowed me to use her computer
27 will make you change your mind
28 (1) looked sad
　　 (2) named the cat Luna

01 감각동사의 보어로 부사는 올 수 없다.

02 allow는 목적격보어로 to부정사를 취하는 동사이다.

03 ③의 a bike는 직접목적어이고, 나머지는 모두 목적격보어이다.

04 make, let, have 등의 사역동사는 목적격보어로 동사원형을 취한다. (→ go)

05 지각동사(see)는 목적격보어로 동사원형이나 현재분사를 취한다.

06 advise는 목적격보어로 to부정사를 취한다.

07 ②에는 for가 들어가고, 나머지에는 to가 들어간다.

08 지각동사(hear)의 목적격보어로는 동사원형이나 현재분사를 쓴다.

09 목적격보어로 to부정사를 취하는 동사는 want, tell, advise이다.

10 〈보기〉와 ④는 직접목적어이고, 나머지는 목적격보어이다.

11 「cook+간접목적어+직접목적어」를 써서 '~에게 …을 요리해 주다'의 의미를 나타내며, 전치사 for를 간접목적어 앞에 써서 두 목적어의 위치를 바꾸어 쓸 수도 있다.

12 ③ ask는 목적격보어로 to부정사를 취하는 동사이다. (carrying → to carry)

13 사역동사(make)는 목적격보어로 동사원형을 취하며, 지각동사(feel)는 목적격보어로 동사원형이나 현재분사를 취한다.

14 ⓓ 사역동사의 목적격보어로는 동사원형이 온다. (to fix → fix)
　　 ⓔ 수여동사 make 다음에 직접목적어가 먼저 오는 경우

15 ⓐ는 4형식 수여동사로 쓰인 make이고, ⓑ, ⓓ는 목적격보어(형용사)를 취하는 5형식 동사로 쓰인 make이다. ⓒ는 '~을 만들다'라는 의미의 3형식 동사로 쓰인 make이다.

16 ④ 지각동사(hear)는 목적격보어로 동사원형이나 현재분사를 쓴다. (→ knock(knocking))

17 ⓐ, ⓒ, ⓓ에는 to가, ⓑ와 ⓔ에는 for가 알맞다.

18 해석 A 너 달라 보여. 무엇을 한 거야?
　　 B 나 머리를 조금 잘랐어.
　　 A 네가 직접 했니?
　　 B 아니, 언니에게 해 달라고 부탁했어.
　　 A 그렇구나. 어쨌든 너의 새로운 머리 모양은 너를 더 나아 보이게 해.
　　 → ⓓ ask는 목적격보어로 to부정사를 취하는 동사이다. (do → to do)

19 「make+간접목적어+직접목적어」는 「make+직접목적어+for+간접목적어」로 바꿔 쓸 수 있다.

20 감각동사 sound 다음에는 보어로 형용사가 온다.

21 지각동사 feel은 목적격보어로 동사원형이나 현재분사를 쓴다.

22 해석 엄마는 나에게 꽃에 물을 주라고 말씀하셨다. 그것에 물을 주는 동안, 나는 누군가가 내 이름을 부르는 것을 들었다. 내가 뒤를 돌아봤을 때, Peter가 나에게 손을 흔들고 있는 것을 보았다.
　　 (1) tell의 목적격보어로는 to부정사를 쓴다.
　　 (2) 지각동사(hear)의 목적격보어로는 동사원형이나 현재분사를 쓴다.

23 '~에게 …을 하라고 조언하다'는 「advise+목적어+to부정사」로 나타낼 수 있다.

24 '~가 …하는 것을 보다'의 의미가 되어야 하므로 「watch+목적어+현재분사」의 어순으로 쓴다.

25 해석 지난 토요일에 나는 친구들과 밤늦게까지 어울려 놀았다. 다음 날 아침, 나는 춥고 몸이 안 좋았다. 엄마는 내가 일찍 일어나기를 원하셨지만, 나는 그럴 수 없었다. 엄마는 내가 침대에 누워 있는 것을 보고 내게 치킨 수프를 만들어 주셨다. 뜨거운 수프는 내가 훨씬 나아지게 해주었다.
　　 → ⓑ want는 목적격보어로 to부정사를 취한다.
　　 ⓓ make는 간접목적어와 직접목적어의 위치를 바꿀 때 간접목적어 앞에 전치사 for를 쓴다.

26 '~가 …을 하게 허락하다'는 「allow+목적어+to부정사」로 나타낸다.

27 '~가 …하게 하다'는 「make+목적어+목적격보어」로 나타낼 수 있고, make가 사역동사이므로 목적격보어로 동사원형을 쓴다.

28 (1) 감각동사 look은 주격보어로 형용사를 취한다.
　　 (2) '~를 …라고 이름 짓다(붙이다)'는 「name+목적어+목적격보어(명사)」로 쓴다.

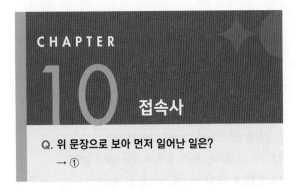

03 when the meeting is over
04 is responsible for the problem
05 you speak loudly
06 Judy and her sister hate insects
07 Chris nor James knows the answer
08 you aren't an adult 또는 you're not an adult
09 and you'll get there
10 so tired that he fell asleep
11 Although(Though, Even though) we lost the game
12 Either Tom or Mia has to

UNIT 01　시간·이유·조건의 접속사

pp. 130~131

시험 point　1 come　2 rains

개념 우선 확인　1 내가 돌아올 때까지　2 비오는 것이 멈추면

A　1 while　2 because　3 that　4 even though
B　1 call　2 because　3 leave　4 graduates
C　1 when you have　2 since I forgot
　　3 Although I was tired
　　4 Unless you are busy

30초 완성 map

① get　② because, so　③ Unless, Although

UNIT 02　명령문 + and / or, 짝을 이루는 접속사

pp. 132~133

시험 point　1 am　2 are

개념 우선 확인　1 Take a taxi, and you won't be late.　2 I like neither summer nor winter.

A　1 or　2 both　3 or　4 likes
B　1 as well as　2 If you go　3 Unless you take
C　1 felt neither, nor　2 Both, and, enjoy
　　3 have either, or　4 Not only, but also, wants

30초 완성 map

① and, or　② are, am, nor

W　서술형 대비 문장 쓰기

p. 134

01 Unless Jack comes 또는 If Jack doesn't come
02 because it was cloudy

시험에 꼭 나오는 출제포인트

p. 135

1　is　고득점 POINT don't help
2　⑤
3　(1) If you do　(2) If you don't study
4　(1) both, and　(2) neither, nor
　　고득점 POINT (1) likes　(2) like

실전 Test

pp. 136~139

01 ③　02 ⑤　03 ④　04 ④　05 ④
06 ④　07 ①　08 ①　09 ②　10 ④
11 ②,③　12 ⑤　13 ①　14 ④　15 ③
16 ④　17 ⑤　18 ④

19 so, that
20 Unless you stop smoking
21 Though my car is old
22 neither read nor speak Chinese
23 Both Chris and Helen were born
24 (1) even though it was raining
　　(2) until the movie ended
　　(3) because it snowed a lot
25 (1) did my homework, watched TV
　　(2) did my homework, watched TV
26 as well as
27 (1) so hungry that I couldn't wait
　　(2) not only fresh but also delicious
28 ⓐ → if it rains
　　ⓓ → Unless you show your ID 또는 If you don't show your ID

---

01 문맥상 '~하는 동안'의 의미를 나타내는 while이 알맞다.
02 문맥상 '~이기 때문에'의 의미를 나타내는 since가 알맞다.
03 문맥상 '~에도 불구하고'의 의미를 나타내는 Although가

알맞다.

04 neither A nor B: A도 B도 아닌

05 「if you ~ not」은 unless나 「명령문, or ~」를 이용하여 같은 의미를 나타낼 수 있다.

06 ④에는 이유를 나타내는 접속사(as, because, since)를 써야 하고, 나머지에는 so가 알맞다.

07 첫 번째 빈칸에는 이유의 접속사가 알맞고, 두 번째 빈칸에는 '~할 때'의 의미인 시간의 접속사가 들어가야 하므로 두 가지 의미로 모두 쓰이는 as가 알맞다.

08 첫 번째 빈칸에는 결과의 접속사 so가 알맞고, 두 번째 빈칸에는 '너무 ~해서 …하다'의 의미인 「so ~ that ....」 구문의 so가 알맞다.

09 'A와 B 둘 다'는 「both A and B」로 나타내고, 'A도 B도 아닌'은 「neither A nor B」로 나타낸다.

10 둘 다 이유를 나타내는 말이 들어가야 한다. 첫 번째 빈칸 뒤에는 절이 오므로 접속사 As가 알맞고, 두 번째 빈칸 뒤에는 명사구가 오므로 전치사구 because of가 알맞다.

11 '우산을 가져가라, 그렇지 않으면 너는 비에 젖게 될 것이다.'라는 뜻이므로 '네가 우산을 가져가지 않으면, 너는 비에 젖을 것이다.'로 바꿔 쓸 수 있다.

12 ⓔ 문맥상 '~하지 않으면'의 의미를 나타내는 unless가 알맞다.

13 ① 시간이나 조건의 부사절에서는 미래의 일을 나타낼 때 현재시제로 쓴다. (→ stops)

14 ④ 「either A or B」가 주어일 때 동사는 B에 일치시킨다. (→ has)

15 ③ '나는 영화를 보는 동안 잠이 들었다.'의 의미가 되어야 하므로 While이 알맞다.

16 both A and B: A와 B 둘 다
neither A nor B: A도 B도 아닌
not only A but also B: A뿐만 아니라 B도

17 해석 A 나는 영어 말하기 시험에 대해 너무 걱정 돼.
B 걱정하지 마. 너는 잘할 거야.
A 너는 영어를 잘 하잖아. 나에게 어떻게 너처럼 영어를 잘할 수 있는지 말해 줘.
B 많이 연습해, 그러면 너는 영어 말하기를 잘하게 될 거야.
→ ⓔ '많이 연습해라, 그러면 너는 영어 말하기를 잘하게 될 것이다.'라는 뜻이 되어야 하므로 or가 아닌 and로 말해야 한다.

18 ④ 「not only A but also B」는 「B as well as A」로 바꿔 쓸 수 있다. 「either A or B」는 'A나 B 둘 중 하나'라는 의미이다.

19 '너무 ~해서 …하다'는 「so+형용사/부사+that ....」 구문을 써서 나타낼 수 있다.

20 '~하지 않으면'은 unless를 써서 나타낼 수 있다.

21 '~에도 불구하고'는 though를 써서 나타낼 수 있다.

22 'A도 B도 아닌'은 「neither A nor B」를 써서 나타낸다.

23 'A와 B 둘 다'는 「both A and B」로 나타내고, 주어로 쓰일 때 복수 취급한다.

24 (1) 비록 비가 오고 있었지만 / 그들은 밖에서 축구를 했다.
(2) 영화가 끝날 때까지 / 나는 내 스마트폰을 켜지 않았다.
(3) 눈이 많이 왔기 때문에 / 우리는 외출하지 않기로 했다.

25 각각 접속사 after(~ 후에)와 before(~ 전에)가 포함된 문장이므로, '숙제를 한 후에 TV를 보았다'와 'TV를 보기 전에 숙제를 했다'는 내용의 문장을 써야 한다.

26 「not only A but also B」는 「B as well as A」로 바꿔 쓸 수 있다.

27 (1) so+형용사/부사+that+주어+can't ...: 너무 ~해서 …할 수 없다
(2) not only A but also B: A뿐만 아니라 B도

28 ⓐ 시간이나 조건의 부사절에서는 미래의 일을 나타낼 때 현재시제로 쓴다.
ⓓ Unless는 부정의 의미가 포함되어 있으므로 not을 함께 쓰지 않는다.

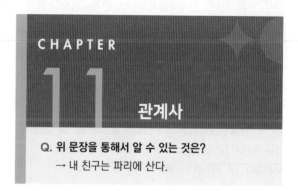

CHAPTER

11

관계사

Q. 위 문장을 통해서 알 수 있는 것은?
→ 내 친구는 파리에 산다.

UNIT 01　　관계대명사의 개념

p. 143

개념 우선 확인　　**1** 책을 읽고 있는 소녀　**2** 내가 만난 소년　**3** 내가 사고 싶은 신발

A **1** 선행사: the people / 관계대명사: who
2 선행사: the bike / 관계대명사: that
3 선행사: the package / 관계대명사: that
4 선행사: the girl / 관계대명사: whom
5 선행사: a man / 관계대명사: whose

B **1** which **2** who **3** that **4** who **5** that

C **1** that[which] **2** who[that] **3** that[which]
4 who[that] **5** that[which]

① who, that ② that, which

UNIT 02 관계대명사의 역할

pp. 144~145

시험 point **1** is **2** have

[개념 우선 확인] **1** the book that I like
2 a man whose father is a doctor
3 people who need help

A **1** who **2** whose **3** lives **4** are

B **1** who **2** whose **3** which **4** whom

C **1** who invented **2** a boy whose dream
3 that(which) we saw **4** a book whose cover

30초 완성 map

① who, 프랑스어를 말할 수 있는 남자를
② that, 잃어버렸던 펜을
③ whose, 어머니가 유명한 배우인 한 소년을

UNIT 03 관계대명사 what, 관계대명사의 생략

p. 147

[개념 우선 확인] **1** 내가 읽은 그 이야기 **2** 내가 원하는 것

A **1** What **2** that **3** that **4** what **5** who

B **1** × **2** that **3** × **4** which **5** who is

C **1** The girl wearing a black jacket is **2** lost the wallet he bought **3** I found an old book written **4** What I want to eat is

30초 완성 map

① that, what ② who is, that

UNIT 04 관계부사

p. 149

[개념 우선 확인] **1** when **2** why **3** where

A **1** where **2** why **3** when

B **1** why **2** when **3** where **4** how

C **1** how he talks to me **2** where we used to ride our bikes **3** when Korea hosted the World Cup

---

30초 완성 map

① when ② where ③ why ④ ×

W 서술형 대비 문장 쓰기

p. 150

01 that(which) he draws
02 what you want
03 who(that) sang
04 why the movie is popular
05 whose owner is a famous actor
06 that he had lost
07 how(the way) I made the cheesecake
08 (where) she parked her car
09 The pants that I bought yesterday
10 a girl whose hair was red
11 the supermarket which is open 24 hours
12 what I know about him

시험에 꼭 나오는 출제포인트

p. 151

1 (1) What (2) what
2 ①
3 (1) that (2) who is
4 This is how(the way) I brush my teeth.
[고득점 POINT] (1) where (2) which

실전 Test

pp. 152~155

01 ③	02 ②	03 ⑤	04 ⑤	05 ①
06 ④	07 ③,⑤	08 ③	09 ④	10 ①
11 ②	12 ③	13 ⑤	14 ④	15 ④
16 ②	17 ④	18 ③		

19 why **20** what
21 a nice restaurant that(which) is open
22 a day when people exchange gifts
23 (1) a photo which was taken in Paris
(2) the hospital where I was born
24 I am watching a movie made in the 1980s.
25 which → when
26 We need someone who(that) can play the drums.
27 The apples that(which) are in the basket are delicious.
28 volunteers who(that) will clean up the beach with them

01 선행사가 a documentary이고 주격 관계대명사가 들어가야 하므로 that이 알맞다.

02 선행사를 포함한 관계대명사가 들어가야 하므로 what이 알맞다.

03 선행사가 a dog이고 관계사절에서 명사 앞에 위치하므로 소유격 관계대명사 whose가 알맞다.

04 선행사가 the place이고 관계사절에서 부사 역할을 하므로 where가 알맞다.

05 선행사 The dream과 관계대명사절 I had last night 사이에 목적격 관계대명사 that 또는 which가 들어가야 한다.

06 두 번째 문장의 소유격 His를 소유격 관계대명사 whose로 바꿔 연결할 수 있다.

07 〈보기〉와 같이 관계대명사로 쓰인 것은 ③,⑤이다. 나머지는 '누구, 누가'의 뜻으로 쓰인 의문사이다.

08 ③은 '무엇'의 뜻으로 쓰인 의문사이고, 나머지는 선행사를 포함하는 관계대명사로 '~하는 것'의 의미이다.

09 첫 번째 빈칸에는 the reason을 선행사로 하는 관계부사 why가 들어가야 한다. 두 번째 빈칸에는 선행사 the way가 생략된 관계부사 how가 알맞다.

10 ①은 명사절을 이끄는 접속사 that이고, 나머지는 관계대명사로 쓰인 that이다.

11 분사(구) 앞의 「주격 관계대명사+be동사」는 생략할 수 있다.

12 ③은 소유격 관계대명사 whose를 써야 하고, 나머지는 관계대명사 who나 that을 쓸 수 있다.

13 ⑤ 관계사 앞에 선행사가 없으므로 선행사를 포함하는 관계대명사 what을 써야 한다.

14 ④ 「주격 관계대명사+be동사」 뒤에 분사가 오는 경우에만 생략할 수 있다.

15 해석 A 너는 저기 걷고 있는 남자와 개를 아니?
B 털이 갈색인 개를 말하는 거야?
A 응, 그래.
B 그는 내 이웃이야. 내가 너에게 옆집으로 이사 온 남자에 대해 말했었지. 그가 바로 저 사람이야.
→ (A) 사람과 동물이 함께 선행사로 쓰였으므로 관계대명사 that이 알맞다.
(B) 명사 앞이므로 소유격 관계대명사 whose가 알맞다.
(C) 사람이 선행사이므로 관계대명사 who나 that이 알맞다.

16 ⓐ the way와 how는 함께 쓸 수 없다.
ⓑ 주어는 선행사를 포함한 관계대명사인 What이 맞다.
ⓔ 목적격 관계대명사절에서는 목적어를 또 쓰지 않아야 하므로 it을 삭제해야 한다.

17 ④ ⓓ에 올 말이 목적어 역할을 하므로 목적격 관계대명사 that이나 which를 써야 한다.

18 ③ 관계부사는 부사구를 대신하므로 live 다음에 전치사를 쓰지 않는다.

19 이유를 나타내는 선행사 the reason 다음에는 관계부사 why를 쓴다.

20 앞에 선행사가 없으므로 선행사를 포함하는 관계대명사 what을 쓴다.

21 a nice restaurant이 선행사이고 뒤 문장에서 주어이므로 that이나 which를 써서 두 문장을 연결한다.

22 a day가 선행사이고 뒤 문장에서 부사구이므로 관계부사 when을 써서 두 문장을 연결한다.

23 (1) 주격 관계대명사 which가 이끄는 절이 선행사 a photo를 수식한다.
(2) 관계부사 where가 이끄는 절이 선행사 the hospital을 수식한다.

24 분사(구) 앞의 「주격 관계대명사+be동사」는 생략 가능하다.

25 선행사 the day가 관계사절에서 부사 역할을 하므로 관계부사 when을 써야 한다.

26 someone을 선행사로 하고 주격 관계대명사 who나 that을 써서 '드럼을 칠 수 있는 누군가'를 나타낸다.

27 선행사(The apples)가 사물이므로 주격 관계대명사 that이나 which를 써서 주어 부분을 쓴다. 이때 문장의 동사는 선행사에 수 일치시킨다.

28 선행사(volunteers)가 사람이므로 관계대명사 who나 that을 이용하여 쓴다.

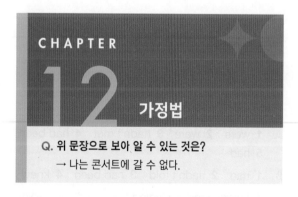

CHAPTER 12 가정법

Q. 위 문장으로 보아 알 수 있는 것은?
→ 나는 콘서트에 갈 수 없다.

UNIT 01 가정법 과거

pp. 158~159

시험 point don't have, can't

개념 우선 확인 1 그는 지금 농구 선수가 아니다.
2 나는 그녀의 전화번호를 모른다.

A **1** were **2** will go **3** went **4** rains
5 could

B **1** weren't, could go **2** had, could give
3 weren't, would start

C **1** were, would challenge
2 asked, might help **3** had, could open

30초 완성 map

① were, 좋다면, 갈 텐데
② doesn't know, can't introduce

UNIT 02 가정법 과거완료

p. 161

개념 우선 확인 **1** 가정법 과거완료 **2** 가정법 과거

A **1** might have seen **2** were **3** had had
4 would have said

B **1** hadn't helped, would have failed
2 had arrived, wouldn't have been
3 hadn't told, could have trusted

C **1** were, would be
2 had snowed, could have made
3 hadn't lost, would have gotten

30초 완성 map

① had arrived, 도착했다면, 만날 수 있었을 텐데
② wasn't, made

UNIT 03 I wish 가정법, as if 가정법

p. 163

개념 우선 확인 **1** 나는 친구가 많지 않다.
2 그는 런던에 산 적이 없다.

A **1** were **2** were **3** hadn't met **4** had been
5 had

B **1** had **2** hadn't told **3** had been **4** knew

C **1** I were good at singing
2 as if she hadn't slept
3 I wish you had watched

30초 완성 map

① were, had slept ② were, had read

 서술형 대비 문장 쓰기

p. 164

01 were, would study
02 had known, could have asked
03 as if, were
04 had learned
05 had a driver's license, could drive
06 didn't snow, didn't go
07 has never(not) been
08 could go
09 as if he understood me
10 I hadn't eaten ice cream
11 were, would be proud of her
12 hadn't been, wouldn't have made a mistake

시험에 꼭 나오는 출제포인트

p. 165

1 (1) had (2) wouldn't
고득점 POINT don't know, can't call

2 (1) couldn't have finished (2) had apologized
고득점 POINT had saved, could have bought

3 ⑤

4 (1) isn't (2) ate

실전 Test

pp. 166~169

01 ③	02 ③	03 ④	04 ④	05 ②
06 ④	07 ③	08 ⑤	09 ②	10 ④
11 ④	12 ⑤	13 ④	14 ③	15 ③
16 ③	17 ④	18 ①		

19 weren't, could help
20 I had a skateboard
21 I had, would give
22 had gotten up, could have had
23 as if he were a doctor
24 had made a reservation
25 as if she hadn't been sick
26 were, could ride
27 as if it were his native language
28 if I had invited him

01 if절의 동사로 보아 가정법 과거 문장이므로 주절의 동사는 「조동사의 과거형＋동사원형」 형태인 could buy가 알맞다.

02 I wish 가정법 과거는 were, 과거완료는 had been으로 쓴다.

03 주절의 동사로 보아 가정법 과거완료 문장이므로 if절의 동사는 「had+p.p.」 형태로 쓴다.

04 과거 일에 대해 반대로 말하는 것이므로 as if 다음에 가정법 과거완료를 쓴다.

05 과거 일에 대한 반대 가정은 가정법 과거완료로 나타내므로, if절의 동사는 「had+p.p.」로 쓴다. (→ had gone)

06 현재의 상황을 가정하는 질문이므로 시제에 맞게 가정법 과거로 대답한다.

07 현재 사실의 반대 가정은 가정법 과거를 써서 나타낸다. 가정법 과거의 be동사는 항상 were로 쓴다.

08 ⑤ 주절의 동사로 보아 가정법 과거완료 문장이므로 if절의 동사는 had snowed로 써야 한다.

09 「I wish+가정법 과거완료」는 과거에 대한 아쉬움이나 유감을 나타내므로 반대 의미의 직설법 과거로 바꿔 쓸 수 있다.

10 현재 사실에 대한 반대 가정이므로 가정법 과거를 써서 나타낸다.

11 첫 번째 문장은 가정법 과거이므로 빈칸에 had가 들어가야 하고, 두 번째 문장은 가정법 과거완료이므로 빈칸에 had been이 들어가야 한다.

12 과거 일에 대한 반대 가정은 가정법 과거완료로 나타내고, 긍정문은 부정문으로 쓴다.

13 as if+가정법 과거: as if+주어+동사의 과거형

14 I wish+가정법 과거완료: I wish+주어+had+p.p.

15 ⓐ was → were   ⓓ didn't lie → hadn't lied
ⓔ are → were

16 ③ '내가 요리를 잘한다면 좋을 텐데.'는 '사실 나는 요리를 못 한다'는 의미이다. (am → am not)

17 [해석] A 무슨 일이야? 너 속상해 보이네.
B 나 Emily와 싸웠어.
A 무슨 일이 있었어?
B 그녀가 나를 비웃었어. 그녀가 나를 비웃지 않았다면 나는 화가 나지 않았을 거야.
A 그렇구나. 내가 너라면 그것에 대해 그녀에게 이야기할 거야.
→ ⓓ는 가정법 과거완료로 써야 하므로 if절의 동사를 「had+p.p.」로 써야 한다. (hasn't → hadn't)

18 ① '~한다면 좋을 텐데'는 「I wish+가정법 과거」로 나타낸다. (had stopped → stopped)

19 현재 사실의 반대 가정은 가정법 과거로 나타내며 「If+주어+동사의 과거형 ~, 주어+조동사의 과거형+동사원형 ...」으로 쓴다.

20 현재 사실에 대한 반대 가정이므로 「I wish+가정법 과거」를 써서 나타낸다.

21 현재 사실에 대한 반대 가정이므로 가정법 과거로 나타낸다.

22 과거 사실에 대한 반대 가정이므로 가정법 과거완료로 나타낸다.

23 실제로는 아니지만 현재 마치 그런 것처럼 가정할 때 쓰는 표현은 「as if+가정법 과거」이다.

24 [해석] 어제 우리 가족은 저녁 식사를 위해 인기 있는 식당에 갔다. 우리는 예약을 하지 않아서, 한 시간을 기다려야 했다.
→ 과거 일에 대한 유감·후회를 나타낼 때는 I wish 다음에 가정법 과거완료를 쓴다.

25 실제로는 아니지만 과거에 마치 그랬던 것처럼 가정할 때 쓰는 표현은 「as if+가정법 과거완료」이다.

26 Emma는 현재 키가 작아서 롤러코스터를 탈 수 없으므로 '키가 더 크다면 롤러코스터를 탈 수 있을 텐데.'의 의미를 나타내는 가정법 과거 문장으로 써야 한다.

27 [해석] 나는 러시아에서 온 친구가 한 명 있다. 그는 서울에 10년째 살고 있고, 한국어를 유창하게 말한다. 그는 마치 그것(한국어)이 모국어인 것처럼 한국어를 말할 수 있다.
→ '(현재 사실과 반대로) 마치 ~한 것처럼'의 의미를 나타낼 때는 「as if+가정법 과거」를 쓰며, 가정법 과거의 be동사는 항상 were를 쓴다.

28 [해석] 어제는 내 생일이었다. 나는 내 친구들을 파티에 초대했지만, 실수로 Jason을 초대하는 것을 잊었다. 내가 그를 초대했다면 그는 파티에 왔을 것이다.
→ 과거 일에 대해 반대로 가정하는 것이므로 가정법 과거완료로 써야 한다.

WORKBOOK ANSWERS

UNIT 01 | 현재시제, 과거시제, 미래시제 pp. 2~3

A **1** scored **2** is **3** are going to visit **4** leaves **5** will meet **6** went **7** cry
8 to attend

B **1** eats **2** will(are going to) take **3** invented **4** will(am going to) learn **5** collects
6 rode

C **1** travels **2** visited **3** will be **4** are going to have 또는 will have **5** started
6 takes **7** discovered **8** gets **9** am going to visit 또는 will visit

D **1** works at a fire station **2** Breakfast will be ready
3 wrote her report at home **4** are going to visit the palace
5 opens at 10 o'clock every morning **6** I stayed home and watched TV
7 I am going to watch a movie

UNIT 02 | 현재진행형, 과거진행형 pp. 4~5

A **1** drinks **2** is talking **3** am studying **4** was meeting **5** have
6 are going **7** were watching **8** likes

B **1** is going **2** belongs **3** were planting **4** was visiting **5** are having
6 was washing

C **1** know **2** has **3** is downloading **4** was running **5** are making **6** was sleeping
7 are going **8** is having

D **1** is going to the bank now **2** was talking to his homeroom teacher
3 are solving math problems **4** are going to the swimming pool
5 What are you hiding **6** were falling to the ground
7 were playing soccer when it started to rain

pp. 6~7

A 1 have lived   2 have cleaned   3 has broken   4 has gone   5 have met
   6 has studied   7 has written   8 has fallen   9 has solved   10 has moved

B 1 has   2 seen   3 sent   4 Have   5 missed   6 has driven   7 haven't
   8 met   9 did you move   10 Have you known

C 1 (부정문) You haven't(have not) learned how to swim.   (의문문) Have you learned how to swim?
   2 (부정문) Amy hasn't(has not) finished the work.   (의문문) Has Amy finished the work?
   3 (부정문) They haven't(have not) prepared a lot of food for the party.
   (의문문) Have they prepared a lot of food for the party?
   4 (부정문) Mr. and Ms. Thomson haven't(have not) traveled overseas.
   (의문문) Have Mr. and Ms. Thomson traveled overseas?

D 1 have watched the movie several times   2 has never ridden a bicycle
   3 moved to LA two years ago   4 Have you already finished
   5 Have you ever eaten sushi before?   6 She has been here since 9 o'clock.

 pp. 8~9

A 1 ㉂   2 ㉖   3 ㉤   4 ㉡   5 ㉖   6 ㉤   7 ㉂   8 ㉡

B 1 has been busy   2 has hurt his leg
   3 has gone to Italy   4 hasn't finished his homework
   5 has worked at a flower shop

C 1 been   2 for   3 has watched   4 has worked   5 has gone
   6 has never been

D 1 has already heard the news   2 Have you gone camping
   3 has worked with us for six months   4 has never seen her before
   5 has lived in Yeosu since 2010   6 have not arrived at the airport yet

CHAPTER ● 2 | 조동사

pp. 10~11

UNIT 01 | can, may, will

A **1** can **2** may **3** will **4** can **5** will be able to **6** may

B **1** 늦을지도 모른다 **2** 참석하지 않을 것이다 **3** 제가 앉아도 될까요 **4** 넣어 주시겠어요

C **1** can play **2** wasn't able to eat **3** will be able to make **4** may not be
5 will be able to pass

D **1** can **2** is able to **3** were able to

E **1** may use my scissors **2** Can I have some cotton candy
3 were not able to play **4** may not agree with your plan
5 You will be able to find your way.

pp. 12~13

UNIT 02 | must, should, had better, used to

A **1** had better **2** go **3** must **4** should **5** don't have to **6** had to

B **1** has to **2** must not **3** used to **4** should **5** doesn't have to **6** had better not
7 had to **8** travel **9** must **10** must not open

C **1** 배고픈 게 틀림없다 **2** 교복을 입어야 했다 **3** 보호해야 한다 **4** 대답할 필요가 없다
5 말하지 않는 게 좋겠다 **6** 요가를 하곤 하셨다

D **1** There used to be a lake **2** should not eat too much
3 will have to change our plans **4** You must be quiet
5 You had better not drive **6** You don't have to pay for

UNIT 01 | to부정사의 명사적 용법

A 1 ㉰ 2 ㉩ 3 ㉯ 4 ㉰ 5 ㉩ 6 ㉩ 7 ㉰ 8 ㉯ 9 ㉩ 10 ㉰

B 1 To live 2 to go 3 where to buy 4 to be 5 not to 6 how 7 It
8 not to do 9 is 10 to reuse

C 1 It, to fix 2 It, to protect 3 It, to swim 4 to get

D 1 It 2 when to leave 3 not to be 4 requires 5 to play

E 1 I like to read books 2 doesn't know how to send emails
3 is not to lose your dream 4 It is wrong to lie to your friends.

UNIT 02 | to부정사의 형용사적·부사적 용법

A 1 ⓑ 2 ⓔ 3 ⓓ 4 ⓒ 5 ⓐ 6 ⓐ 7 ⓔ 8 ⓓ

B 1 to pass 2 to be 3 write with 4 to hear 5 live in 6 to have
7 something cold 8 to learn 9 to tell 10 to visit

C 1 읽을 무언가가 2 앉을 의자를 3 그녀를 도와주다니

D 1 to find 2 to have 3 to write on 4 to become

E 1 left early to avoid 2 a lot of toys to play with
3 be wise to give such good advice 4 was glad to win the final match

UNIT 03 | to부정사의 의미상 주어, to부정사 구문

A 1 for you 2 of her 3 of him 4 for them 5 for me 6 too 7 hard enough to
8 too 9 enough 10 small enough

B 1 too, to 2 It, of, to 3 tall enough to 4 for you to 5 enough to move
6 too, for, to

C 1 of you 2 to play 3 for us 4 Amy is rich enough to buy the new car.

D 1 too fast, me, catch 2 comfortable enough, to wear 3 so, that, could notice
4 so, that, couldn't help

E 1 of you to talk to your parents 2 too worried to sleep
3 brave enough to try that 4 natural for you to get angry

UNIT 01 동명사의 역할

pp. 20~21

A 1 ㈜ 2 ㉫ 3 ㈜ 4 ㈜ 5 ㉫ 6 ㉲ 7 ㈜ 8 ㉫ 9 ㉫ 10 ㉲

B 1 Having 2 speaking 3 meeting 4 Being 5 is 6 saying 7 playing
8 becoming 9 requires 10 listening

C 1 자전거를 타는 것은 2 그림을 그리는 것이다 3 하느라 바쁘다 4 먹고 싶지 않다
5 너를 보기를 고대하고 있다

D 1 is 2 drawing 3 to getting 4 practicing 5 buying 6 drinking

E 1 this is worth buying 2 couldn't help crying
3 Going out at night is dangerous 4 spent all afternoon helping her mom

UNIT 02 동명사와 to부정사

pp. 22~23

A 1 to be 2 playing 3 seeing 4 to take 5 talking 6 to see 7 to learn
8 going

B 1 갔던 2 갈 것을 3 조깅을 하려고 노력했다 4 열어보려고 했지만 5 전화할 것을
6 보냈던 것을 7 우는 것을 멈췄다

C 1 watching 2 to move 3 to send 4 walking 5 to go 6 doing 7 to do
8 to turn

D 1 enjoy walking to 2 I remembered meeting him
3 promised to clean his room 4 forgot to attend the meeting
5 tried to get up early 6 decided to take a walk every day
7 Would you mind closing the window?

UNIT 01 현재분사와 과거분사
pp. 24~25

A 1 ⑧ 2 ⑲ 3 ⑲ 4 ⑧ 5 ⑧ 6 ⑲ 7 ⑲ 8 ⑧ 9 ⑲

B 1 삶은 2 날고 있는 3 연주하고 있는 4 칠해진 5 지루한 6 만들어진
   7 흥미가(관심이) 있다 8 흥미로웠다 9 충격적이었다 10 충격을 받았다

C 1 amazing 2 lost 3 surprised 4 exciting 5 shining

D 1 written 2 standing 3 built 4 dancing 5 interested

E 1 buy things made in Korea 2 a boy living in the jungle was exciting
   3 Reading books written in English 4 He was disappointed at the news.
   5 The documentary about Africa was amazing.

UNIT 02 분사구문
pp. 26~27

A 1 Having 2 Living 3 Leaving your car 4 Waving to us 5 Knowing him well
   6 Being in a hurry

B 1 ⓔ 2 ⓑ 3 ⓕ 4 ⓓ 5 ⓐ 6 ⓒ

C 1 시간이 없었기 때문에 2 보면서 3 그를 보았을 때

D 1 Being sick 2 Talking on the phone 3 smiling brightly 4 Finishing my homework

E 1 Seeing me in the park 2 After reading her email
   3 Watching TV, he had dinner. 4 Getting up late, I couldn't get to school on time.

UNIT 01 | 수동태의 기본 개념

pp. 28~29

A 1 ㈜   2 ㉤   3 ㈜   4 ㉤   5 ㈜   6 ㈜

B 1 attacked   2 was   3 were injured   4 will be fixed   5 is cooked   6 were invited

C 1 was played   2 was stolen by   3 will be employed by

D 1 were written   2 by her   3 was painted   4 are spoken   5 solved   6 will be held
7 was cleaned   8 was built   9 reads

E 1 was made in Germany   2 was bitten by the dog
3 was stopped because of the rain   4 is grown by farmers
5 will be punished by   6 The window was broken by a stone.
7 Small fish are eaten by larger fish.

UNIT 02 | 수동태의 여러 가지 형태

pp. 30~31

A 1 was not   2 can be recycled   3 may be finished   4 was the telescope
5 should be carried   6 Was this flower watered

B 1 Is, spoken   2 was not   3 were, by   4 When were   5 not be

C 1 was not canceled   2 was   3 will visit   4 can't be understood   5 should be taken
6 can be paid

D 1 is not provided   2 was, used by   3 should be closed   4 weren't answered by him
5 may not be needed

E 1 Was your bike repaired by   2 must be followed by all of us
3 What languages are spoken   4 The project should be completed
5 will be translated into Korean   6 When was the planet discovered?
7 The promise may not be kept.

UNIT 03 | 주의해야 할 수동태

pp. 32~33

A 1 doesn't fit   2 with   3 has   4 at   5 is looked up to   6 appeared

B 1 was laughed at   2 was tired of   3 will arrive   4 is worried about
5 resemble   6 is covered with

C 1 interested in   2 turned on by   3 satisfied with   4 be put off   5 filled with

D 1 is taken care of by   2 was brought up by   3 was pleased with   4 be satisfied with
5 were turned off

E 1 are interested in K-pop   2 was looked after by neighbors
3 I'm tired of doing the same thing   4 was looked up to by many people
5 was not surprised at the result   6 The airport is crowded with tourists.
7 Are you worried about the environment?

UNIT 01 부정대명사 I (one, another, other)

pp. 34~35

A **1** one **2** it **3** ones **4** them **5** the others **6** Some **7** another, the other
8 One, the other

B **1** one **2** ones **3** the others **4** another, the other **5** others

C **1** Some, the others **2** One, another, the other **3** One, the other **4** Some, others

D **1** one **2** it **3** ones **4** others **5** the other **6** another **7** the others

UNIT 02 부정대명사 II (each, every, both, all, some, any)

pp. 36~37

A **1** Each **2** Both **3** every **4** consists **5** wear **6** Both of **7** are **8** side
9 was **10** some **11** student gets **12** any

B **1** Both **2** any **3** Every **4** All **5** some **6** each

C **1** Both of them **2** some butter **3** Every room **4** all my books **5** have to

D **1** don't have any money **2** Each member has the right
3 Every room in the house has **4** All our money was stolen
5 Both of them are very cute. **6** We need some new ideas to solve the problem.

UNIT 03 재귀대명사

pp. 38~39

A **1** myself **2** herself **3** him **4** yourself **5** himself **6** yourself **7** himself
8 herself

B **1** myself **2** yourself **3** ourselves **4** themselves **5** myself **6** themselves

C **1** make yourself at home **2** Help yourself to
3 by myself **4** enjoyed myself

D **1** should believe in yourself **2** had to finish the work by himself
3 looked at herself in the mirror **4** I don't like chocolate itself
5 help yourself to some cheesecake **6** do you talk to yourself
7 himself played the piano at the party

CHAPTER 8 | 비교

pp. 40~41

UNIT 01 원급, 비교급, 최상급

A 1 longer, longest 2 bigger, biggest 3 prettier, prettiest 4 taller, tallest
5 worse, worst 6 more famous, most famous 7 more important, most important
8 heavier, heaviest 9 better, best 10 less, least

B 1 as 2 large 3 stronger 4 yours 5 much 6 warm 7 better
8 the highest 9 of 10 most

C 1 hot 2 more expensive 3 wiser 4 most popular 5 tallest

D 1 much happier 2 as small as 또는 smaller than 3 than 4 more expensive
5 much(even, a lot, far) sweeter 6 the largest planet

E 1 even lighter than those ones 2 not as brave as his brother
3 the most important thing in life 4 is much colder than last winter
5 is the longest river in the world

pp. 42~43

UNIT 02 다양한 비교 표현

A 1 three times 2 twice as big 3 three times faster 4 tests 5 better and better
6 the most popular 7 The more, the wiser 8 more and more
9 four times more expensive 10 The harder, the better

B 1 fatter and fatter 2 three times larger 3 more and more 4 The higher
5 the most beautiful places 6 hotter and hotter 7 one of the nicest rooms
8 the kindest people 9 the more easily 10 twice as heavy as

C 1 worse and worse 2 twice as thick 3 sooner, better 4 more and more important
5 the most famous cities

D 1 one of the most important skills 2 the days get shorter and shorter
3 twice as long as elephants do 4 three times more money than he did
5 The more books you read, the smarter 6 one of the richest people in the world

UNIT 01 감각동사, 수여동사

pp. 44~45

A 1 soft 2 serious 3 to students 4 me 5 Lily a magazine 6 me 7 nervous
8 to 9 looks like 10 for her

B 1 to him 2 for me 3 to the children 4 a Christmas present 5 potato chips

C 1 sad 2 felt 3 different 4 for me 5 to foreigners 6 bad 7 looks like
8 to them 9 us dinner 또는 dinner for us 10 some hot tea for you 또는 you some hot tea

D 1 tastes bitter and sweet 2 looked like an angel
3 lent his comic book to me 4 showed us his old diary, showed his old diary to us
5 made Jessy a card, made a card for Jessy

UNIT 02 목적격보어가 필요한 동사

pp. 46~47

A 1 her, class president 2 him, look different 3 my room, warm 4 us, to exercise
regularly 5 him, to be happy 6 me, clean my desk 7 my heart, beating faster
8 him, sing 9 me, to wash the dishes 10 my dog, playing with a ball

B 1 her cat Momo 2 you healthy 3 to read 4 jump 5 know 6 go
7 blowing 8 warm 9 had 10 watched

C 1 sing(singing) 2 to brush 3 move(moving) 4 play 5 clean

D 1 Kelly 2 to learn 3 cry(crying) 4 fresh 5 fall(falling)

E 1 elected Mr. Keating captain 2 found the math homework difficult
3 told us to keep quiet 4 had him wash his hands
5 heard Jessica read a book aloud

CHAPTER 10 접속사

UNIT 01 시간·이유·조건의 접속사

pp. 48~49

A 1 when 2 Before 3 jogs 4 as 5 unless 6 Though 7 because 8 Since 9 that 10 until

B 1 When 2 unless 3 while 4 Although 5 if 6 because

C 1 그녀는 졸업한 후에 2 목이 매우 말랐기 때문에 3 (비록) 그는 중국 출신이지만 4 문을 닫지 않으면

D 1 is 2 so 3 get 4 takes 5 so

E 1 As the sun is bright 2 brush your teeth after you eat something 3 said nothing while I was talking 4 had a great time even though it rained 5 so crowded that I couldn't find a seat

UNIT 02 명령문+and/or, 짝을 이루는 접속사

pp. 50~51

A 1 and 2 or 3 or 4 nor 5 and 6 either 7 as 8 has 9 are 10 are

B 1 and 2 Unless, or 3 neither, nor 4 as well as

C 1 그러면 너는 기분이 더 나아질 거야 2 코트나 재킷 둘 중 하나를 3 그러지 않으면 회의에 늦을 거야 4 한국에서뿐만 아니라 미국에서도

D 1 or 2 neither 3 like 4 that 5 is

E 1 both good news and bad news 2 and your dream will come true 3 or you can't get on the plane 4 not only easy to cook but also delicious

pp. 52~53

UNIT 01 | 관계대명사의 개념

A 1 선행사: the girl 관계대명사절: who painted the picture
2 선행사: the tree 관계대명사절: which my grandfather planted
3 선행사: food 관계대명사절: which is hot and spicy
4 선행사: the girl 관계대명사절: that is wearing a blue hat
5 선행사: the police officer 관계대명사절: who helped you
6 선행사: the deer 관계대명사절: that are drinking water
7 선행사: the house 관계대명사절: whose door is painted blue
8 선행사: a book 관계대명사절: that is about jazz
9 선행사: the boy 관계대명사절: who you met in Paris

B 1 ③ 2 ② 3 ① 4 ③ 5 ② 6 ② 7 ③ 8 ② 9 ②

C 1 that 2 whose 3 who 4 that 5 that

D 1 설거지를 할 수 있는 로봇을 2 내가 텔레비전에서 봤던 소년 3 내가 좋아하지 않는 노래를
4 생일이 오늘인 학생을

E 1 a house which has big windows 2 a dog whose name is Baekgu
3 the teacher whom I respect 4 is a person who doesn't tell the truth

pp. 54~55

UNIT 02 | 관계대명사의 역할

A 1 ㈜ 2 ㈜ 3 ㈐ 4 ㈑ 5 ㈜ 6 ㈜ 7 ㈑ 8 ㈐ 9 ㈜ 10 ㈑

B 1 which 2 who 3 who 4 which 5 whose 6 that 7 that 8 visited
9 barks 10 live

C 1 who(m)(that) 2 that(which) 3 whose

D 1 that(which) 2 who(m)(that) 3 whose 4 that(which) I watched 5 who(that) loves

E 1 an uncle who lives in Canada 2 a dog whose tail is short
3 heroes whom we must remember 4 have a brother who is 10 years old
5 use the natural soap that Mom made

UNIT 03 관계대명사 what, 관계대명사의 생략

A 1 ○ 2 × 3 ○ 4 ○ 5 × 6 × 7 ○ 8 × 9 ○ 10 ×

B 1 what 2 What 3 we saw 4 talking 5 what 6 that 7 which 8 written
9 playing 10 directed

C 1 내가 말하는 것을 2 아이스크림을 먹고 있는 저 소년은 3 이탈리아에서 만들어진 탁자를

D 1 what 2 what 3 cooked 또는 that(which) is cooked 4 eating 또는 that(which) are
eating 5 what 또는 the things that(which)

E 1 Remember what the teacher said 2 The thing that we need most
3 the man who is standing at the gate 4 What she ate for lunch was
5 bought a cake decorated with fruit

UNIT 04 관계부사

A 1 when 2 why 3 where 4 how 5 where 6 when 7 why 8 the way
9 the season 10 the island

B 1 where 2 when 3 why 4 where 5 how

C 1 런던에 살았던 날들을 2 그녀가 오디션에 합격한 방법 3 우리가 종종 산책을 하는 장소

D 1 when 2 why 3 where 4 the way 또는 how 5 when the class starts

E 1 the time when we have lunch 2 the house where I was born
3 is the way I stay healthy 4 is the reason why I was late
5 showed us how the native Americans lived

UNIT 01 | 가정법 과거
p. 60

A **1** were **2** had **3** were **4** can **5** could **6** rains **7** could save
8 will be **9** would **10** had

B **1** knew, could introduce **2** came, could watch **3** weren't, could go
4 were, could meet **5** isn't, can't feed **6** don't have, can't go

UNIT 02 | 가정법 과거완료
p. 61

A **1** had seen **2** had been **3** could have opened **4** might have arrived
5 had practiced **6** had taken **7** had told **8** had snowed **9** would have ridden
10 had won

B **1** hadn't been, would have had **2** wasn't, couldn't come
3 didn't take, couldn't solve **4** had done, would have gotten
5 had been, would have seen **6** didn't watch, went

UNIT 01-02 | 가정법 과거와 가정법 과거완료
pp. 62~63

A **1** 가정법 과거 **2** 가정법 과거 **3** 가정법 과거완료 **4** 가정법 과거 **5** 가정법 과거완료

B **1** went **2** had come **3** would play **4** could have gone **5** were
6 would have joined

C **1** would know **2** had **3** would have regretted **4** would taste **5** had studied

D **1** liked, would get **2** had spoken, wouldn't have communicated **3** were, could have
4 didn't stay, didn't clean **5** didn't drink, couldn't fall **6** had watched, would have had

E **1** I could have made a snowman **2** we could help the environment
3 If she had been home **4** If I were you, I would buy
5 If he had spoken, you could have understood

UNIT 03 | I wish 가정법, as if 가정법
p. 64

A **1** ate **2** lied **3** bought **4** had visited **5** were **6** had bought **7** were not
8 could run **9** hadn't eaten **10** were flying

B **1** wish, hadn't lost **2** as if, hadn't slept **3** wish, knew **4** as if, were
5 wish, hadn't fought **6** as if, had cleaned

동아출판 영어 교재 가이드

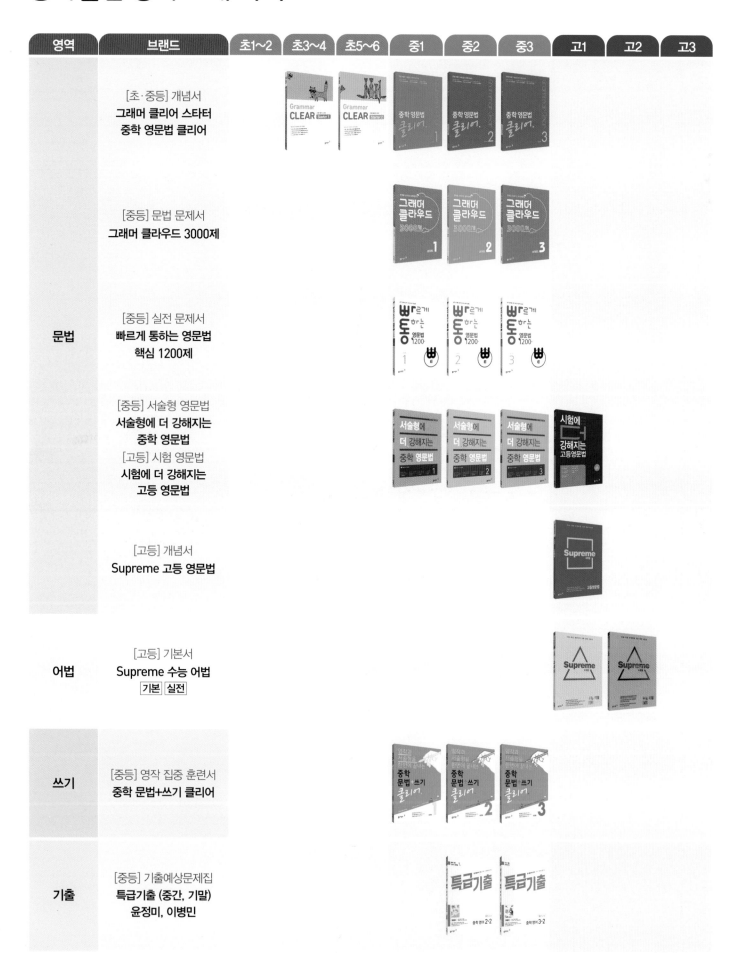

영역	브랜드	초1~2	초3~4	초5~6	중1	중2	중3	고1	고2	고3
문법	[초·중등] 개념서 그래머 클리어 스타터 중학 영문법 클리어		Grammar CLEAR Starter 1	Grammar CLEAR Starter 2	중학 영문법 클리어 1	중학 영문법 클리어 2	중학 영문법 클리어 3			
	[중등] 문법 문제서 그래머 클라우드 3000제				그래머 클라우드 3000제 LEVEL 1	그래머 클라우드 3000제 LEVEL 2	그래머 클라우드 3000제 LEVEL 3			
	[중등] 실전 문제서 빠르게 통하는 영문법 핵심 1200제				빠르게 통하는 영문법 1200 1	빠르게 통하는 영문법 1200 2	빠르게 통하는 영문법 1200 3			
	[중등] 서술형 영문법 서술형에 더 강해지는 중학 영문법 [고등] 시험 영문법 시험에 더 강해지는 고등 영문법				서술형에 더 강해지는 중학 영문법 1	서술형에 더 강해지는 중학 영문법 2	서술형에 더 강해지는 중학 영문법 3	시험에 더 강해지는 고등영문법		
	[고등] 개념서 Supreme 고등 영문법							Supreme 고등영문법		
어법	[고등] 기본서 Supreme 수능 어법 기본 실전							Supreme 기본	Supreme 실전	
쓰기	[중등] 영작 집중 훈련서 중학 문법+쓰기 클리어				중학 문법+쓰기 클리어 1	중학 문법+쓰기 클리어 2	중학 문법+쓰기 클리어 3			
기출	[중등] 기출예상문제집 특급기출 (중간, 기말) 윤정미, 이병민					특급기출 중학 영어 2-2	특급기출 중학 영어 3-2			

문법 개념과 내신을 한번에 끝내다

| 문장 구조 시각화로
핵심 문법 개념 CLEAR! | 시험포인트 및 비교포인트로
헷갈리는 문법 CLEAR! | 더 확대된 실전테스트로
학교 시험 대비 CLEAR!

Grammar clear

중학 영문법

클리어.

WORKBOOK

문장 구조 시각화로
핵심 문법 개념 CLEAR!　시험포인트 및 비교포인트로
헷갈리는 문법 CLEAR!　더 확대된 실전테스트로
학교 시험 대비 CLEAR!

동아출판

Level 2

중학 영문법 클리어.

Level 2

WORKBOOK

UNIT 01 현재시제, 과거시제, 미래시제

Answers p. 24

A
어법 선택

괄호 안에서 알맞은 것을 고르시오.

1 He (scores / scored) two goals in the 2002 World Cup.

2 Hot air (is / will be) lighter than cold air.

3 We (visited / are going to visit) the museum next weekend.

4 The plane (leaves / left) in an hour. Hurry up!

5 My teacher (met / will meet) my parents tomorrow.

6 Judy (goes / went) shopping with her mom yesterday.

7 Babies (cry / are crying) when they are hungry.

8 Who is going (attend / to attend) the meeting this afternoon?

B
빈칸 완성

우리말과 일치하도록 괄호 안의 말을 알맞은 형태로 바꿔 빈칸에 쓰시오.

1 Annie는 매일 아침에 바나나 한 개를 먹는다.

→ Annie _____ a banana every morning. (eat)

2 우리는 내일 영어 시험을 볼 것이다.

→ We _____ an English exam tomorrow. (take)

3 중국인들이 최초의 지폐를 발명했다.

→ The Chinese _____ the first paper money. (invent)

4 나는 여름방학 동안 수영을 배울 것이다.

→ I _____ to swim during summer vacation. (learn)

5 Steve는 오래된 만화책을 수집한다.

→ Steve _____ old comic books. (collect)

6 Amy는 오늘 아침에 자전거를 탔다.

→ Amy _____ her bike this morning. (ride)

C

어법 수정

밑줄 친 부분을 어법에 맞게 고쳐 쓰시오.

1 Light is traveling faster than sound.   → _____

2 My sister and I visit Tokyo last year.   → _____

3 I think it is sunny tomorrow.   → _____

4 We are going have a party for Julia.   → _____

5 The concert starts five minutes ago.   → _____

6 She take the bus to school every day.   → _____

7 Newton discovers the law of gravity.   → _____

8 My dad is getting up early every morning.   → _____

9 I going to visit Paris next month.   → _____

D

영작

우리말과 일치하도록 괄호 안의 말을 배열하여 문장을 완성하시오.

1 Michael은 소방서에서 일한다. (at, a fire station, works)

→ Michael _____ .

2 아침 식사가 곧 준비될 것이다. (will, ready, breakfast, be)

→ _____ soon.

3 Susan은 어제 집에서 보고서를 썼다. (at home, wrote, her report)

→ Susan _____ yesterday.

4 우리는 11시에 궁전을 방문할 계획이다. (going, visit, to, the palace, are)

→ We _____ at 11 o'clock.

5 그 식당은 매일 아침 10시에 문을 연다. (every morning, opens, 10 o'clock, at)

→ The restaurant _____ .

6 나는 하루 종일 집에 있으면서 TV를 봤다. (watched TV, stayed home, and, I)

→ _____ all day long.

7 나는 오늘 밤에 David와 함께 영화를 볼 것이다. (a movie, going, I, watch, to, am)

→ _____ with David tonight.

UNIT 02 현재진행형, 과거진행형

Answers p. 24

A 어법 선택

괄호 안에서 알맞은 것을 고르시오.

1 He (drinks / is drinking) a glass of water every morning.

2 He (is talking / was talking) on the phone. Can you wait for a minute?

3 I (studying / am studying) for the test now.

4 She (is meeting / was meeting) him at that time.

5 Dogs (have / are having) a great sense of smell.

6 They (are going / are going to go) to the science museum now.

7 We (are watching / were watching) TV when he came.

8 My brother (likes / is liking) playing online games.

B 빈칸 완성

우리말과 일치하도록 빈칸에 들어갈 말을 〈보기〉에서 골라 알맞은 형태로 쓰시오.

보기	plant	wash	have	go	visit	belong

1 그녀는 지금 백화점에 가고 있다.

→ She _____ to the department store now.

2 이 책은 내 여동생의 소유이다.

→ This book _____ to my sister.

3 그들은 마당에서 꽃을 심고 있는 중이었다.

→ They _____ flowers in the yard.

4 나는 그때 런던을 방문 중이었다.

→ I _____ London at that time.

5 Amy와 Jess는 함께 점심 식사를 하는 중이다.

→ Amy and Jess _____ lunch together.

6 아빠는 그때 세차를 하는 중이셨다.

→ My dad _____ his car at that time.

C

어법 수정

밑줄 친 부분을 어법에 맞게 고쳐 쓰시오.

1 I am knowing what you mean. → _____

2 Mike is having a brand-new video game. → _____

3 He was downloading a music file now. → _____

4 When I saw Jason, he is running down the road. → _____

5 Mom and I am making sandwiches now. → _____

6 Tom is sleeping when I called him. → _____

7 My brother and I am going to the gym now. → _____

8 Jennifer was having dinner at the restaurant now. → _____

D

영작

우리말과 일치하도록 괄호 안의 말을 배열하여 문장을 완성하시오.

1 엄마는 지금 은행에 가는 중이다. (going, the bank, is, to, now)

→ My mom _____ .

2 John은 담임 선생님과 이야기하고 있었다. (his homeroom teacher, to, was, talking)

→ John _____ .

3 학생들은 수학 문제를 풀고 있다. (solving, are, math problems)

→ The students _____ .

4 우리는 내일 수영장에 갈 것이다. (are, the swimming pool, to, going)

→ We _____ tomorrow.

5 너는 등 뒤에 무엇을 숨기고 있니? (you, what, are, hiding)

→ _____ behind your back?

6 나뭇잎들이 땅으로 떨어지고 있었다. (the ground, were, to, falling)

→ Leaves _____ .

7 비가 오기 시작했을 때 우리는 축구를 하고 있었다.

(it, playing soccer, to rain, when, started, were)

→ We _____ .

UNIT 3 현재완료의 개념

Answers p. 25

A 빈칸 완성

주어진 동사를 이용하여 현재완료 문장을 완성하시오.

1 I _____ here for five years. (live)

2 We _____ the house. (clean)

3 Somebody _____ the vase. (break)

4 Mr. Smith _____ to Brazil. (go)

5 Joe and Ann _____ three times. (meet)

6 Jenny _____ Japanese. (study)

7 My aunt _____ two novels. (write)

8 My smartphone _____ into the water. (fall)

9 John _____ this problem. (solve)

10 My best friend _____ to another city. (move)

B 어법 선택

괄호 안에서 알맞은 것을 고르시오.

1 My uncle (have / has) gone to China.

2 I have (saw / seen) you on TV.

3 Paul (sent / has sent) me a text message yesterday.

4 (Do / Have) you ever eaten Korean food?

5 Olivia has just (missed / missing) the bus.

6 My dad (drove / has driven) this car since 2015.

7 I (haven't / hasn't) read the book yet.

8 I (met / have met) Sally for the first time in 2014.

9 When (did you move / have you moved) to Seoul?

10 (Did you know / Have you known) her for a long time?

주어진 문장을 괄호 안의 지시대로 바꿔 쓰시오.

1 You have learned how to swim.

→ (부정문) _____

→ (의문문) _____

2 Amy has finished the work.

→ (부정문) _____

→ (의문문) _____

3 They have prepared a lot of food for the party.

→ (부정문) _____

→ (의문문) _____

4 Mr. and Ms. Thomson have traveled overseas.

→ (부정문) _____

→ (의문문) _____

D

영작

우리말과 일치하도록 괄호 안의 말을 배열하여 문장을 완성하시오.

1 나는 그 영화를 여러 번 봤다. (the movie, have, several times, watched)

→ I _____.

2 내 여동생은 자전거를 타 본 적이 없다. (a bicycle, never, ridden, has)

→ My sister _____.

3 그의 가족은 2년 전에 LA로 이사 갔다. (LA, two years ago, to, moved)

→ His family _____.

4 너는 벌써 점심 식사를 끝마쳤니? (you, finished, have, already)

→ _____ your lunch?

5 너는 전에 초밥을 먹어 본 적이 있니? (you, before, have, sushi, eaten, ever)

→ _____

6 그녀는 9시 이후로 여기에 있었다. (since, here, has, 9 o'clock, been, she)

→ _____

UNIT 04 현재완료의 쓰임

Answers p. 25

A 개념 확인

밑줄 친 현재완료의 쓰임에 ✔ 표시하시오.

계속: 계 경험: 경 완료: 완 결과: 결

1 I have been abroad twice.   계 경 완 결

2 He has taught English for ten years.   계 경 완 결

3 Jimmy has gone to Canada.   계 경 완 결

4 Have you done the work yet?   계 경 완 결

5 John hasn't called me since February.   계 경 완 결

6 Emily has lost her diary.   계 경 완 결

7 Have you ever seen a rainbow?   계 경 완 결

8 We have just returned from our summer vacation.   계 경 완 결

B 문장 전환

〈보기〉와 같이 두 문장을 한 문장으로 바꿔 쓰시오.

> 보기   He lived in Daegu two years ago. He still lives in Daegu.
> → He has lived in Daegu for two years.

1 She was busy last week. She is still busy now.

→ She _____ since last week.

2 Jason hurt his leg. He is still in pain.

→ Jason _____.

3 My brother went to Italy. He isn't here now.

→ My brother _____.

4 Mark didn't finish his homework. He is still doing his homework.

→ Mark _____ yet.

5 Judy started working at a flower shop three months ago. She still works there.

→ Judy _____ for three months.

우리말과 일치하도록 밑줄 친 부분을 어법에 맞게 고쳐 쓰시오.

1 너는 파리에 가 본 적이 있니?

Have you <u>gone</u> to Paris?　　　　　　　　　　→ _____

2 그 비행기는 12시간 동안 비행했다.

The plane has flown <u>since</u> twelve hours.　　　→ _____

3 내 남동생은 지금까지 그 만화를 세 번 봤다.

My brother <u>watches</u> the cartoon three times so far.　→ _____

4 그녀는 오랫동안 이곳에서 일해왔다.

She <u>works</u> here for a long time.　　　　　　　→ _____

5 Sam은 호주에 가 버려서 지금 여기에 없다.

Sam <u>goes</u> to Austrialia, so he is not here now.　→ _____

6 그는 학교에 지각해 본 적이 없다.

He <u>is never</u> late for school.　　　　　　　　　→ _____

우리말과 일치하도록 괄호 안의 말을 배열하여 문장을 완성하시오.

1 Rebecca는 이미 그 소식을 들었다. (heard, has, already, the news)

→ Rebecca _____.

2 너는 최근에 캠핑을 간 적이 있니? (gone camping, have, you)

→ _____ lately?

3 Emily는 6개월 동안 우리와 함께 일하고 있다. (with us, has, for, worked, six months)

→ Emily _____.

4 James는 전에 그녀를 본 적이 없다. (never, her, before, has, seen)

→ James _____.

5 그는 2010년 이후로 여수에서 살고 있다. (since 2010, lived, in Yeosu, has)

→ He _____.

6 우리는 아직 공항에 도착하지 않았다. (arrived, at the airport, not, yet, have)

→ We _____.

UNIT 01 can, may, will

Answers p. 26

A 개념 확인

우리말과 일치하도록 괄호 안에서 알맞은 것을 고르시오.

1 그 어린 남자아이는 영어를 말하고 읽을 수 있다.

→ The little boy (can / may) speak and read English.

2 Jason은 요즘 무척 바쁠지도 모른다.

→ Jason (will / may) be very busy these days.

3 우리 가족은 다음 주말에 캠핑을 갈 것이다.

→ My family (will / may) go camping next weekend.

4 너는 내 선글라스를 써도 돼.

→ You (can / will) wear my sunglasses.

5 로봇은 모든 것을 할 수 있을 것이다.

→ Robots (will can / will be able to) do everything.

6 너는 들어와서 여기서 기다려도 돼.

→ You (will / may) come in and wait here.

B 해석 완성

밑줄 친 부분에 유의하여 해석을 완성하시오.

1 I <u>may be late</u> for the party tonight.

나는 오늘 밤 파티에 _____.

2 I <u>won't attend</u> the meeting tomorrow.

나는 내일 회의에 _____.

3 <u>Can I sit</u> on this chair?

이 의자에 _____?

4 <u>Could you put</u> my bag in the trunk?

트렁크에 제 가방을 _____?

밑줄 친 부분을 어법에 맞게 고쳐 쓰시오.

1 Dave <u>can plays</u> the electric guitar.　　　　　→ _____

2 She <u>isn't able to eat</u> anything yesterday.　　→ _____

3 You <u>will can make</u> new friends at school.　　→ _____

4 I <u>may be not</u> here when you arrive.　　　　　→ _____

5 I hope he <u>will able to pass</u> the exam.　　　→ _____

주어진 문장과 의미가 같도록 빈칸에 알맞은 말을 쓰시오.

1 You may use this room for a while.

→ You _____ use this room for a while.

2 My brother can drive a car.

→ My brother _____ drive a car.

3 We could play the beautiful music together.

→ We _____ play the beautiful music together.

우리말과 일치하도록 괄호 안의 말을 배열하여 문장을 완성하시오.

1 너는 내 가위를 사용해도 된다. (use, my scissors, may)

→ You _____.

2 엄마, 제가 솜사탕을 먹어도 되나요? (I, can, cotton candy, have, some)

→ _____, Mom?

3 John과 나는 부상 때문에 경기를 할 수 없었다. (play, to, not, able, were)

→ John and I _____ because of injuries.

4 그녀는 네 계획에 동의하지 않을지도 모른다. (agree with, your plan, not, may)

→ She _____.

5 너는 너의 길을 찾을 수 있을 것이다. (find, be, to, able, your way, will, you)

→ _____

UNIT 02 must, should, had better, used to

Answers p. 26

A 개념 확인

우리말과 일치하도록 괄호 안에서 알맞은 것을 고르시오.

1 너는 그 수업을 듣는 게 좋겠어.

→ You (had better / used to) take the class.

2 그는 매일 아침 조깅을 하러 가곤 했다.

→ He used to (go / going) jogging every morning.

3 어떤 착오가 있는 게 틀림없다.

→ There (must / should) be some mistake.

4 너는 좋은 점수를 받기 위해서 열심히 공부해야 한다.

→ You (should / would) study hard to get good grades.

5 너는 지금 그 돈을 지불할 필요가 없다.

→ You (must not / don't have to) pay the money now.

6 그녀는 더 주의해야 했다.

→ She (must / had to) be more careful.

B 어법 선택

괄호 안에서 알맞은 것을 고르시오.

1 Emma (have to / has to) practice the piano.

2 You (must not / don't have to) smoke in public places.

3 There (would / used to) be a park near my house.

4 I think you (should / would) apologize to her.

5 She (don't have to / doesn't have to) finish it today.

6 You (had better not / had not better) say anything.

7 We (must / had to) go there yesterday.

8 My family used to (travel / traveling) a lot when I was a kid.

9 It (must / has to) be really hot outside.

10 You (must not open / don't must open) the mail.

밑줄 친 부분에 유의하여 해석을 완성하시오.

1 Steve must be hungry.

Steve는 _____.

2 I had to wear a school uniform at primary school.

나는 초등학교 때 _____.

3 We should protect the environment.

우리는 환경을 _____.

4 David doesn't have to answer the questions.

David은 그 질문들에 _____.

5 You had better not tell the secret to anybody.

너는 누구에게도 그 비밀을 _____.

6 My mom used to do yoga every morning.

엄마는 매일 아침 _____.

우리말과 일치하도록 괄호 안의 말을 배열하여 문장을 완성하시오.

1 이곳에 호수가 있었다. (a lake, used, be, there, to)

→ _____ here.

2 너는 밤에 너무 많이 먹지 말아야 한다. (eat, not, too much, should)

→ You _____ at night.

3 우리는 계획을 변경해야 할 것이다. (change, to, will, our plans, have)

→ We _____.

4 너는 도서관에서 조용히 해야 한다. (be, you, must, quiet)

→ _____ in the library.

5 너는 오늘 밤에 운전하지 않는 게 좋겠다. (drive, not, better, you, had)

→ _____ tonight.

6 너는 영화표 값을 지불할 필요가 없다. (have, don't, pay for, you, to)

→ _____ the movie ticket.

UNIT 01 to부정사의 명사적 용법

Answers p. 27

A 개념 확인

밑줄 친 to부정사의 역할에 ✔ 표시하시오.

주어: ㉧ 목적어: ㉤ 보어: ㉦

1 <u>To sing</u> together is fun. ㉧ ㉤ ㉦

2 I want <u>to eat</u> something spicy like *tteokbokki*. ㉧ ㉤ ㉦

3 His goal is <u>to save</u> $500. ㉧ ㉤ ㉦

4 <u>To drink</u> too much soda is bad for your health. ㉧ ㉤ ㉦

5 Can you tell me <u>when to start</u>? ㉧ ㉤ ㉦

6 He decided not <u>to leave</u> his hometown. ㉧ ㉤ ㉦

7 <u>What to eat</u> is a common question. ㉧ ㉤ ㉦

8 My plan is <u>to travel</u> around the world. ㉧ ㉤ ㉦

9 Jane knows <u>how to play</u> the game. ㉧ ㉤ ㉦

10 It's important <u>to keep</u> your promises. ㉧ ㉤ ㉦

B 어법 선택

괄호 안에서 알맞은 것을 고르시오.

1 (Live / To live) without water is impossible.

2 We decided (go / to go) on a picnic in the park.

3 I don't know (where to buy / to buy where) the book.

4 My brother's dream is (be / to be) an actor.

5 My teacher told me (not to / to not) give up.

6 Please tell me (how / what) to solve the problem.

7 (It / That) is hard to make new friends.

8 He promised (not to do / to not do) it again.

9 To play board games (are / is) fun.

10 It is a good way (reuse / to reuse) plastic bags.

주어진 문장과 의미가 같도록 문장을 완성하시오.

1 To fix computers is very difficult.

→ _____ is very difficult _____ _____ computers.

2 To protect the environment is important.

→ _____ is important _____ _____ the environment.

3 To swim in the river can be dangerous.

→ _____ can be dangerous _____ _____ in the river.

4 Can you tell me how I should get to the museum?

→ Can you tell me how _____ _____ to the museum?

밑줄 친 부분을 어법에 맞게 고쳐 쓰시오.

1 <u>This</u> is hard to write in a diary every day. → _____

2 We have to decide <u>when leave</u>. → _____

3 I told him <u>to not be</u> late for school. → _____

4 To speak a foreign language <u>require</u> lots of practice. → _____

5 I want <u>play</u> soccer with my friends after school. → _____

우리말과 일치하도록 괄호 안의 말을 배열하여 문장을 완성하시오.

1 나는 도서관에서 책을 읽는 것을 좋아한다. (like, read, I, to, books)

→ _____ in the library.

2 나의 할머니는 이메일 보내는 방법을 모르신다. (doesn't, how, send emails, to, know)

→ My grandmother _____.

3 가장 중요한 일은 너의 꿈을 잃지 않는 것이다. (is, your, not, dream, lose, to)

→ The most important thing _____.

4 네 친구들에게 거짓말하는 것은 잘못되었다. (to, wrong, to, is, lie, it, your friends)

→ _____

to부정사의 형용사적·부사적 용법

Answers p. 27

A
개념 확인

밑줄 친 to부정사의 용법을 〈보기〉에서 찾아 기호를 쓰시오.

보기　ⓐ 형용사적 용법　　ⓑ 부사적 용법 〈판단의 근거〉　　ⓒ 부사적 용법 〈결과〉
　　　ⓓ 부사적 용법 〈목적〉　　ⓔ 부사적 용법 〈감정의 원인〉

1 I was stupid to believe that news. _____

2 She was glad to get her son's letter. _____

3 I went to the market to buy some apples. _____

4 My grandfather lived to be 80 years old. _____

5 Do you have a friend to talk with? _____

6 He has a large family to support. _____

7 I was pleased to eat such delicious food. _____

8 I turned on the TV to watch the news. _____

B
어법 선택

괄호 안에서 알맞은 것을 고르시오.

1 She studied hard (pass / to pass) the exam.

2 Einstein grew up (be / to be) a famous scientist.

3 I don't have a pencil to (write / write with).

4 I was very sad (to hear / to heard) the news.

5 He bought a small house to (live / live in).

6 She must be rich (to have / to having) that expensive car.

7 I need (something cold / cold something) to drink.

8 My grandmother wants (to learn / learning) English.

9 He was silly (to tell / to telling) everyone his password.

10 There are many places (to visit / to visit there) in Korea.

밑줄 친 부분에 유의하여 해석을 완성하시오.

1 Is there anything to read in your room?

네 방에 _____ 있니?

2 She wants a chair to sit on.

그녀는 _____ 원한다.

3 You are kind to help her.

_____ 너는 친절하구나.

주어진 문장과 의미가 같도록 to부정사를 이용하여 빈칸에 알맞은 말을 쓰시오.

1 I found my lost watch, so I was glad.

→ I was glad _____ my lost watch.

2 I wanted to have lunch, so I went to the cafeteria.

→ I went to the cafeteria _____ lunch.

3 I need some paper, and I will write on it.

→ I need some paper _____ .

4 The girl grew up, and she became a nurse.

→ The girl grew up _____ a nurse.

우리말과 일치하도록 괄호 안의 말을 배열하여 문장을 완성하시오.

1 우리는 교통 혼잡 시간을 피하기 위해 일찍 출발했다. (avoid, early, to, left)

→ We _____ rush hour.

2 나는 가지고 놀 장난감을 많이 가지고 있다. (toys, play, a lot of, to, with)

→ I have _____ .

3 그런 좋은 조언을 하다니 그는 현명한 게 틀림없다. (to, be, wise, advice, such, give, good)

→ He must _____ .

4 그녀는 결승전을 이겨서 기뻤다. (the final match, glad, win, was, to)

→ She _____ .

UNIT 3 to부정사의 의미상 주어, to부정사 구문

Answers p. 27

A 어법 선택

괄호 안에서 알맞은 것을 고르시오.

1 It is natural (for you / of you) to worry sometimes.

2 It was careless (for her / of her) to do such a thing.

3 It was foolish (for him / of him) to believe that.

4 It's impossible (for them / of them) to finish the work today.

5 It is difficult (for me / of me) to carry the boxes alone.

6 We arrived (too / so) late to catch the train.

7 He studied (hard enough to / enough hard to) pass the test.

8 Mina is (very / too) busy to go for a walk.

9 Mike is strong (so / enough) to lift the desk.

10 This is (enough small / small enough) for you to carry.

B 문장 완성

우리말과 일치하도록 to부정사를 이용하여 문장을 완성하시오.

1 나는 어젯밤에 너무 졸려서 숙제를 할 수 없었다.

→ I was _____ sleepy _____ do my homework last night.

2 제 가방을 들어주시다니 친절하시군요.

→ _____ is kind _____ you _____ carry my bag.

3 수진이는 시계에 닿을 만큼 키가 크다.

→ Sujin is _____ _____ _____ reach the clock.

4 당신은 외국어 하나는 배울 필요가 있다.

→ It is necessary _____ _____ _____ learn a foreign language.

5 그는 혼자서 탁자를 옮길 만큼 힘이 세다.

→ He is strong _____ _____ _____ the table alone.

6 이 문제는 너무 어려워서 내가 풀 수 없다.

→ This problem is _____ difficult _____ me _____ solve.

밑줄 친 부분을 어법에 맞게 고쳐 쓰시오.

1 It is foolish <u>for you</u> to trust her. → _____

2 The game was too difficult for them <u>play</u>. → _____

3 The room is too small <u>of us</u> to sleep in. → _____

4 Amy is <u>enough rich to buy</u> the new car. (고쳐서 완전한 문장으로 다시 쓰시오.)

→ _____

주어진 문장과 의미가 같도록 문장을 완성하시오.

1 The rabbit is so fast that I can't catch it.

→ The rabbit is _____ _____ for _____ to _____.

2 These sneakers are so comfortable that you can wear them all day.

→ These sneakers are _____ _____ for you _____ _____ all day.

3 Sam was smart enough to notice the mistake.

→ Sam was _____ smart _____ he _____ _____ the mistake.

4 Mom was too busy to help me.

→ Mom was _____ busy _____ she _____ _____ me.

우리말과 일치하도록 괄호 안의 말을 배열하여 문장을 완성하시오.

1 부모님께 그렇게 말하다니 너는 무례하구나. (to, you, to your parents, of, talk)

→ It is rude _____ like that.

2 나는 너무 걱정이 돼서 어젯밤에 잘 수가 없었다. (worried, to, too, sleep)

→ I was _____ last night.

3 나의 남동생은 그것을 시도할 만큼 용감하다. (to, enough, try, brave, that)

→ My brother is _____.

4 네가 화를 내는 것은 당연하다. (to, get angry, you, for, natural)

→ It is _____.

UNIT 1 동명사의 역할

Answers p. 28

A 개념 확인

밑줄 친 동명사의 역할에 ✔ 표시하시오.

주어: ㈜ 목적어: ㉱ 보어: ㉲

1 <u>Learning</u> foreign languages is not easy.   ㈜ ㉱ ㉲

2 It began <u>snowing</u> this morning.   ㈜ ㉱ ㉲

3 <u>Winning</u> the race won't be easy.   ㈜ ㉱ ㉲

4 <u>Playing</u> the violin is very fun.   ㈜ ㉱ ㉲

5 Jennifer is good at <u>skating</u>.   ㈜ ㉱ ㉲

6 My hobby is <u>baking</u> cakes.   ㈜ ㉱ ㉲

7 <u>Eating</u> fast food is bad for your health.   ㈜ ㉱ ㉲

8 I enjoy <u>reading</u> mystery books.   ㈜ ㉱ ㉲

9 Thank you for <u>taking</u> care of my cat.   ㈜ ㉱ ㉲

10 My mother's job is <u>teaching</u> children.   ㈜ ㉱ ㉲

B 어법 선택

괄호 안에서 알맞은 것을 고르시오.

1 (Have / Having) breakfast is important for your health.

2 I'm scared of (speaking / speak) in public.

3 We are looking forward to (meet / meeting) you soon.

4 (Be / Being) kind to others is important.

5 Taking pictures (is / are) one of his hobbies.

6 She went home without (to say / saying) good-bye to us.

7 My hobby is (play / playing) the guitar.

8 I dreamed of (becoming / become) a popular movie star.

9 Being a musician (require / requires) practice and effort.

10 I thought (listened / listening) to classical music would be boring.

밑줄 친 부분에 유의하여 해석을 완성하시오.

1 Riding a bike is fun. _____ 재미있다.

2 My hobby is drawing pictures. 내 취미는 _____.

3 Jane is busy doing her homework. Jane은 그녀의 숙제를 _____.

4 I don't feel like eating anything. 나는 아무것도 _____.

5 Amy is looking forward to seeing you. Amy는 _____.

밑줄 친 부분을 어법에 맞게 고쳐 쓰시오.

1 Playing mobile games are fun. → _____

2 John often reads books about to draw. → _____

3 My brother is used to get up early. → _____

4 If you keep to practice, you'll get better. → _____

5 He spent a lot of money to buy a new car. → _____

6 I quit to drink soda to lose weight. → _____

우리말과 일치하도록 괄호 안의 말을 배열하여 문장을 완성하시오.

1 내 생각에 이것은 살 만한 가치가 있다. (buying, is, worth, this)

→ I think _____.

2 나는 그 소식을 듣고 울지 않을 수 없었다. (help, couldn't, crying)

→ I _____ at the news.

3 뉴욕에서 밤에 외출하는 것은 위험하다. (dangerous, is, at night, going out)

→ _____ in New York.

4 그녀는 오후 내내 엄마를 도우며 보냈다. (spent, her mom, all afternoon, helping)

→ She _____.

A
어법 선택

괄호 안에서 알맞은 것을 고르시오.

1 Do you want (to be / being) a member of our club?

2 He practiced (to play / playing) the cello every day.

3 I remember (to see / seeing) the girl before.

4 Don't forget (to take / taking) the medicine tomorrow morning.

5 Stop (to talk / talking) and listen to him.

6 I didn't expect (to see / seeing) her again.

7 My sister plans (to learn / learning) how to ski.

8 Do you enjoy (to go / going) camping?

B
해석 완성

밑줄 친 부분에 유의하여 해석을 완성하시오.

1 I remembered <u>going</u> there last winter.
  나는 작년 겨울에 그곳에 _____ 것이 기억났다.

2 Remember <u>to go</u> to the post office after school.
  방과 후에 우체국에 _____ 기억해.

3 He tried <u>to jog</u> every day for his health.
  그는 건강을 위해 매일 _____.

4 He <u>tried opening</u> the door, but he couldn't.
  그는 그 문을 _____, 열 수 없었다.

5 Don't forget <u>to call</u> me in the evening.
  저녁에 나에게 _____ 잊지 마.

6 I forgot <u>sending</u> the email to her.
  나는 그녀에게 이메일을 _____ 잊고 있었다.

7 The baby suddenly <u>stopped crying</u>.
  그 아기는 갑자기 _____.

밑줄 친 부분을 자연스러운 문장이 되도록 고쳐 쓰시오.

1 I don't enjoy to watch TV. → _____

2 We decided moving to the city. → _____

3 Don't forget sending her flowers next Sunday. → _____

4 He stopped to walk and looked back. → _____

5 My brother plans going swimming. → _____

6 Jessica finished to do her homework. → _____

7 I always try doing my best. → _____

8 Remember turning off the lights when you leave the room.

→ _____

우리말과 일치하도록 괄호 안의 말을 배열하여 문장을 완성하시오.

1 나는 학교에 걸어가는 것을 즐긴다. (walking, enjoy, to)

→ I _____ school.

2 나는 공원에서 그를 만났던 것이 기억났다. (meeting, remembered, him, I)

→ _____ in the park.

3 그는 자신의 방을 청소하기로 약속했다. (clean, promised, his room, to)

→ He _____.

4 그녀는 그 회의에 참석해야 하는 것을 잊었다. (forgot, the meeting, attend, to)

→ She _____.

5 나는 일찍 일어나려고 노력했지만, 할 수 없었다. (early, tried, get up, to)

→ I _____, but I couldn't.

6 그녀는 매일 산책하기로 결심했다. (decided, every day, take a walk, to)

→ She _____.

7 창문 좀 닫아주시겠어요? (closing, mind, the window, you, would)

→ _____

UNIT 1 현재분사와 과거분사

Answers p. 29

A 개념 확인

밑줄 친 부분의 쓰임에 ✔ 표시하시오.

현재분사: (현) 동명사: (동)

1 <u>Walking</u> in the forest is good for your health.　　(현)　(동)

2 He was <u>walking</u> along the beach.　　(현)　(동)

3 The boy <u>sleeping</u> on the sofa is my son.　　(현)　(동)

4 I need a tent and a <u>sleeping</u> bag.　　(현)　(동)

5 She practiced <u>singing</u> for the audition.　　(현)　(동)

6 Do you know the girl <u>singing</u> on the stage?　　(현)　(동)

7 Catching <u>falling</u> leaves will bring good luck.　　(현)　(동)

8 My favorite activity is <u>going</u> camping.　　(현)　(동)

9 Mr. and Mrs. Smith are <u>going</u> to the theater.　　(현)　(동)

B 해석 완성

밑줄 친 부분에 유의하여 해석을 완성하시오.

1 I ate a <u>boiled</u> egg for breakfast.　　나는 아침으로 ＿＿＿＿＿＿＿＿ 달걀을 먹었다.

2 Look at the bird <u>flying</u> in the sky.　　하늘에서 ＿＿＿＿＿＿＿＿ 새를 봐.

3 I know the girl <u>playing</u> the piano.　　나는 피아노를 ＿＿＿＿＿＿＿＿ 소녀를 안다.

4 The room <u>painted</u> green is mine.　　소록색으로 ＿＿＿＿＿＿＿＿ 방이 내 방이다.

5 I don't like <u>boring</u> stories.　　나는 ＿＿＿＿＿＿＿＿ 이야기를 좋아하지 않는다.

6 He bought a car <u>made</u> in Germany.　　그는 독일에서 ＿＿＿＿＿＿＿＿ 차를 샀다.

7 I am <u>interested</u> in pop art.　　나는 팝 아트에 ＿＿＿＿＿＿＿＿.

8 His new movie <u>was interesting</u>.　　그의 새 영화는 ＿＿＿＿＿＿＿＿.

9 The rumor <u>was shocking</u>.　　그 소문은 ＿＿＿＿＿＿＿＿.

10 We <u>were shocked</u> by his death.　　우리는 그의 죽음에 ＿＿＿＿＿＿＿＿.

괄호 안에서 알맞은 것을 고르시오.

1 Yesterday was an (amazing / amazed) day.

2 She is looking for her (losing / lost) pencil.

3 I was (surprising / surprised) to see my aunt at the mall.

4 The amusement park is full of (exciting / excited) rides.

5 You can see a lot of (shining / shined) stars in the countryside.

괄호 안의 말을 알맞은 분사로 바꿔 빈칸에 쓰시오.

1 I bought a book _____ by a famous poet. (write)

2 The man _____ in front of me was very tall. (stand)

3 They live in a house _____ in 1960. (build)

4 Everyone was looking at the girl _____ on the stage. (dance)

5 I am _____ in science and math. (interest)

우리말과 일치하도록 괄호 안의 말을 배열하여 문장을 완성하시오. (필요시 형태를 바꿀 것)

1 나는 한국에서 만들어진 물건들을 사고 싶다. (things, in Korea, make, buy)

→ I want to _____.

2 정글에 사는 소년에 대한 그 영화는 흥미진진했다. (in the jungle, was, a boy, live, excite)

→ The movie about _____.

3 영어로 쓰인 책을 읽는 것은 영어를 배우는 좋은 방법이다. (books, in English, reading, write)

→ _____ is a good way to learn English.

4 그는 그 소식을 듣고 실망했다. (disappoint, at, he, the news, was)

→ _____

5 아프리카에 관한 그 다큐멘터리는 놀라웠다. (was, Africa, amaze, about, the documentary)

→ _____

UNIT 2 분사구문

Answers p. 29

A 문장 전환

주어진 문장을 분사구문으로 바꿀 때, 빈칸에 알맞은 말을 쓰시오.

1 As I had her address, I was able to write to her.

→ _____ her address, I was able to write to her.

2 While I was living in Paris, I made a lot of friends.

→ _____ in Paris, I made a lot of friends.

3 When you leave your car in a parking lot, you should lock the doors.

→ _____ _____ _____ in a parking lot, you should lock the doors.

4 As she was waving to us, she left the train station.

→ _____ _____ _____, she left the train station.

5 Because I knew him well, I didn't believe the story.

→ _____ _____ _____, I didn't believe the story.

6 Because I was in a hurry, I left my umbrella at home.

→ _____ _____ _____ _____, I left my umbrella at home.

B 문장 완성

자연스러운 문장이 되도록 〈보기〉에서 가장 알맞은 말을 골라 빈칸에 기호를 쓰시오. (한 번씩만 사용할 것)

보기	ⓐ Listening to music	ⓑ Driving on the road
	ⓒ Fating dinner together	ⓓ Leaving the room
	ⓔ Being very shy	ⓕ Knowing her phone number

1 _____, he had few friends.

2 _____, my mother listened to the radio.

3 _____, I can call her.

4 _____, he turned the lights off.

5 _____, she sat on the bench.

6 _____, they talked about the food.

밑줄 친 부분에 유의하여 해석을 완성하시오.

1 Having no time, I couldn't help her.

_____ 나는 그녀를 도울 수 없었다.

2 John was sitting in the park, looking at the trees.

나무를 _____ John은 공원에 앉아 있었다.

3 Seeing him at the airport, I was pleased.

공항에서 _____, 나는 기뻤다.

우리말과 일치하도록 괄호 안의 말을 이용하여 문장을 완성하시오.

1 아팠기 때문에 그는 파티에 갈 수 없었다. (sick)

→ _____ _____, he couldn't go to the party.

2 통화를 하면서, 그는 역으로 걸어갔다. (talk on the phone)

→ _____ _____ _____ _____, he walked to the station.

3 그녀는 밝게 웃으면서 나와 악수를 했다. (smile brightly)

→ She shook hands with me, _____ _____.

4 숙제를 끝낸 후에 나는 보드 게임을 했다. (finish my homework)

→ _____ _____ _____, I played board games.

우리말과 일치하도록 괄호 안의 말을 배열하여 문장을 완성하시오.

1 공원에서 나를 보자 그는 내 이름을 불렀다. (me, in the park, seeing)

→ _____, he called my name.

2 그녀의 이메일을 읽은 후, 나는 그녀의 생각을 이해했다. (email, reading, her, after)

→ _____, I understood her idea.

3 TV를 보면서 그는 저녁을 먹었다. (had, he, TV, dinner, watching)

→ _____

4 늦게 일어나서 나는 제시간에 학교에 갈 수 없었다.

(late, I, on time, get, couldn't, getting up, to school)

→ _____

UNIT 1 수동태의 기본 개념

Answers p. 30

A
개념 확인

밑줄 친 부분에 주의하여 문장이 능동태인지 수동태인지 ✔ 표시하시오.   능동태: 능 수동태: 수

1 The lost children <u>were found</u> by the police.   능 수

2 The thief <u>stole</u> her diamond necklace.   능 수

3 The windows <u>are cleaned</u> on Saturdays.   능 수

4 Kelly <u>is painting</u> the wall now.   능 수

5 The coffee <u>is served</u> by the waitress.   능 수

6 Rice <u>is eaten</u> in many countries.   능 수

B
어법 선택

괄호 안에서 알맞은 것을 고르시오.

1 The rabbit was (attacked / attacking) by the lion.

2 The room (was / were) decorated by them.

3 Two people (injured / were injured) in the accident.

4 This machine (was fixed / will be fixed) tomorrow.

5 Keep the pan warm until the spaghetti (is cooked / was cooked).

6 Linda and I (are invited / were invited) to the party yesterday.

C
문장 전환

주어진 문장을 수동태로 바꿀 때, 빈칸에 알맞은 말을 쓰시오.

1 Jessica played the song on the guitar.

→ The song _____ _____ on the guitar by Jessica.

2 Someone stole my bike.

→ My bike _____ _____ _____ someone.

3 The company will employ five people.   *employ 고용하다

→ Five people _____ _____ _____ _____ the company.

밑줄 친 부분을 어법에 맞게 고쳐 쓰시오.

1 These books <u>was written</u> in Chinese. → _____

2 This picture was taken <u>by she</u>. → _____

3 The *Mona Lisa* <u>painted</u> by Leonardo da Vinci. → _____

4 French and English <u>are speaking</u> in Canada. → _____

5 Nobody <u>was solved</u> the problem. → _____

6 The meeting <u>will held</u> in Seoul next week. → _____

7 The kitchen <u>is cleaned</u> yesterday. → _____

8 This tower <u>is built</u> in 2000. → _____

9 My mother <u>is read</u> poems every morning. → _____

우리말과 일치하도록 괄호 안의 말을 배열하여 문장을 완성하시오.

1 이 카메라는 독일에서 만들어졌다. (made, in Germany, was)

→ This camera _____ .

2 Tony는 그 개에게 물렸다. (by, was, the dog, bitten)

→ Tony _____ .

3 그 경기는 비 때문에 중단되었다. (stopped, because of, was, the rain)

→ The game _____ .

4 그 커피는 농부들에 의해 브라질에서 재배된다. (by, is, farmers, grown)

→ The coffee _____ in Brazil.

5 그 소년은 그의 선생님에 의해 벌을 받을 것이다. (be, by, punished, will)

→ The boy _____ his teacher.

6 그 창문이 돌멩이에 의해 깨졌다. (a stone, was, the window, by, broken)

→ _____

7 작은 물고기는 더 큰 물고기에 의해 잡아먹힌다. (larger fish, are, by, eaten, small fish)

→ _____

UNIT 2 수동태의 여러 가지 형태

Answers p. 30

A 어법 선택

괄호 안에서 알맞은 것을 고르시오.

1 The letter (was not / did not) written by Emma.

2 Paper (can recycle / can be recycled).

3 The work (may be finishing / may be finished) early by Tony.

4 When (did the telescope / was the telescope) invented?

5 Glasses (should be carried / should are carried) carefully.

6 (Was this flower watered / Did this flower water) yesterday?

B 빈칸 완성

우리말과 일치하도록 빈칸에 알맞은 말을 쓰시오.

1 태국에서 영어가 쓰이니? (speak)
→ _____ English _____ in Thailand?

2 다행히도 그는 심하게 다치지 않았다.
→ Luckily, he _____ _____ hurt badly.

3 우리는 그 이야기에 감동을 받았다.
→ We _____ moved _____ the story.

4 그 쿠키는 언제 구워졌니?
→ _____ _____ the cookies baked?

5 어떤 사실들은 잊혀져서는 안 된다.
→ Some facts must _____ _____ forgotten.

C 어법 수정

밑줄 친 부분을 어법에 맞게 고쳐 쓰시오.

1 The show not was canceled. → _____

2 Why did the plan changed? → _____

3 Millions of people will be visited the new museum. → _____

4 The book is difficult, so it can't understand easily. → _____

5 The medicine should is taken twice a day. → _____

6 The bill can paid by credit card. → _____

주어진 문장과 의미가 같도록 문장을 완성하시오.

1 The hotel does not provide breakfast.

→ Breakfast _____ _____ _____ by the hotel.

2 When did Jack use your computer?

→ When _____ your computer _____ _____ Jack?

3 You should close the doors at night.

→ The doors _____ _____ _____ at night (by you).

4 He didn't answer the questions.

→ The questions _____ _____ _____ _____ .

5 We may not need more food for the party.

→ More food _____ _____ _____ _____ (by us) for the party.

우리말과 일치하도록 괄호 안의 말을 배열하여 문장을 완성하시오.

1 너의 자전거는 Tom에 의해 고쳐졌니? (by, your bike, was, repaired)

→ _____ Tom?

2 교통 규칙은 우리 모두에 의해 지켜져야만 한다. (must, followed, all of us, be, by)

→ The traffic rules _____ .

3 캐나다에서는 어떤 언어가 쓰이니? (are, what languages, spoken)

→ _____ in Canada?

4 그 프로젝트는 1년 안에 완료되어야 한다. (be, completed, the project, should)

→ _____ within a year.

5 이 책은 한국어로 번역될 것이다. (translated, will, into, Korean, be)

→ This book _____ .

6 그 행성은 언제 발견되었나요? (the planet, was, when, discovered)

→ _____

7 그 약속은 지켜지지 않을지도 모른다. (be, may, kept, not, the promise)

→ _____

UNIT 3 주의해야 할 수동태

Answers p. 30

A 어법 선택

괄호 안에서 알맞은 것을 고르시오.

1 This hat (doesn't fit / isn't fitted) me.

2 The jar is filled (by / with) sweet honey.

3 The man (has / is had) an expensive car.

4 They were surprised (at / with) the news.

5 The teacher (looks up to / is looked up to) by her students.

6 The bus (appeared / was appeared) around the corner.

B 어법 수정

밑줄 친 부분을 어법에 맞게 고쳐 쓰시오.

1 The boy laughed at by his friends. → _____

2 He was tired by shopping online. → _____

3 The train will be arrived soon. → _____

4 My family is worried for my grandfather's health. → _____

5 The twins are resembled each other. → _____

6 The top of the mountain covers with snow. → _____

C 문장 완성

자연스러운 문장이 되도록 괄호 안의 말을 이용하여 문장을 완성하시오.

1 I am not _____ _____ math. (interest)

2 His cell phone was _____ _____ _____ someone. (turn on)

3 He is _____ _____ his current job. (satisfy)

4 The meeting may _____ _____ _____ until Friday. (put off)

5 The room was _____ _____ smoke. (fill)

다음 문장을 수동태로 바꿔 쓰시오.

1 Julia takes care of the cat.

→ The cat _____ Julia.

2 His aunt brought up him.

→ He _____ his aunt.

3 My present pleased my mother.

→ My mother _____ my present.

4 His idea will satisfy everyone.

→ Everyone will _____ his idea.

5 My dad turned off the lights.

→ The lights _____ by my dad.

우리말과 일치하도록 괄호 안의 말을 배열하여 문장을 완성하시오.

1 많은 외국인들이 K-pop에 관심을 가지고 있다. (are, K-pop, interested, in)

→ Many foreigners _____ .

2 그 아이는 이웃들에 의해 돌봄을 받았다. (neighbors, by, looked, was, after)

→ The child _____ .

3 나는 매일 같은 일을 하는 것이 지겹다. (the same thing, tired, doing, I'm, of)

→ _____ every day.

4 그 지도자는 많은 사람들의 존경을 받았다. (up, was, by, to, many people, looked)

→ The leader _____ .

5 그녀는 그 결과에 놀라지 않았다. (at, not, the result, was, surprised)

→ She _____ .

6 공항은 여행객들로 붐빈다. (crowded, tourists, with, is, the airport)

→ _____

7 당신은 환경에 대해 걱정하나요? (about, you, the environment, worried, are)

→ _____

UNIT 1 부정대명사 I (one, another, other)

Answers p. 31

A 어법 선택

괄호 안에서 알맞은 것을 고르시오.

1 This box is too big. I need a smaller (it / one).

2 Jack gave me a novel. I will read (it / one) tonight.

3 These clothes are too small. I need to buy bigger (one / ones).

4 **A** Where are my sunglasses? **B** I saw (them / ones) on the table.

5 On the stage, some students are singing and (the other / the others) are dancing.

6 I have a lot of foreign friends in Korea. (Some / Another) are from China, and the others are from Japan.

7 There are three kinds of Olympic medals. One is gold, (another / the other) is silver, and (the other / the others) is bronze.

8 Ms. May bought two cakes. (One / Some) is a cheesecake and (the other / another) is a chocolate cake.

B 빈칸 완성

빈칸에 알맞은 말을 〈보기〉에서 골라 쓰시오. (단, 한 번씩만 사용할 것)

보기	one	ones	another	others	the other	the others

1 I want a pet. Do you have _____?

2 Brad doesn't like black pants. He wants blue _____.

3 There were seven pieces of candy. I ate some, and I put _____ back in the box.

4 There are three ways to go to school. One is by bus, _____ is by bicycle, and _____ is on foot.

5 There are a lot of people in the theater. Some are ordering popcorn and _____ are looking at the posters.

C 우리말과 일치하도록 빈칸에 알맞은 말을 쓰시오.
문장 완성

1 나는 일곱 마리의 반려동물이 있다. 몇몇은 햄스터이고, 나머지는 모두 이구아나이다.

→ I have seven pets. _____ are hamsters, and _____ are iguanas.

2 Kate는 세 가지의 악기를 연주할 수 있다. 하나는 피아노, 다른 하나는 기타, 나머지 하나는 플루트이다.

→ Kate can play three musical instruments. _____ is the piano, _____ is the guitar, and _____ is the flute.

3 탁자 위에 두 개의 가방이 있다. 하나는 검은색 여행 가방이고, 나머지 하나는 파란색 배낭이다.

→ There are two bags on the table. _____ is a black suitcase, and _____ is a blue backpack.

4 나는 공원에서 많은 사람들을 보았다. 몇몇은 자전거를 타고 있었고, 다른 몇몇은 산책을 하고 있었다.

→ I saw a lot of people in the park. _____ were riding bikes, and _____ were taking a walk.

D 밑줄 친 부분을 어법에 맞게 고쳐 쓰시오.
어법 수정

1 I don't have a black pen. Do you have it? → _____

2 I have read the book. I want to read one again. → _____

3 She needs more socks.
She is going to buy some new one. → _____

4 The kids like fruit.
Some prefer apples, and another prefer bananas. → _____

5 Ms. Smith has two daughters.
One has brown eyes, and another has blue eyes. → _____

6 There are three old trees in the town.
One is 200 years old, other is 250 years old, and the other is 500 years old.

→ _____

7 In our class, some students wear glasses, and others don't.

→ _____

UNIT 2 부정대명사 II (each, every, both, all, some, any)

Answers p. 31

A
어법 선택

괄호 안에서 알맞은 것을 고르시오.

1   (Each / All) person has his or her own habits.

2   He has two daughters. (Both / Each) of them live in London.

3   You should attend (every / all) class.

4   Each group (consist / consists) of five members.

5   All the students in the class (wear / wears) glasses.

6   I have two sisters. (Both / Both of) them are interested in fashion.

7   All of the stores here (is / are) closed every Sunday.

8   There are tall trees on each (side / sides) of the street.

9   All the money in his wallet (was / were) gone.

10 I bought (some / any) toast for breakfast.

11 Every (student gets / students get) a laptop from school.

12 There isn't (some / any) milk left in the refrigerator.

B
빈칸 완성

빈칸에 알맞은 말을 〈보기〉에서 골라 쓰시오. (단, 한 번씩만 사용할 것)

보기	each	every	both	all	some	any

1   _____ of my parents were born in Busan.

2   I don't have _____ plans for this weekend.

3   _____ country has a national flag.

4   _____ the passengers have to fasten their seat belts.

5   A Would you like _____ chocolate?   B No thanks.

6   The girl is holding an ice cream cone in _____ hand.

C

어법 수정

우리말과 일치하도록 밑줄 친 부분을 바르게 고쳐 쓰시오.

1 나는 자전거가 두 대 있다. 그것들 둘 다 고장 났다.

I have two bikes. <u>Some of them</u> are broken. → _____

2 나는 버터를 좀 사러 슈퍼마켓에 갔다.

I went to the supermarket to buy <u>any butter</u>. → _____

3 그 호텔의 모든 객실이 예약되었다.

<u>Each room</u> in the hotel was booked. → _____

4 나는 올해 내 책을 모두 읽을 것이다.

I am going to read <u>all my book</u> this year. → _____

5 우리 모두는 그 질문에 대답해야 한다.

All of us <u>has</u> to answer the question. → _____

D

영작

우리말과 일치하도록 괄호 안의 말을 바르게 배열하여 문장을 완성하시오.

1 나는 지금 당장 돈을 조금도 갖고 있지 않다. (have, money, don't, any)

→ I _____ right now.

2 각 회원은 회의에서 투표할 권리를 가지고 있다. (the right, has, each, member)

→ _____ to vote in meetings.

3 그 집의 모든 방에는 큰 창문이 있다. (has, room, in, every, the house)

→ _____ a large window.

4 공항에서 우리의 모든 돈을 도둑맞았다. (our, all, was, stolen, money)

→ _____ at the airport.

5 Sally는 강아지 두 마리가 있다. 그들 둘 다 아주 귀엽다. (are, of, both, them, very cute)

→ Sally has two puppies. _____

6 우리는 그 문제를 해결하기 위해 새로운 아이디어가 좀 필요하다.

(to solve, we, ideas, new, some, the problem, need)

→ _____

UNIT 3 재귀대명사

Answers p. 31

A
어법 선택

괄호 안에서 알맞은 것을 고르시오.

1 I said to (me / myself), "I can do it."

2 She repaired her bike (herself / himself).

3 Yesterday I sent an email to (him / himself).

4 Please help (yourself / ourselves) to this salad.

5 Mark (itself / himself) wrote the poem.

6 The oven is very hot. Be careful not to burn (you / yourself).

7 Jack is proud of (herself / himself).

8 Emma took the pictures (itself / herself).

B
빈칸 완성

우리말과 일치하도록 빈칸에 알맞은 재귀대명사를 쓰시오.

1 나는 요리를 하다가 베었다.

→ I cut _____ while I was cooking.

2 네가 이 쿠키를 직접 만들었니?

→ Did you make these cookies _____?

3 우리는 학교 축제에서 즐거운 시간을 보냈다.

→ We enjoyed _____ at the school festival.

4 아이들은 옷 입는 법을 배워야 한다.

→ Kids should learn how to dress _____.

5 여러분에게 제 소개를 하겠습니다.

→ I'd like to introduce _____ to everyone.

6 어떤 사람들은 오직 자신들만을 생각한다.

→ Some people think only of _____.

C

문장 완성

빈칸에 알맞은 말을 〈보기〉에서 골라 알맞은 형태로 바꿔 쓰시오.

보기	by oneself	enjoy oneself
	help oneself to	make oneself at home

1 Take off your coat and _____.

2 Are you hungry, Minho? _____ some doughnuts.

3 A Did you clean up the house?

    B Yes. I did it _____.

4 A How was your trip?

    B It was great. I _____ very much.

D

영작

우리말과 일치하도록 괄호 안의 말을 바르게 배열하여 문장을 완성하시오.

1 너는 네 자신을 믿어야 한다. (should, in, yourself, believe)

  → You _____.

2 그는 혼자서 그 일을 끝내야만 했다. (by, the work, finish, had to, himself)

  → He _____.

3 그녀는 거울에 비친 자기 모습을 보았다. (in, at, looked, the mirror, herself)

  → She _____.

4 나는 초콜릿 자체는 좋아하지 않지만 초콜릿 아이스크림은 좋아한다. (itself, I, like, chocolate, don't)

  → _____, but I like chocolate ice cream.

5 치즈케이크를 마음껏 드세요. (some, help, yourself, cheesecake, to)

  → Please _____.

6 당신은 얼마나 자주 혼잣말을 하나요? (talk, yourself, do, to, you)

  → How often _____?

7 그 파티에서 Chris가 직접 피아노를 연주했다. (at, himself, played, the party, the piano)

  → Chris _____.

UNIT 1 원급, 비교급, 최상급

Answers p. 32

A 개념 확인

주어진 단어의 비교급과 최상급 형태를 쓰시오.

원급	비교급	최상급
1 long		
2 big		
3 pretty		
4 tall		
5 bad		
6 famous		
7 important		
8 heavy		
9 good		
10 little		

B 어법 선택

괄호 안에서 알맞은 것을 고르시오.

1 The book is as exciting (as / than) the movie.

2 Africa isn't as (large / larger) as Asia.

3 I am (more strong / stronger) than you.

4 My bag is a lot bigger than (you / yours).

5 Paul is (very / much) taller than Laura.

6 Today is as (warm / warmer) as yesterday.

7 My new computer is (better / best) than my old one.

8 Mt. Everest is (highest / the highest) mountain in the world.

9 Brian is the smartest (of / in) the 20 students.

10 She is the (more / most) beautiful of the three sisters.

C

빈칸 완성

괄호 안의 말을 알맞은 형태로 바꿔 빈칸에 쓰시오.

1 It is as _____ as last week. (hot)

2 This jacket is _____ than that one. (expensive)

3 He is much _____ than his brother. (wise)

4 It is the _____ toy in this store. (popular)

5 James is the _____ basketball player in America. (tall)

D

어법 수정

밑줄 친 부분을 어법에 맞게 고쳐 쓰시오.

1 You look <u>much happy</u> than I do. → _____

2 This apple is not <u>as smaller as</u> that one. → _____

3 He always eats much more <u>to</u> I do. → _____

4 His shoes are <u>most expensive</u> than mine. → _____

5 This cake is <u>very sweeter</u> than that one. → _____

6 Jupiter is <u>largest planet</u> in the solar system. → _____

E

영작

우리말과 일치하도록 괄호 안의 말을 바르게 배열하여 문장을 완성하시오.

1 이 상자들은 저 상자들보다 훨씬 더 가볍다. (than, even, those, lighter, ones)

→ These boxes are _____.

2 그는 그의 형만큼 용감하지 않다. (his brother, as, as, not, brave)

→ He is _____.

3 돈이 인생에서 가장 중요한 것은 아니다. (thing, the, important, in life, most)

→ Money is not _____.

4 올 겨울이 작년 겨울보다 훨씬 더 춥다. (is, last winter, than, colder, much)

→ This winter _____.

5 아마존 강은 세상에서 제일 긴 강이다. (the, is, the world, longest, river, in)

→ The Amazon River _____.

UNIT 02 다양한 비교 표현

Answers p. 32

A 어법 선택

괄호 안에서 알맞은 것을 고르시오.

1 My mother is (three / three times) older than me.

2 This bag is (twice as big / big as twice) as that one.

3 John can run (faster three times / three times faster) than Mike.

4 This is one of the most important (test / tests) in my life.

5 His condition is getting (good and good / better and better).

6 Soccer is one of (the popular / the most popular) sports in Korea.

7 (The many / The more) we think, (the wise / the wiser) we will be.

8 The game is becoming (many and more / more and more) exciting.

9 Watermelons are (four times more expensive / four times expensive) than apples.

10 (Harder / The harder) you practice, (better / the better) you can play the piano.

B 어법 수정

밑줄 친 부분을 어법에 맞게 고쳐 쓰시오.

1 My cat becomes fat and fat these days. → _____

2 This pumpkin is three times large than that one. → _____

3 Snow White became much and much beautiful. → _____

4 The high we climb, the colder it gets. → _____

5 Jeju-do is one of the beautiful places in Korea. → _____

6 The earth is getting hot and hotter. → _____

7 It is one of the nicest room in the hotel. → _____

8 Chris is one of the kindest person in our company. → _____

9 The more tired you are, the easily you catch a cold. → _____

10 My older brother is as twice heavy as me. → _____

C

문장 완성

우리말과 일치하도록 괄호 안의 말을 이용하여 문장을 완성하시오.

1 그의 건강은 점점 더 나빠지고 있다. (bad)

→ His health is getting _____ _____ _____ .

2 이 책이 저 책의 두 배만큼 두껍다. (thick)

→ This book is _____ _____ _____ as that one.

3 우리가 더 빨리 도착할수록, 우리의 자리가 더 좋을 것이다. (soon, good)

→ The _____ we arrive, the _____ our seats will be.

4 인터넷은 점점 더 중요해졌다. (important)

→ The Internet has become _____ _____ _____ _____ .

5 경주는 한국에서 가장 유명한 도시들 중 하나이다. (famous)

→ Gyeongju is one of _____ _____ _____ _____ in Korea.

D

영작

우리말과 일치하도록 괄호 안의 말을 바르게 배열하여 문장을 완성하시오.

1 읽기는 학생들에게 가장 중요한 기술들 중 하나이다. (skills, of, most, the, one, important)

→ Reading is _____ for students.

2 가을에는 낮이 점점 더 짧아진다. (shorter, get, and, shorter, the days)

→ In autumn, _____ .

3 거북이는 코끼리의 두 배만큼 오래 산다. (as, elephants, twice, as, do, long)

→ Turtles live _____ .

4 나는 그보다 세 배 더 많은 돈을 지불했다. (more, than, three times, he did, money)

→ I paid _____ .

5 네가 더 많은 책을 읽을수록, 너는 더 똑똑해질 것이다. (the, books, more, read, the, you, smarter)

→ _____ you will become.

6 그는 세계에서 가장 부유한 사람들 중 한 명이다. (in, the, of, people, one, the world, richest)

→ He is _____ .

UNIT 1 감각동사, 수여동사

Answers p. 33

A 어법 선택

괄호 안에서 알맞은 것을 고르시오.

1 The cotton blanket feels (soft / softly).

2 Jake sounded (serious / seriously) on the phone.

3 Mr. Park taught science (students / to students).

4 Paul bought (me / for me) some clothes.

5 I brought (Lily a magazine / a magazine Lily).

6 Could you hand (me / to me) the menu, please?

7 The singer looks (nervous / nervously) on the stage.

8 I gave my toys (to / for) my little sister.

9 The cake (looks / looks like) a large ship.

10 The chef made a special dish (to her / for her).

B 문장 완성

주어진 문장과 같은 의미가 되도록 빈칸에 알맞은 말을 쓰시오.

1 They lent him some money.

→ They lent some money _____ .

2 My mother bought me a red baseball cap.

→ My mother bought a red baseball cap _____ .

3 We gave the children cookies and cake.

→ We gave cookies and cake _____ .

4 I sent a Christmas present to Jessica.

→ I sent Jessica _____ .

5 Jenny made potato chips for her friends.

→ Jenny made her friends _____ .

C

어법 수정

밑줄 친 부분을 어법에 맞게 고쳐 쓰시오.

1 The music sounds very <u>sadly</u>. → _____

2 I <u>felt like</u> sleepy after lunch. → _____

3 The twins look very <u>differently</u>. → _____

4 My aunt bought a new pair of shoes <u>to me</u>. → _____

5 Mr. Kim teaches Korean history <u>foreigners</u>. → _____

6 The milk on the table smells <u>badly</u>. → _____

7 The cloud <u>looks</u> a rabbit. → _____

8 She told the story of her life <u>for them</u>. → _____

9 Dad cooks <u>dinner us</u> every day. → _____

10 I'll make <u>some hot tea to you</u>. → _____

D

영작

우리말과 일치하도록 괄호 안의 말을 바르게 배열하여 문장을 완성하시오.

1 초콜릿은 쓰고 단맛이 난다. (and, sweet, tastes, bitter)

→ Chocolate _____ .

2 그녀는 그 하얀 드레스를 입으니 천사처럼 보였다. (an, like, angel, looked)

→ She _____ in that white dress.

3 Brad는 나에게 그의 만화책을 빌려주었다. (me, comic book, lent, his, to)

→ Brad _____ .

4 Alan은 우리에게 그의 오래된 일기장을 보여 주었다.

→ Alan _____ . (us, his old diary, showed)

→ Alan _____ . (to, his old diary, us, showed)

5 나는 Jessy에게 카드를 만들어 주었다.

→ I _____ . (a card, Jessy, made)

→ I _____ . (for, a card, Jessy, made)

UNIT 2 목적격보어가 필요한 동사

Answers p. 33

A 개념 확인

문장에서 목적어와 목적격보어를 찾아 쓰시오.

		목적어	목적격보어
1	We elected her class president.		
2	Tom's new hat makes him look different.		
3	I always keep my room warm.		
4	Anna advised us to exercise regularly.		
5	I want him to be happy.		
6	She had me clean my desk.		
7	Can you feel my heart beating faster?		
8	Have you ever heard him sing?		
9	Mom told me to wash the dishes.		
10	I saw my dog playing with a ball.		

B 어법 선택

괄호 안에서 알맞은 것을 고르시오.

1 Nicole named (her cat Momo / Momo her cat).

2 Drinking water every morning keeps (healthy you / you healthy).

3 Sally asked him (read / to read) the book about animals.

4 I saw a man (jump / to jump) into the river.

5 Please let me (know / knowing) if you need help.

6 Mom made me (go / to go) to bed early.

7 I can hear the wind (to blow / blowing).

8 These gloves keep our hands (warm / warmly) in winter.

9 Ms. Scott (told / had) her son take part in the contest.

10 We (watched / had) the birds flying away.

괄호 안의 말을 알맞은 형태로 바꿔 빈칸에 쓰시오.

1 I saw him _____ on the stage. (sing)

2 She told me _____ my teeth before going to bed. (brush)

3 I felt something _____ in the dark. (move)

4 Mom let me _____ the computer games. (play)

5 Dad had me _____ the table after dinner. (clean)

밑줄 친 부분을 어법에 맞게 고쳐 쓰시오.

1 They named their baby to Kelly. → _____

2 My dad wanted me learning how to swim. → _____

3 Sam heard someone to cry in the street. → _____

4 The refrigerator keeps the vegetables freshly. → _____

5 Sue watched raindrops to fall on her hand. → _____

우리말과 일치하도록 괄호 안의 말을 바르게 배열하여 문장을 완성하시오.

1 그들은 Keating 선생님을 선장으로 선출했다. (elected, captain, Mr. Keating)

→ They _____.

2 Anna는 그 수학 숙제가 어렵다는 것을 알았다. (the, math, difficult, homework, found)

→ Anna _____.

3 사서는 우리에게 조용히 하라고 말했다. (keep, us, to, quiet, told)

→ The librarian _____.

4 Henry의 엄마는 식사 전에 그에게 손을 씻게 했다. (wash, had, his hands, him)

→ Henry's mom _____ before meals.

5 나는 Jessica가 큰 소리로 책을 읽는 것을 들었다. (Jessica, a book, heard, read, aloud)

→ I _____.

UNIT 01 시간·이유·조건의 접속사

Answers p. 34

A 어법 선택

괄호 안에서 알맞은 것을 고르시오.

1 Mom made me chicken soup (when / until) I was very sick.

2 (After / Before) you buy something, think twice about it.

3 Sam will take a shower after he (jogs / will jog).

4 I smelled the flowers (if / as) I was taking a walk.

5 I can't read the book (if / unless) I put my glasses on.

6 (If / Though) penguins are birds, they can't fly.

7 Yuri was happy (so / because) she found her lost dog.

8 (Though / Since) I enjoy skiing and skating, I love winter.

9 This soup is so hot (as / that) I can't eat it now.

10 Let's wait (as / until) the rain stops.

B 빈칸 완성

빈칸에 알맞은 말을 〈보기〉에서 골라 쓰시오.

보기	unless	while	when

1 _____ I looked up at the sky, there was a UFO!

2 He doesn't look like a police officer _____ he is in uniform.

3 I washed the dishes _____ Dad was cleaning the house.

보기	if	because	although

4 _____ he was really tired, he couldn't fall asleep until late at night.

5 What should I do _____ my eyes turn red?

6 You should drive carefully _____ the road is slippery.

C 해석 완성 **밑줄 친 부분에 유의하여 해석을 완성하시오.**

1 She started to work in a bank after she graduated.

_____ 은행에서 일하기 시작했다.

2 Jack drank a bottle of water, as he was very thirsty.

Jack은 _____ 물 한 병을 마셨다.

3 Even though he's from China, he can speak English very well.

_____ 영어를 매우 잘한다.

4 Unless you close the door, the cold air will come in.

_____ 차가운 공기가 들어올 것이다.

D 어법 수정 **밑줄 친 부분을 어법에 맞게 고쳐 쓰시오.**

1 I'll wait here until the concert will be over. → _____

2 He was driving, because he couldn't answer the phone. → _____

3 Unless you don't get enough sleep, you'll be tired. → _____

4 Jenny will get better if she will take the medicine. → _____

5 The problem was as difficult that we couldn't solve it. → _____

E 영작 **우리말과 일치하도록 괄호 안의 말을 바르게 배열하여 문장을 완성하시오.**

1 햇빛이 눈부시니 너는 선글라스를 쓰는 게 좋겠다. (bright, is, the sun, as)

→ _____, you'd better put on sunglasses.

2 너는 무언가를 먹은 후에 이를 닦아야 한다. (after, something, your teeth, eat, brush, you)

→ You have to _____.

3 내가 말하는 동안 Jessica는 아무 말도 하지 않았다. (I, was, said, talking, while, nothing)

→ Jessica _____.

4 비록 비가 왔지만 우리는 즐거운 시간을 보냈다. (a great time, it, even though, rained, had)

→ We _____.

5 지하철이 너무 붐벼서 나는 자리를 찾지 못했다. (I, so, find a seat, that, crowded, couldn't)

→ The subway was _____.

UNIT 2 명령문 + and/or, 짝을 이루는 접속사

Answers p. 34

A 어법 선택

괄호 안에서 알맞은 것을 고르시오.

1 Drink more water, (and / or) you'll be healthier.

2 Hurry up, (and / or) you will miss the school bus.

3 Take an umbrella, (and / or) you'll get wet.

4 I have been to neither Busan (or / nor) Mokpo.

5 I'm interested in both science (and / or) math.

6 They will visit the museum (either / neither) today or tomorrow.

7 You can buy the raincoat as well (as / so) the sweater.

8 Either you or Jenny (have / has) to wash the dishes.

9 Not only Emma but also her sisters (is / are) good at sports.

10 I think both learning and playing (is / are) important.

B 문장 완성

주어진 문장과 의미가 같도록 빈칸에 알맞은 말을 쓰시오.

1 If you practice hard, you will play the piano well.

→ Practice hard, _____ you will play the piano well.

2 If you don't apologize to her, she won't forgive you.

→ _____ you apologize to her, she won't forgive you.

→ Apologize to her, _____ she won't forgive you.

3 Jason doesn't like horror movies. He doesn't like action movies, either.

→ Jason likes _____ horror movies _____ action movies.

4 The actor is good at not only acting but also singing.

→ The actor is good at singing _____ _____ _____ acting.

밑줄 친 부분에 유의하여 해석을 완성하시오.

1 Get some fresh air, <u>and you'll feel better</u>.

바람 좀 쐬어, _____ .

2 I'll buy <u>either a coat or a jacket</u>.

나는 _____ 살 것이다.

3 Take the subway, <u>or you will be late for the meeting</u>.

지하철을 타, _____ .

4 Her song is very popular <u>not only in Korea but also in America</u>.

그녀의 노래는 _____ 매우 인기 있다.

밑줄 친 부분을 어법에 맞게 고쳐 쓰시오.

1 Be careful, <u>and</u> you will make a mistake.　　　　→ _____

2 She looked <u>either</u> surprised nor worried.　　　　→ _____

3 Both Anna and Jake <u>likes</u> to read mysteries.　　　→ _____

4 She was so tired <u>as</u> she fell asleep.　　　　　　→ _____

5 Either you or Ellen <u>are</u> telling a lie.　　　　　　→ _____

우리말과 일치하도록 괄호 안의 말을 바르게 배열하여 문장을 완성하시오.

1 나에게 좋은 소식과 나쁜 소식 둘 다 있다. (good news, bad news, and, both)

→ I have _____ .

2 포기하지 마, 그러면 너의 꿈은 이루어질 거야. (will, and, come true, your dream)

→ Don't give up, _____ .

3 여권을 가져 와, 그러지 않으면 너는 비행기를 탈 수 없어. (get on, you, or, the plane, can't)

→ Bring your passport, _____ .

4 라면은 요리하기 쉬울 뿐만 아니라 맛있다. (to cook, delicious, but also, not only, easy)

→ Instant noodles are _____ .

UNIT 1 관계대명사의 개념

Answers p. 35

A 개념 확인   〈보기〉와 같이 선행사에는 동그라미, 관계대명사절에는 밑줄로 표시하시오.

> 보기   I have (a friend) who wants to be a scientist.

1   I know the girl who painted the picture.

2   This is the tree which my grandfather planted.

3   Kate likes food which is hot and spicy.

4   I know the girl that is wearing a blue hat.

5   Is this the police officer who helped you?

6   Look at the deer that are drinking water.

7   Look at the house whose door is painted blue.

8   Emma is reading a book that is about jazz.

9   Do you remember the boy who you met in Paris?

B 개념 확인   괄호 안의 관계대명사가 들어갈 위치로 알맞은 곳을 고르시오.

1   He (①) is (②) a man (③) I can trust (④). (whom)

2   That is (①) the dog (②) helps (③) the blind man (④). (that)

3   She bought a jacket (①) color (②) is (③) dark grey (④). (whose)

4   I cannot (①) forget (②) the song (③) they played (④) last night. (that)

5   This is (①) the girl (②) comes (③) from Spain (④). (that)

6   The Thames (①) is a river (②) runs (③) through London (④). (which)

7   What's (①) the name (②) of the girl (③) hair is (④) very long? (whose)

8   I'd like to be (①) a singer (②) can make (③) many people (④) happy. (who)

9   He (①) is the actor (②) I've really wanted (③) to meet (④). (who)

괄호 안에서 알맞은 것을 고르시오.

1 She joined a club (who / that) shows a movie every week.

2 I saw a sick animal (which / whose) life was in danger.

3 Maria is a cheerful girl (which / who) everybody likes.

4 This is the apple pie (who / that) Jack made for you.

5 He is the movie star (that / which) I met last night.

밑줄 친 부분에 유의하여 해석을 완성하시오.

1 I want a robot that can do the dishes.

나는 _____ 원한다.

2 This is the boy whom I saw on television.

이 아이는 _____ 이다.

3 Jenny is singing a song that I don't like.

Jenny는 _____ 부르고 있다.

4 Do you know the student whose birthday is today?

너는 _____ 아니?

우리말과 일치하도록 괄호 안의 말을 바르게 배열하여 문장을 완성하시오.

1 그들은 커다란 창문이 있는 집에서 산다. (has, a house, big, which, windows)

→ They live in _____ .

2 Sally는 이름이 백구인 개에게 먹이를 주고 있다. (a dog, Baekgu, name, whose, is)

→ Sally is feeding _____ .

3 White 씨는 내가 존경하는 선생님이다. (whom, I, the teacher, respect)

→ Mr. White is _____ .

4 거짓말쟁이는 진실을 말하지 않는 사람이다. (tell the truth, doesn't, who, a person, is)

→ A liar _____ .

UNIT 02 관계대명사의 역할

Answers p. 35

A 개념 확인

밑줄 친 관계대명사의 역할에 ✔ 표시하시오.

주격: ㈜   소유격: ㈜   목적격: ㈜

1 Read the book <u>which</u> is on the table.   ㈜ ㈜ ㈜

2 I have a friend <u>who</u> always helps me.   ㈜ ㈜ ㈜

3 I have a dog <u>whose</u> fur is white.   ㈜ ㈜ ㈜

4 The shirt <u>that</u> you are wearing today looks nice.   ㈜ ㈜ ㈜

5 Kate has two cats <u>that</u> have blue eyes.   ㈜ ㈜ ㈜

6 Jessy doesn't like desserts <u>that</u> are too sweet.   ㈜ ㈜ ㈜

7 The man <u>who</u> you saw was a famous actor in China.   ㈜ ㈜ ㈜

8 Look at the house <u>whose</u> door is painted blue.   ㈜ ㈜ ㈜

9 The cafe is popular with people <u>that</u> love to take pictures. ㈜ ㈜ ㈜

10 I'd like to see my aunt <u>that</u> I haven't seen for a long time. ㈜ ㈜ ㈜

B 어법 선택

괄호 안에서 알맞은 것을 고르시오.

1 This is the story (which / whom) I heard from my mother.

2 People (who / whom) travel a lot are usually open-minded.

3 The girl (who / which) we helped yesterday is Sue's sister.

4 The apples (who / which) we bought at the store are good.

5 The woman (who / whose) name was Elizabeth died in 1603.

6 I've lost the storybook (that / who) Jane lent me.

7 What's the name of the boy (that / which) called you?

8 That is the museum which I (visited / visited it) last week.

9 Anna has a puppy that always (barks / it barks) at me.

10 The people who (live / lives) on the island are very friendly.

알맞은 관계대명사를 넣어 두 문장을 한 문장으로 바꿔 쓰시오.

1 Mr. Miller is the man. I visited him in London.

→ Mr. Miller is the man _____ I visited in London.

2 Please tell me the name of the shop. It sells good fruit.

→ Please tell me the name of the shop _____ sells good fruit.

3 We found a lake. Its water was quite blue.

→ We found a lake _____ water was quite blue.

밑줄 친 부분을 어법에 맞게 고쳐 쓰시오.

1 Fish are a kind of animal <u>who</u> lives in the water. → _____

2 He is the actor <u>which</u> I interviewed last Friday. → _____

3 Peter likes a girl <u>that</u> hobby is taking pictures. → _____

4 I remember the movie <u>who I watched it</u> with Paul. → _____

5 He is a scientist <u>who love</u> art and music. → _____

우리말과 일치하도록 괄호 안의 말을 바르게 배열하여 문장을 완성하시오.

1 나에게는 캐나다에 사는 삼촌이 있다. (in Canada, who, lives, an uncle)

→ I have _____.

2 Sam은 꼬리가 짧은 개를 돌보고 있다. (is, a dog, tail, whose, short)

→ Sam is taking care of _____.

3 우리가 기억해야 하는 영웅들이 있다. (we, whom, must, heroes, remember)

→ There are _____.

4 나에게는 10살인 남동생이 있다. (a brother, have, 10 years old, who, is)

→ I _____.

5 우리는 엄마가 만든 천연 비누를 사용한다. (the natural soap, that, Mom, use, made)

→ We _____.

Answers p. 36

UNIT 3 관계대명사 what, 관계대명사의 생략

A 개념 확인

밑줄 친 부분을 생략할 수 있으면 ○, 생략할 수 없으면 ×를 쓰시오.

1 The teacher <u>whom</u> I respect is very kind. _____

2 I have a cat <u>whose</u> eyes are blue. _____

3 Do you know the girl <u>who is</u> playing the flute? _____

4 Everything <u>that</u> he said was true. _____

5 Many people still love <u>what</u> he wrote. _____

6 Daniel likes a girl <u>who</u> is kind and smart. _____

7 This is a castle <u>which was</u> built in the early 1800s. _____

8 He drew a house <u>that</u> was made of chocolate. _____

9 There is nothing <u>that</u> I can do for him. _____

10 <u>What</u> she is looking at now is a painting by Van Gogh. _____

B 어법 선택

괄호 안에서 알맞은 것을 고르시오.

1 I can't understand (that / what) you're saying.

2 (That / What) I like is taking a walk with my dog.

3 The movie (we saw / we saw it) last week was exciting.

4 Do you know the girl (talking / is taking) to Eric?

5 I will never forget (that / what) you did for me.

6 The story (that / what) he told me was not true.

7 Do the things (which / what) you'd like to do.

8 I read a book (written / that written) by Charles Dickens.

9 The kids (play / playing) at the beach look happy.

10 Jenny likes the movies (direct / directed) by Steven Spielberg.

밑줄 친 부분에 유의하여 해석을 완성하시오.

1 My sister believes <u>what I say</u>.

내 여동생은 _____ 믿는다.

2 <u>The boy eating ice cream</u> looks happy.

_____ 행복해 보인다.

3 She bought <u>a table made in Italy</u>.

그녀는 _____ 샀다.

밑줄 친 부분을 어법에 맞게 고쳐 쓰시오.

1 Can you understand <u>which</u> I'm saying? → _____

2 This hat is exactly <u>that</u> I want. → _____

3 Food <u>is cooked</u> by my mother is always delicious. → _____

4 Look at the rabbits <u>are eating</u> carrots. → _____

5 Please tell me <u>the things what</u> you know about Tom. → _____

우리말과 일치하도록 괄호 안의 말을 바르게 배열하여 문장을 완성하시오.

1 선생님이 환경에 관해 말한 것을 기억해라. (said, the teacher, what, remember)

→ _____ about the environment.

2 우리가 가장 필요로 하는 것은 충분한 시간이다. (need, the thing, we, most, that)

→ _____ is enough time.

3 너는 정문에 서 있는 남자를 아니? (is, who, standing, the man, at the gate)

→ Do you know _____ ?

4 그녀가 점심식사로 먹은 것은 양파 수프였다. (she, what, ate, was, for lunch)

→ _____ onion soup.

5 Emily는 과일로 장식된 케이크를 샀다. (a cake, decorated, with, bought, fruit)

→ Emily _____ .

UNIT 04 관계부사

Answers p. 36

A 어법 선택

괄호 안에서 알맞은 것을 고르시오.

1 Sunday is the day (where / when) Ms. White is free.

2 I want to know the reason (why / how) you're angry with me.

3 This is a museum (when / where) people can see modern art.

4 The Internet has changed (how / why) we communicate.

5 Turkey is a country (how / where) the East meets the West.

6 I can't wait for the day (how / when) the summer vacation starts.

7 May I ask you the reason (why / how) you made that decision?

8 I want to learn (the way / the way how) you made the soup.

9 Spring is (the season / the reason) when many people go on picnics.

10 That is (the summer / the island) where I spent my vacation.

B 문장 전환

알맞은 관계부사를 넣어 두 문장을 한 문장으로 바꿔 쓰시오.

1 Do you know the store? I bought my raincoat there.

→ Do you know the store _____ I bought my raincoat?

2 Now is the time. Dave has to go to bed at this time.

→ Now is the time _____ Dave has to go to bed.

3 What was the reason? You stopped playing the game for that reason.

→ What was the reason _____ you stopped playing the game?

4 This is the place. I lost my dog here.

→ This is the place _____ I lost my dog.

5 It was the way. The children celebrated Christmas in that way.

→ It was _____ the children celebrated Christmas.

밑줄 친 부분에 유의하여 해석을 완성하시오.

1 I always miss <u>the days when I lived in London</u>.

나는 _____ 항상 그리워한다.

2 This is <u>how she passed the audition</u>.

이것이 _____이다.

3 Olympic Park is <u>the place where we often take walks</u>.

올림픽 공원은 _____이다.

밑줄 친 부분을 어법에 맞게 고쳐 쓰시오.

1 March is the month <u>where</u> the trees become green.   → _____

2 He finally told me the reason <u>how</u> he was so upset.   → _____

3 A library is a place <u>when</u> you can borrow books.   → _____

4 Tell me <u>the way how</u> you cooked this beef.   → _____

5 I don't know the time <u>when the class starts at</u>.   → _____

우리말과 일치하도록 괄호 안의 말을 바르게 배열하여 문장을 완성하시오.

1 정오는 우리가 점심을 먹는 시간이다. (we, lunch, the time, have, when)

→ Noon is _____.

2 여기는 내가 태어난 집이다. (the house, born, where, was, I)

→ This is _____.

3 수영은 내가 건강을 유지하는 방법이다. (is, stay, the way, healthy, I)

→ Swimming _____.

4 늦게 일어난 것이 내가 늦은 이유이다. (was, I, the reason, late, is, why)

→ Getting up late _____.

5 그 다큐멘터리는 아메리카 원주민들이 살았던 방식을 우리에게 보여 주었다.

(us, lived, how, showed, the native Americans)

→ The documentary _____.

UNIT 1 가정법 과거

Answers p. 37

A
어법 선택

괄호 안에서 알맞은 것을 고르시오.

1 If I (am / were) a millionaire, I would live in Beverly Hills.

2 If he (has / had) a car, he would go for a drive every weekend.

3 If I (was / were) you, I would not lend him money.

4 If you look in the refrigerator, you (can / could) find the milk.

5 If Minho spoke English, he (can / could) make foreign friends.

6 If it (rains / rained), the festival will be canceled.

7 If you turned off the lights, you (saved / could save) energy.

8 You (were / will be) healthy if you don't eat junk food.

9 What (will / would) you do if you were a superhero?

10 If I (have / had) more time, I would visit the museum.

B
문장 전환

직설법은 가정법으로, 가정법은 직설법으로 바꿔 쓰시오.

1 As I don't know Jay, I can't introduce him to you.

→ If I _____ Jay, I _____ him to you.

2 As she doesn't come home early, she can't watch the TV show.

→ If she _____ home early, she _____ the TV show.

3 As Maria is sick, she can't go out with her friends.

→ If Maria _____ sick, she _____ out with her friends.

4 As I'm not in New York, I can't meet you.

→ If I _____ in New York, I _____ you.

5 If Andrew were home, he could feed his dog.

→ As Andrew _____ home, he _____ his dog.

6 If I had a time machine, I could go to the future.

→ As I _____ a time machine, I _____ to the future.

UNIT 2 가정법 과거완료

A
어법 선택

괄호 안에서 알맞은 것을 고르시오.

1 If I (saw / had seen) you, I would have said hello.

2 If it (were / had been) warmer, we might have gone swimming.

3 If she had had a key, she (can open / could have opened) the door.

4 If they hadn't missed the train, they (may arrive / might have arrived) on time.

5 The boy could have done better if he (practiced / had practiced) more.

6 If Tom (took / had taken) his coat, he might not have caught a cold.

7 If you (told / had told) me the truth, I would have helped you.

8 What would you have done if it (snowed / had snowed) last Christmas?

9 If it had been sunny, we (had ridden / would have ridden) our bikes.

10 Mary would have been very happy if she (won / had won) first prize.

B
문장 전환

직설법은 가정법으로, 가정법은 직설법으로 바꿔 쓰시오.

1 As he was busy, he didn't have lunch with us.

→ If he _____ busy, he _____ lunch with us.

2 If the party had been on Saturday, Peter could have come.

→ As the party _____ on Saturday, Peter _____.

3 If she had taken my advice, she could have solved the problem.

→ As she _____ my advice, she _____ the problem.

4 As Jenny didn't do her homework, she didn't get an A.

→ If Jenny _____ her homework, she _____ an A.

5 As you weren't there, you didn't see the accident.

→ If you _____ there, you _____ the accident.

6 If I had watched the weather forecast, I might not have gone out.

→ As I _____ the weather forecast, I _____ out.

Answers p. 37

UNIT 1-2 가정법 과거와 가정법 과거완료

A 개념 확인
해당되는 가정법의 종류에 ✔ 표시하시오.

		가정법 과거	가정법 과거완료
1	If I had a spaceship, I could fly to the moon.	☐	☐
2	If we didn't have language, we couldn't communicate easily.	☐	☐
3	If I had had time, I could have visited you.	☐	☐
4	If I were a teacher, I would never give tests.	☐	☐
5	If Ted had known about it, he would have helped us.	☐	☐

B 어법 선택
괄호 안에서 알맞은 것을 고르시오.

1 If Dave (goes / went) there, he would love that place.

2 If he (came / had come) earlier, he would have met Stella.

3 We (would play / would have played) tennis if it stopped raining.

4 If we had stayed in Florida, we (could go / could have gone) to the beach.

5 If Bob (were / had been) healthy, he could travel around the world.

6 I (would join / would have joined) the band if I had played the guitar well.

C 어법 수정
밑줄 친 부분을 어법에 맞게 고쳐 쓰시오.

1 If you listened carefully, you <u>will know</u> about it.　　→ _____

2 If I <u>have</u> more time, I would stay longer in Vienna.　　→ _____

3 If we hadn't come here, we <u>will regret</u> it.　　→ _____

4 The soup <u>will taste</u> better if you added some salt.　　→ _____

5 If she <u>studies</u> harder, she would have passed the exam.
　　→ _____

직설법은 가정법으로, 가정법은 직설법으로 바꿔 쓰시오.

1 As Jeff doesn't like Jessica, he doesn't get along with her.

→ If Jeff _____ Jessica, he _____ along with her.

2 As I didn't speak Italian, I communicated with body gestures.

→ If I _____ Italian, I _____ with body gestures.

3 As the weather isn't warm, we can't have lunch on the grass.

→ If the weather _____ warm, we _____ lunch on the grass.

4 If he had stayed home, he would have cleaned the house.

→ As he _____ home, he _____ the house.

5 If Aaron had drunk warm milk, he could have fallen asleep.

→ As Aaron _____ warm milk, he _____ asleep.

6 As you didn't watch the horror movie, you didn't have nightmares.

→ If you _____ the horror movie, you _____ nightmares.

우리말과 일치하도록 괄호 안의 말을 배열하여 문장을 완성하시오.

1 눈이 많이 왔다면, 나는 눈사람을 만들 수 있었을 텐데. (have, could, made, a snowman, I)

→ If it had snowed a lot, _____.

2 우리가 이 캔을 재활용하면, 우리는 환경을 도울 수 있을 텐데. (the environment, we, help, could)

→ If we recycled these cans, _____.

3 그녀가 집에 있었다면, 우리는 같이 저녁을 먹었을 텐데. (had, if, she, home, been)

→ _____, we would have had dinner together.

4 내가 너라면, 그 신발을 살 텐데. (if, I, would, buy, you, I, were)

→ _____, _____ the shoes.

5 그가 천천히 말했다면, 너는 그의 말을 이해할 수 있었을 텐데.
(if, he, could, had, have, spoken, you, understood)

→ _____ slowly, _____ him.

UNIT 3 I wish 가정법, as if 가정법

Answers p. 37

A 어법 선택

괄호 안에서 알맞은 것을 고르시오.

1 I wish my sister (eats / ate) more salad.

2 It seems as if Maria (lies / lied) to me.

3 I wish I (buy / bought) the blue jeans.

4 Sora talks as if she (visited / had visited) London last year.

5 She talks as if she (is / were) from Australia.

6 I wish Mom (has bought / had bought) me the jacket.

7 Mary is smiling as if she (is not / were not) sad.

8 I wish I (can run / could run) faster.

9 I feel sick. I wish I (had eaten / hadn't eaten) so much ice cream.

10 Nick feels as if he (is flying / were flying) through the air.

B 문장 완성

우리말과 일치하도록 괄호 안의 말을 이용하여 문장을 완성하시오.

1 내가 지갑을 잃어버리지 않았다면 좋을 텐데. (lose)

→ I _____ I _____ my wallet.

2 하영이는 마치 며칠 동안 잠을 자지 않았던 것처럼 보였다. (sleep)

→ Hayeong looked _____ she _____ for days.

3 내가 나의 새 이웃들을 알면 좋을 텐데. (know)

→ I _____ I _____ my new neighbors.

4 그녀는 마치 자기가 주방장인 것처럼 행동한다. (be)

→ She acts _____ she _____ a chef.

5 내가 Harry와 싸우지 않았다면 좋을 텐데. (fight)

→ I _____ I _____ with Harry.

6 유리는 마치 그녀가 그녀의 방을 청소했던 것처럼 말한다. (clean)

→ Yuri talks _____ she _____ her room.

중학 영문법 클리어.

Level **2**

WORKBOOK

영역	브랜드	초1~2	초3~4	초5~6	중1	중2	중3	고1	고2	고3
독해	[중등] 기본서 READING CLEAR				READING CLEAR 1	READING CLEAR 2	READING CLEAR 3			
	[중등] 수능 대비서 **수작 중학 비문학 영어 독해**				수능시작 비문학 영어 독해	수능시작 비문학 영어 독해	수능시작 비문학 영어 독해			
	[고등] 기본서 **Supreme 구문독해 / 유형독해**							Supreme 구문독해	Supreme 유형독해	
	[중·고등] 문장독해 **공식으로 통하는 문장독해** 기본 완성							공통문 기본	공통문 완성	
듣기	[중등] 듣기모의고사 LISTENING CLEAR 중학영어 듣기모의고사				LISTENING CLEAR 1	LISTENING CLEAR 2	LISTENING CLEAR 3			
	[고등] 듣기모의고사 **Supreme 수능 영어 듣기 모의고사** 기본 실전							Supreme 기본	Supreme 실전	
어휘	[초·중·고등] 영단어, 영숙어 **뜯어먹는 시리즈**	뜯어먹는 필수 영단어 1	뜯어먹는 필수 영단어 2		뜯어먹는 중학 기본 영단어 1200	뜯어먹는 중학 영단어 1800	뜯어먹는 중학 영어 1000	뜯어먹는 수능 1800	뜯어먹는 수능 1800	뜯어먹는 수능 1200
	[중·고등] 영단어 **보카클리어**				보카클리어 중등 기본편	보카클리어 중등 실력편	보카클리어 고등 입문편	보카클리어 고등실력편	보카클리어 수능편	

영어 실력과 내신 점수를 함께 높이는
중학 영어 클리어 시리즈

문법 영문법 클리어 | LEVEL 1~3

최신 개정판

문법 개념과 내신을 한 번에 끝내다!

- 중등에서 꼭 필요한 핵심 문법만 담아 시각적으로 정리
- 시험에 꼭 나오는 출제 포인트부터 서술형 문제까지 내신 완벽 대비

쓰기 문법+쓰기 클리어 | LEVEL 1~3

영작과 서술형을 한 번에 끝내다!

- 기초 형태 학습부터 문장 영작까지 단계별로 영작 집중 훈련
- 최신 서술형 유형과 오류 클리닉으로 서술형 실전 준비 완료

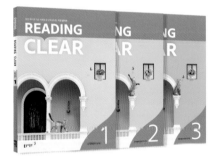

독해 READING CLEAR | LEVEL 1~3

문장 해석과 지문 이해를 한 번에 끝내다!

- 핵심 구문 32개로 어려운 문법 구문의 정확한 해석 훈련
- Reading Map으로 글의 핵심 및 구조 파악 훈련

듣기 LISTENING CLEAR | LEVEL 1~3

듣기 기본기와 듣기 평가를 한 번에 끝내다!

- 최신 중학 영어듣기능력평가 완벽 반영
- 1.0배속/1.2배속/받아쓰기용 음원 별도 제공으로 학습 편의성 강화